BF
692
.R79   Rubin, Jerry.

       The war between the
       sheets

Cop. 6

© THE BA

D1174434

THE WAR BETWEEN THE SHEETS

Also by Jerry Rubin

Do It!
We Are Everywhere
Vote! (With Abbie Hoffman and Ed Sanders)
Growing (Up) At 37

THE WAR BETWEEN THE SHEETS

JERRY RUBIN & MIMI LEONARD

FOREWORD BY PAUL LOWINGER, M.D.
PREFACE BY GEORGE LEONARD

RICHARD MAREK PUBLISHERS
NEW YORK

Cop. 6

The authors wish to thank the following for permission to quote from the sources listed:

Bernard Apfelbaum for "Does Turning on Mean Always Saying Yes?"; for "The Enemy in the Bedroom, or Say I Love You"; and for "On the Etiology of Sexual Dysfunction." *Journal of Sex and Marital Therapy*, vol. 3, no. 1 (Spring, 1977).

Harcourt Brace Jovanovich, Inc., for *The Philosophy of Andy Warhol* by Andy Warhol.

Alfred A. Knopf, Inc., for *Combat in the Erogenous Zone* by Ingrid Bengis, copyright © 1972 by Ingrid Bengis.

Macmillan Publishing Company, Inc., for *The Hite Report* by Shere Hite, copyright © 1976 by Shere Hite.

Ms. Magazine, for quote by Venable Herndon in the April 1978 issue.

W. W. Norton & Company, Inc., for *Love and Will* by Rollo May, copyright © 1969 by W. W. Norton & Company, Inc.

Richard Pryor for his movie, *Richard Pryor, Live*.

G. P. Putnam's Sons for *Cruel Shoes* by Steve Martin, copyright © 1979 by Steve Martin.

Michael Rossman for "Masturbation and Consciousness-Raising Groups as Adjunctive Therapy in the the Treatment of Male Sexual Dysfunction."

Charles Scribner's Sons for *The Moveable Feast* by Ernest Hemingway, copyright © 1964 by Ernest Hemingway, Ltd.

Library of Congress Cataloging in Publication Data

Rubin, Jerry.
    The war between the sheets.

    1. Sex (Psychology) 2. Men—Sexual behavior.
3. Intimacy (Psychology) I. Leonard, Mimi,
joint author. II. Title.
BF692.R79   155.3'4   80-16541
ISBN 0-399-90093-4

Printed in the United States of America

Acknowledgments

We want to thank the hundreds of people who participated in our sex-and-relationships survey. The sincere and intense responses from more than 500 people from all over the country provided us with the information, insights and support to write the book. Although we have changed the identities of everyone whom we quote, you may find yourself in here somewhere. Thank you.

We also want to thank the individual men and women who permitted us to interview them on their romantic and sexual lives. The in-depth grilling sometimes lasted up to four hours, and was essential in both generating and refining the theoretical perspective of the book.

Although parts of the book describe actual events, the identities of the people have been changed to make any resemblance to real people purely coincidental. We thank Donald Porter, whose excellent writing workshop assisted us greatly. We thank Steven Gaines, who worked on the earliest, personal first-draft of the manuscript. We acknowledge literary agent Francis Greenburger for his patience and support during our endless rewriting. And we want to thank our editor Joyce Engelson, who had the insight and creativity to recognize the importance of our message, and the courage and perseverance to stand by it through its many versions. We deeply appreciate Joyce's originality, her open mind and open heart, and we credit her with any success the book may achieve.

We are deeply grateful to those people who read and critiqued one or more drafts of this book, although they bear no responsibility for the limitations or point of view of the final version. In particular, we want to thank Warren Farrell, Lynn Hollyn, Judy Orringer, George Leonard, Ben Zablocki, Mary Schoonmaker, Suni Paz, Tom Jackson, Ellen Frankfort, Bob Fitch, Philip Nobile, Laurie Frank, Jerelle Kraus, Lillie Leonard, Michael Kennedy, Tom Benenson, Barry Samuels, Stuart Samuels, Barry Michaels, Dharoni Bluestone, Paul Bowles, Roger Ressemeyer, Richard Summers, Linda Rubin, Martin Garbus, Ivan Liberman, Mike Sussel, John Gruber, Frank Van Stirum, David Fenton and Michael Hernstadt. We also want to thank the professionals who took the time to read and comment on the book: John Bush, Leonard Gross, Terry Starker and Michael Quagland.

MIMI LEONARD, JERRY RUBIN

Dedicated with Love to
Mimi
from Jerry

Dedicated with Love to
Jerry
from Mimi

CONTENTS

A Note from Mimi Leonard   17
Foreword by Paul Lowinger, M.D.   19
Preface by George Leonard   22

1
Sexual Knots

A STRANGE TWIST IN THE SAGA OF MALE
SEXUAL COMPETITION   27

REPORT FROM THE SEXUAL BATTLEFIELD   31

THE MALE SEXUAL PEP TALK   33

BREAKING THE CONSPIRACY OF MALE SEXUAL SILENCE   36

A SECOND LOOK AT "SEX THERAPY" AND
WOMEN'S LIBERATION   38

11

2

The Female Orgasm Upsets the Sexual Balance of Power

SEXUAL TECHNOLOGY   43

THE SEXUAL COWBOY'S "BLUE BALLS"   44

THE GOOD GIRL AND THE BAD GIRL   46

THE SEXUAL REVOLUTION DOES NOT REVOLUTIONIZE SEX   47

THE COWBOY MEETS THE CLITORIS   48

MEN TAKE THEIR BRIEFCASES TO BED   51

THE NEW FEMALE "PERFORMANCE ANXIETY"   53

IS THERE SEX FOR MEN AFTER THE WOMEN'S MOVEMENT?   55

THE FEMALE LIBERATION OF MASTURBATION   59

FREUD TURNS OVER IN HIS GRAVE   61

3

Men and Women Change Positions (Or Do They?)

SHOOTOUT IN THE BEDROOM   65

CONTRADICTIONS WITHIN CONTRADICTIONS   70

HAL'S PENIS DEFEATS JERRY'S PENIS, 1–0   72

MEN MAKE WOMEN THE JUDGES OF THEIR MANHOOD   74

PENIS WARS   76

THE (SHH!) MALE VIRGIN   78

COMPETITION INVADES THE NONMACHO WORLD   79

GOOD SEX, NO FEELING!   80

4

Not for Men Only

MEN ARE SEXUALLY MORE VULNERABLE THAN WOMEN   89

THE MELTDOWN OF MASCULINITY   90

THE POLITICS OF POTENCY   93

"YOUR MIND IS WILLING BUT YOUR BODY ISN'T"   94

THE DUTIFUL ERECTION   97

HUGE TREES, TINY TWIGS   101

THE FEMALE JUDGE STRIKES AGAIN   106

BUT OTHER WOMEN . . .   110

AN ESSENTIAL PROP OF MANHOOD?   111

THREE RESPONSES TO PREMATURE EJACULATION   113

5

Relationship Training: Become the Right Person

OH SO HEALTHY   117

HOW TO FREE YOURSELF FROM YOUR PARENTS   119

HOW TO FREE YOURSELF FROM A BAD RELATIONSHIP   124

FINDING INTIMACY: THE POWER TO GIVE UP POWER   126

MEETING MS. RIGHT   128

SHARING YOUR SEXUAL SECRETS   132

6

Asexuality: The Hottest Game in Town

THE ASEXUAL REVOLUTION   137

SEX WHEN YOU WANT IT (AND NOT WHEN YOU DON'T)   139

THE NEW MALE HEADACHE   140

FEAR OF FAILURE, FEAR OF SUCCESS   144

WORKAHOLISM AS A SUBSTITUTE FOR SEX   146

IS ASEXUALITY HARMFUL TO YOUR HEALTH?   147

7

The Rubin-Leonard Non-Method for Feeling Good Sexually

HOW TO TEACH YOURSELF TO BECOME A GOOD LOVER   151

KEYS TO SEXUAL DESIRE   152

ZEN PARADOXES ABOUT THE ERECTION   155

WELCOME HOME, MR. ANXIETY   159

HOW TO RESPOND TO A NONHAPPENING   160

FEMALE GOSSIP AND SYMPATHY   161

TELLING THE TRUTH IN BED—IS IT POSSIBLE?   162

SHY MEN   165

DOES "ROGER" KNOW BEST?   166

ANOTHER PETER PRINCIPLE   169

8

What Women Really Want in Bed

LOVE ME, LOVE MY PUSSY   175

LEARNING FROM LESBIANS   178

THE "RIGHT" AND "WRONG" FEMALE ORGASM   179

SECRETS OF FEMALE AROUSAL   183

THE PERFORMING TONGUE   186

THREE CHEERS FOR THE TONGUE AND THE FINGER   187

YOU DON'T NEED AN ERECTION TO HAVE FUN IN BED   188

9

A New Sexuality

EQUALITY IN BED   195

JONATHAN   196

PEOPLE LIBERATION   198

I AND THOU IN BED   200

TAKING-TURNS SEX   202

THE SEXUAL RADICALS HAVE BECOME
SEXUAL CONSERVATIVES   204

WHO MAKES THE FIRST SEXUAL MOVE?   206

THE FEMALE VIBRATOR AND THE MALE EGO   208

RESOLVING THE MALE-FEMALE CRISIS OVER
TIME OF ORGASM   209

ECSTASY AND BASEBALL SCORES   212

FIVE WAYS MASTURBATION WITH ANOTHER ADDS TO EQUALITY
AND ECSTASY IN SEX   215

YOU DON'T NEED AN ORGASM TO HAVE FUN IN BED   216

EROTIC CUDDLING   221

Questionnaire for Men
on Sexuality   222
Bibliography   224

A Note from Mimi Leonard

In 1977, Jerry decided to write a book that would help men and women understand and deal with the new sexual pressures that have arisen in the past decade. The first year, Jerry wrote a very personal first draft—300 pages getting out his experiences and thoughts on the subject. By the time he completed the draft, I had already involved myself in the project with countless hours of discussion about the book. At this point, I entered the project as a coauthor. However we both wanted to maintain one of the most significant features of the book, that it is an honest, personal expression about love and sex *from a man*. And after a decade that produced quite a few excellent books on this subject from women, neither of us felt it would be innovative for me to write my personal story. Therefore, I decided that my work on the book should focus on its theoretical development, discussion of secondary and primary research, editing, and structuring the material. We used segments from Jerry's first draft to add the personal revelations we feel will contribute to the lives of other men and women, and the rest of the book is by both of us.

Foreword

In spite of the so-called sexual revolution, there is still a great deal of secrecy about men and their sexuality. Openness about sexual anxiety is still something of a taboo, out of age-old culturally born shames. Embarrassment and secrecy still surround the subject of male sexual problems. Doctors say that women should not be superfamiliar with some of the medical techniques developed because "it's a man's problem."

In an era in which we have seen women, quite properly, demanding their own sexual satisfactions, we still see many men made anxious, even disabled, by the sense that they are the ones who have to produce these satisfactions. A revolution will not be much of a success if it produces more anxiety, more secrecy and less satisfaction.

Mimi Leonard and Jerry Rubin think that "a man's problem" should be freely discussed. And they have written a thoughtful and helpful book on the subject, viewed through the lens of Jerry's personal sexual history, including his own anxieties and how he dealt with them. Based on a wide sampling of men and women who have been very frank about their needs and dissatisfactions as well as their pleasures and satisfactions, plus the advice of many experts in the field, this is a coherent "how to do it" guide for puzzled men and the women who are their partners. The specific advice and reassurance in this book, based not only on helpful information but also on the sharing of so many other people's experience ("we are not alone"), will help end the conspiracy of silence surrounding the frustration, the needs and anxieties concerning men's sexuality.

Jerry and Mimi have looked to the heart of what not only they themselves but so many hundreds of others had been seeking—a caring relationship in which to develop each person's own kind of sexuality. For the pains born of this new era have led to a relationship crisis in this country: many people have been giving up on the search for sexual satisfaction and a loving relationship.

I got to knwo Jerry Rubin in 1975 when the two of us were on one of the early political tours of the People's Republic of China. Before this, I had observed Jerry only from a distance as one of the leaders of the antiwar movement, a star of many dramatic confrontations. On the China trip, during the many hours we spent in conversation on the train (traveling the vast distances from one commune to another), I became familiar with the less public side of his personauty and saw his intense interest in people and their feelings—himself included. Many of his perceptive, even impertinent questions in China about the quality of life and sexual behavior there elicited answers that helped me to understand Chinese society. At the time of this trip, his book, *Growing (Up) At 37*, an invetigation of his life experience, touching somewhat on his sexual problems, was on press.

As a psychiatrist in practice for thirty years, I know how few of the men I see want to discuss their sexual problems. When men come to me for treatment, they avoid that issue because admitting that they do have even some sexual anxiety violates the universal myth that all men possess an ever-ready and powerful sexuality. Other therapists find, as I do, that men come seeking help for career difficulties, inappropriately passive or aggressive behavior, trouble in "getting along with women," problems with alcohol and drugs, psychosomatic complaints, and so on. They may have significant worries about or trouble in sexual performance but are too often unwilling to mention that.

Psychiatrists are also aware that men looking for help, men with questions about erection, for instance, will usually go to their family doctors or urologists, and when referred by them to therapists, seldom go. And if a man does go for therapy, the secrecy of communication between patient and therapist may only reinforce the patient's feeling that his problem is one that he cannot share with anyone but his therapist. He may feel that he and his therapist have a "gentleman's agreement" about not revealing his problem, the implication being that the therapist agrees that any revelations would harm the patient—who must save face at all costs. But this is exactly what cuts off the possibility of frank discussions with other men—and women—exchanges that might very well decrease both anxiety and depression, and would certainly reduce the sense of being alone with such questions in the face of an unsympathetic male and female audience.

Sex therapy—which is almost entirely for couples only—is another and usually more helpful approach, but here too the veil of silence descends and the problems that men may have never get beyond the consulting room. Even though the man's sexual partner and a male and female therapist may share the "secret," other men, similarly bothered, may never realize how common the problem is. The locker room mentality perseveres beyond the sexual revolution.

There are many books about men's liberation and about male–female relationships, so why another? Because the man with problems, the man bewildered by the new sexual era, even the man who simply has questions, needs accessible, personalized help. That's the most practical kind. And these authors are practical. They list, for instance, not one but several kinds of solutions for the most common male experiences: premature ejaculation, erectile difficulties, etc.

Of course, for many men and women, sexuality is spontaneous, and the only manuals they may want are erotic films or books about the joy of sex. But too many men—and women—cannot yet feel entirely spontaneous about sex, and they suffer from the sense that everyone in the universe but themselves is sexually carefree. In fact, this is not true, and the mental anguish that arises from such ignorance is enormous. The message of this book, so free of jargon and yet so scientifically accurate, will encourage men to feel more comfortable about discussing their sexual questions and bewilderments (about themselves and about their lovers) with other men and women, in seeking help, and in helping others too. One hopes that the authors' proposals will have a significant influence on attitudes toward what is considered acceptable and desirable in male sexual response. Eventually, this book will affect the approach to sex therapy. The important point is that *The War Between the Sheets* should reach and help an audience that may never get to the therapist or even the family doctor for help or advice. This book is a must for men with or without sexual problems, for men and women who have any questions about sexuality and about what is happening in other beds today.

PAUL LOWINGER, M.D.

Preface

Piano legs were concealed beneath dust ruffles lest the sight of them should inflame the venereal passions. Books by female and male authors were kept on separate shelves out of similar considerations. Libidinal excess between husband and wife (more than once a month for the healthy and robust; less or none at all for the sickly and sedentary) was thought to cause various maladies, ranging from pulmonary consumption to blindness, insanity and early death of offspring.

Fear of masturbation became even more hysterical. Sex experts such as Sylvester Graham, inventor of the graham cracker, advised normal adults to sleep with their hands tied. Respected physicians recommended more extreme measures: circumcision, clitoridectomy, infibulation (putting a silver wire through the foreskin), wearing of chastity belts or spiked penile rings, blistering the penis with red mercury ointment, cauterization of the spine and genitals, surgical denervation of the penis and, in extreme cases, removal of both penis and testes.

Compared to these horrors of the Victorian age, our present attitude toward sex seems incredibly advanced and free. But the nineteenth century, apogee of a 2,500-year Western flight from eros, is not so easily dismissed. In our more daring lunges toward sexual freedom, we are still tied to the Victorians. Seeking the final taboo to break, our X-rated films, magazines and stand-up comics are driven to a kind of kinkiness that is curiously Victorian in tone. Couples try group sex or bisexuality because they think they *should*, and another kind of ethic is loosed upon the waterbeds of the West. Liberal writers on the new sexuality, borrowing what is prissy and ponderous from the language of popular sociology, assure us that anything we freely choose to do, so long as it doesn't harm others, is perfectly all right, healthy, good. (This sentence from *Intimate Friendships* by James Ramey is not atypical: "Accept the premise that sometimes an outside relationship will impinge on the primary relationship time frame; this is not catastrophic, but is akin to the similar incursions of career and children.") The sex reformers' advice on masturbation, anal intercourse, multiple orgasm, you name it, is enlightened, humane, and just as predictable as was that of Sylvester Graham.

In pursuit of sexual liberation, we have arrived instead at a new sexual ideology, by no means as frightening and punitive as that of the Victorians, but no less effective in sabotaging any free and easy expression of the erotic. The new constraints are, in one respect, more insidious than the old; whereas the sex code of the nineteenth century was largely proscriptive, our modern ideology tends to be prescriptive. Masturbation is a sin, said the Victorians, a threat to health and sanity. You should not masturbate. No, say the reformers, masturbation is natural and good, especially for women—recreation, therapy, *duty*. And throughout the land there is a hum of vibrators as liberated women recreationally, therapeutically or dutifully seek the cataclysmic orgasm they have been reading so much about in recent years. Women should not enjoy sex, said our Victorian forebears, but rather grit their teeth and think about England. No, say the reformers; women are capable of boundless arousal and pleasure. Multiple orgasm is the order of the day. And throughout the land, our liberated men struggle dutifully, with every instrumentality at hand, to incite the lengthy, perhaps endless series of female climaxes that will, at last, prove their own erotic worth. And now another prescription: multiple *male* orgasms! "Old fashioned religious moralism," says philosopher Sam Keen, "was permissive indeed compared to our hip erotic methodism."

Into this arena of veiled dogma and unacknowledged anxiety comes a new book, *The War Between the Sheets*. I am hardly a disinterested party in this matter, for the authors are my multitalented, indeed protean daughter, Mimi Leonard, and her husband, the once and future revolutionary, Jerry Rubin. Not only is there the familial connection; I myself am currently completing a book on the subject of love and sex. But if my viewpoint on this volume is biased, it is also informed, and I must say I have come across no other book that can do more to relieve the confusion, anxiety and pain associated with the sexual revolution.

Mimi and Jerry started off by advertising for men who would be willing to fill out a questionnaire on male sexual anxieties. Less than a hundred men responded to the first wave of ads. But more than 300 *women* wrote in, eager to reveal themselves on just this subject. Of the men who did fill out the questionnaires, most were highly guarded about their experiences. The women, on the other hand, were generally quite open; they "poured out their hearts about relating to men." This unexpected response is not definitive, but strongly suggests that the American male has been stunned into defensive silence by the demands of sexual freedom. And, for me, it alone proves the need for this book.

The authors persisted in their search for men willing to speak openly about sex. The interviews they obtained are both instructive and poignant, revealing a thin veneer of male bravado covering depths of bewilderment and unease, *machismo* put to rout by sexually awakened, multiorgasmic women. Reading the words of women as well as men, we are led to a somber conclusion: if this is a war, it is a war without victors. The defeat of *machismo* may be an occasion for celebration, but the destruction of male sexual confidence and ease is a loss for members of both sexes.

Mimi and Jerry's purpose here is not just to chronicle the war, but also to point the way to sexual peace and happiness. By example and induction, they would turn us from conquest to relationship, from performance to intimacy, from results in lovemaking to the joys and fascinations of the process itself. Beyond the sexual revolution, the authors tell us, there could be an era of free but discriminating choice of sexual partners, along with the responsibilities and rewards of long-term commitment.

Asking self-disclosure and vulnerability in other males, Jerry Rubin has chosen to reveal himself and make himself vulnerable in these pages. For me, his revelations are truly humane and helpful. For who among us has not, at one time or another, been locked in a prison of silence about our own sexual fears and misadventures? And how relieving, how life-giving it is to learn that someone else has experienced similar feelings.

Ultimately, we must learn to communicate with one another—openly, honestly and with good will. And we might bear in mind that, in matters of the passions, communication begins with self-disclosure. *The War Between the Sheets* opens the kind of dialogue that holds the key to peace in the current sexual conflict. And it reminds us of one sure thing: where there is no communication, there will always be war.

GEORGE LEONARD
Author of *Education and Ecstasy*
and *The Ultimate Athlete*

SEXUAL KNOTS

A Strange Twist in the Saga of Male
Sexual Competition

Boom! Men have been kicked out of their director's chair in sex. Women are becoming coproducers of the entire event, initiating and controlling the action. To suddenly be the one manipulated can be humiliating. After all, I thought that I was *doing* it to her. All my predecessors—from the caveman with his club to the elegant European rake—are saying in my Jungian unconscious: *Conquer her!*

The conflict between men and women is going on underneath the sheets every night in America and the rest of the post-industrial world. Many men are still defending their positions by automatic repetition of old macho behavior.

An eighteen-year-old San Diego journalist writes, "My boyfriend has remained the aggressor and dominant partner in lovemaking. It is necessary for him to believe he is in control of the situation. When my sexual abilities and appetites grew to match his own, he became almost nervous about sleeping together, fearing he may not be able to perform as expected. He could not cope with a sex partner who could keep up with him or demand more from him."

Historically the purpose of sex has been for reproduction rather than recreation. In the reproductive definition of sex, the male orgasm is the central act. A man needs to come to conceive, while a woman doesn't. So sex is built and structured around the all-crucial male ejaculation of sperm into the vagina.

The pill and other birth-control measures, and the women's consciousness movement of the 1960s and 1970s have changed all that.

The male rules for sexuality ended when the resexualized woman met the Sexual Revolution. Equality is now the name of the game. In the popular indoor recreation, the female orgasm has moved to center stage. And it's thrown competitive man for a sexual loop.

The man's function on the planet has been to provide. Molded into the psyche of every man is the thought: To be a man is to be the provider. The Protestant ethic joined the Sexual Revolution in the hay, and the man now has to provide orgasms for himself *and* his woman. A man feels like more of a man if he can make his woman come.

Men used to fulfill the requirements of masculinity by devirginizing women, but the Sexual Revolution created new frontiers for sexual skill and accomplishment. Today there is a growing shortage of female virgins. The new male sexual frontier is the quantity and quality of female orgasm. In the post-feminist era, man claims he can give orgasms to a woman better than the next man. Big! Bigger! Best!

The new song of Competitive Man is: "I can last longer! I can satisfy her with my incredible tongue tricks! I can show her moves she's never felt. I can be more sensitive, more delightfully vulnerable, and more communicative than her last lover! I can give her a night she'll never forget!"

"The woman's orgasm, newly discovered," writes Berkeley sex therapist Michael Rossman in an unpublished paper, "has immediately become an obligatory goal for the man to 'make happen,' putting his own 'selfish' pleasure aside—and reinforcing dysfunction—in a curious convolution of undiminished sexism."

The New Man wants to leave his woman totally satisfied—she is the consumer and he is the seller—because in the new consumer sex game of the liberated seventies and eighties, the women have their union—they talk together, they share stories, they have their rating systems.

It's no longer, "How many times did you do it to her last night?" Now it's, "How many times did she get off?" The man now says, "Did she get an orgasm? She got eighty-five orgasms in eighty-five seconds! Nonstop!" "Louise hasn't stopped screaming!"

Men no longer go to bed for their pleasure, for themselves, for their selfish orgasm. Men go to bed to give women pleasure. This creates enormous pressure on the female who has got to produce an orgasm to make the man feel like a man and on the man who can't even enjoy himself anymore. He performs in sex so he can fulfill his male conditioning and brag to other men when the subject comes up. And if boasting is not his style, a little wink will do.

Sex therapists report a fascinating development. Males are coming to them in droves, and the major complaint is a new one: "I fear that I cannot satisfy the woman." As one California sex therapist commented, "It's hard to find a selfish man anymore. Men are more interested in their partner's pleasure than in their own."

The need to prove sexual expertise was so great for some men we interviewed that they said to us, "I promise you I'm really good in sex. Let me give you my girlfriend's phone number; call her and find out if you don't believe me."

Competition builds poison into every sexual relationship with the fear: There will always be another man down the block who can satisfy her more!

Another man! More!

In these transitional times, men and women are sexually confused. First-night sex is tense, because nobody knows the other, and mind-reading often fails. Short-time sex becomes performance sex. Sustaining a positive sexual relationship becomes even more difficult.

Unhappiness reigns in this anarchic era of musical beds. Along with every other crisis, we are living through a relationship crisis in the resolution of the power changes between men and women. Sex is confused and pressured, so often asexuality becomes the most popular form of sexual communication. Even the sexual radicals have reappeared as sexual conservatives, seeking meaning in their body communications.

Male sexual behavior received a great deal of criticism in the seventies from women. They said that "Men come too quickly and then stop." "They don't want to just play and cuddle in bed." "Sex is too businesslike for them." At the same time, men felt under pressure to have The Constant Erection and to be sexually in charge.

Although men still dominate, sexually as well as otherwise, the pendulum is beginning to swing the other way. Roles, goals and images are beginning to change. The power of media increases communication and information flow. Changes that ordinarily would take centuries can now occur in decades. With that speed of change in media-dominant America, the switch in expectations taking place in bed is capable of liberating us over the next years from our past sexual-emotional prisons into new expressions of loving.

We are at a historic juncture in the history of human sexuality, going from centuries-old domination of the male orgasm to emphasis in the 1970s on female orgasm to the future—a period of equality of orgasm and intimacy between people unclouded by old sexual myths and false expectations.

The Sexual Revolution, a positive step for humanity, is incomplete. The Female Sexual Revolution contributed to the potential for sexual equality. A change in *male* consciousness and in the meaning of sexuality is needed to complete the promise of the Sexual Revolution, and to move away from the exaggerated emphasis on sex to an emphasis on relationship.

Men are in a bind. Everyone concentrates on women's problems, and nobody pays attention to men's internal concerns. Men are unable to talk with one another about sex because of their enormous sensitivity to the subject, and their identification of sex with masculinity and self-worth.

An entire literature of female sexual communication has transformed the country in the past fifteen years. Writers like Germaine Greer, Shere Hite, Ellen Frankfort, Ingrid Bengis, Ellen Willis, Erica Jong, Nancy Friday, Sandra Hochman, Robin Morgan, Betty Friedan, Alix Shulman, and thousands of unknown but equally eloquent women have changed the quality of female sexual conversation.

Today many more women talk with one another about sex. Women have turned each other into a huge support group. Women have shared themselves with each other.

Men have not.

Men are buddies, but they do not talk honestly with each other about sex. (The only exception is the very small, but important men's consciousness network that exists across the country.) Most men discuss their sexual accomplishments—few ever discuss their problems or fears—with other men.

There's the compulsion to keep up a good front. "I am considered by most people to be a highly successful rack partner," writes M.B. of Punta Gorde, Florida. "The frequency of my sexual escapades is said to be very high—but believe me it certainly isn't. I have *all* the sexual fears and anxieties and some that aren't documented. But you'd never know it. I have built a wall that no one can climb and I rarely let anyone see through its portals."

Men today are going to sex therapists more than ever before. Male sexual problems are on a steady incline. Male sexual worry, avoidance, feelings of failure and lack of satisfaction flourish.

"You think I'm going to be found sitting in a sex doctor's office? People would look at me and say what are you doing here?" said Phil Donahue, illustrating the embarrassment of male sexual problems, on his nationally syndicated TV show.

Male sexual fears are everywhere—in the Pentagon, Congress, Hollywood, on Wall Street, on television, throughout the offices, farms, and factories of America. Although some evidence exists to suggest that these fears increase in men as educational level rises, sexual paranoia is not tied to socioeconomic level. Our status as lovers is completely intertwined with our sense of self-worth; masculinity for all men is, in the words of sexologist John Money, "the kingpin of your identity, the anchor of your emotional health." Most men equate their ability to give a good sexual performance with their masculinity.

Men have not focused on their problems because they could always blame the woman: She is too frigid, too rejecting, too uptight, too distant. Now that women have exploded the myths of female sexuality, the spotlight falls on men. As sex researcher Edward Brecher pointed out in 1969, "As typhoid fever disappeared . . . a whole series of other kinds of fever previously mistaken for typhoid fever came into view. It is my personal belief that we are on the brink of such a development in the field of human sexuality. Many cases of *male sexual inadequacy (sic) now mistakenly attributed to female frigidity* are likely to come to diagnosis as preventive and therapeutic measures gradually whittle away the frigidity problem." (Italics ours.)

More than ten years later, many men are living lives of quiet sexual desperation, and communication about sex is at a low point. Male sexual anxiety abounds: the man who worries, "What does she think?"; the man who brags, "I'm the best lover in town," but fears he's not; the man who feels he's failed in bed. Other men are confused, not knowing what others expect of him or even what he should expect of himself. In the 1980s male sexuality must be rethought, much as female sexuality was in the 1970s.

Report from the Sexual Battlefield

This book climaxes my nine-year study of sexuality, beginning in the early 1970s, when disturbed by occasional nonerection, petrified by the word "impotence," and overwhelmed by the demands of the Male Sexual Credo, I began a special therapy and health program. I visited therapists, read sex books, took workshops, interviewed men and women, and learned everything I could about men and sex. As a cultural historian, I felt that my pressures were not mine alone, but reflected the dramatic changes in sexual expectations of the past twenty years.

I realized how sexually ignorant I was at the beginning. How many myths I entertained! I could not be that unique—my fears were shared by many men.

A man in desperate search of his sexuality can find himself in some very funny situations. Did you ever feel that your life was a Woody Allen comedy, only sometimes without the humor? I go into bookstores and turn to the index and read every word written about "impotence" and "premature ejaculation" and "anxiety." I learn very little.

In *Growing (Up) At 37*, I described some of my experiences with yoga, Zen, Fischer-Hoffman psychic therapy, est, Reichian therapy, jogging, bioenergetics, health foods, sex therapy, massage, acupuncture, and rolfing. But it was the thirteen pages that I wrote about sex that created the most interest for readers, particularly because it is the rare man who admits that he is not a killer in bed, who shares publicly his experiences with nonerection, premature ejaculation, asexuality, apathy, sexual confusion and awkwardness about pleasing a woman. Men wrote to thank me for discussing the unmentionable. I wrote:

I am a typically obsessed American male—obsessed about performance, the size of my cock, competition, jealousy, and control . . . In bed with my lover I lay the heaviest head trip of

all on my body: How well am I *performing?* . . . Because I have
judged myself in bed and am scared that I may go soft, I have
often avoided sexual contact.

Women responded even more positively to this open discussion
about male sexuality because, after all, it is women who spent time with
our male defenses in bed. Women have as much to gain as men when it
comes to the potential liberation of male consciousness.

I began writing this book as my personal sexual story—my
evolution from a sexual "loser" to "winner." I concluded that my story
touched on themes of a common experience, and I asked Mimi Leonard
to help conceive and to coauthor the book with me, as a general cultural
study, and as a kind of self-help book, too. We used my experiences
and those of other men and women as illustrations of general themes.

Much has been written about the modern dilemma of the woman.
Little has been written sensitively about the sexual drama from a man's
point of view. Since men have historically been the researchers of sex,
we seem to believe that we are beyond study. Very little nonmacho
writing has been done by men on sex.

Mimi and I think the unusual contribution of this self-help book is
that it comes from experience. It doesn't come from the detached expert
who drops advice and instant analysis, while he's nowhere to be seen.
He says that men must be more vulnerable and intimate with their
inner selves, yet he never reveals his inner self, because self-revealing
would be inconsistent with the style of professor, psychiatrist, expert,
therapist—or man. You hear what should be done for your problems,
but you never imagine that your expert has any problems.

Mimi and I created the Male Sexual Anxiety Research Project,
distributing a long questionnaire about men and sex to Howard Smith's
column in the *Village Voice*, letters in *Forum, Crawdaddy, Playgirl, New
Sun, New Dawn* and the *Berkeley Barb*. We also handed out copies of the
questionnaire at some of my lectures on college campuses. We
distributed questionnaires to workshops we did together on sex and
intimacy at the Association for Humanistic Psychology in Princeton,
New Jersey, and for the AHP chapter in Washington, D.C.

We received more than five hundred essay responses. They came
from every part of the country and from all social strata, were often
written in longhand, often anonymously, and revealed the intense
desire to communicate about aspects of sex that everyone thinks about
but few dare mention.

For Mimi and myself, the responses to the questionnaire revealed
the necessity for the book. More than 60% of the respondents to a
questionnaire about men were from women! Women poured out their

hearts about relating to men. The minority of men who wrote revealed emotional vulnerability—a direction men may be headed for in the 1980s.

"I am impotent," writes David, twenty-one, from Toronto. Yet David says that he cannot talk about the problem with girlfriends, male friends or parents. He pours out his heart to us for five pages and then writes, "So! Thanks for listening! It's sure good to tell someone!"

We have quoted liberally throughout the book from these people and told some of their stories. We make no correlations with age, occupation, class. The significance of the responses is not statistical or scientific. The purpose is to end the mystique of sexual secrets and to break certain taboos about sexual conversation.

In addition, our research included thirty in-depth interviews with men and women on the subject of male-female sexual communication. The pattern was the same: Women are open and men closed-mouthed on the sensitive subjects of male sexual vulnerability. In this book, women tell men what they really want sexually. And that makes sense, because women are the true experts on male sexuality: a woman can experience more than one man. Heterosexual men generally have seen and experienced only one man—themselves.

Our goal is to describe an important ongoing sexual reality in the United States. Our emphasis is on men and women and heterosexuality, not homosexuality. This report from the sexual battlefield has as its purpose the discovery of the tools that people can use to free themselves from oppression, so that we can take control of our intimate lives, and begin relating to each other.

The Male Sexual Pep Talk

A forty-five-year-old man sat in a New York coffee shop and revealed his experience after his divorce. He moved into a condominium in Florida full of single and divorced women in their thirties and forties and "I became convinced that it was my male responsibility to fuck every day. If I missed a day, I felt like I was not a man."

When he came back to New York he began hanging around with the guys at the Athletic Club. They greeted him, "How you been doing? You getting laid?" He began talking about his exploits until, while boasting, he realized it was all a big charade and he neither enjoyed the fucking nor the talking about it, but was doing it to be "one of the guys."

"I said that I was finally tired of sex, because it was no fun anymore, it was a performance and it was expected of me. One by one over the next few weeks, the men came up to me quietly, so the others wouldn't hear them, and told me they agreed: sex was too much of a performance. It finally convinced me that locker-room talk is a lot of bull, and we men are all sexual liars. We are scared shitless of being thought of as failures in the sack."

In sex, men have a tendency to view their penises as objects separate from themselves. And then to compare them in competition with other men. Ted, a twenty-two-year-old researcher in a laboratory in Cleveland, never gave much thought to the size of his penis. One day, as he describes it, "I was doing errands with a friend's girlfriend. We were talking about penis sizes and she pleasantly recounted an encounter with a nine-inch prick. It made me nervous; I had never been so voluptuous. I wondered: Is my penis too small? Has this ever gone noticed but unspoken with any of my lovers? Could this mean sexual inadequacy?"

That night Ted could not sleep. He reviewed all of his previous relationships and how they ended, and was overcome with paranoia. He began to torture himself: "Am I sexually inadequate?" As he explained later, "I have yet to meet a man willing to discuss—or even admit to—these concerns. Of course, it is difficult to broach the subject in the first place."

Feeling lonely and scared, Ted got out of bed, went into the kitchen, and got a yardstick. He went to the mirror and measured. "The reading was four inches or a shade less, limp. I felt that was all right. I relaxed and finally fell asleep. But I still worry: Am I sexually adequate? And it's these kind of worries that keep me up at night."

And then the embarrassment of premature ejaculation. Jim became very turned on in the mattress room at Plato's Retreat. He had one of those giant erections, and shortly was embracing and kissing the neck of Rayann, a juicy woman who looked to him like Sophia Loren. Bodies pulsated all around. Jim became suddenly anxious and began losing his erection. Rayann did everything she could to keep him hard. She sucked, bathed, tickled, tantalized. And she won! Jim got his erection.

But then he lost it again. He galloped on top of Rayann and lying on her, humped and humped, and back came his erection. This time Jim was taking no chances.

He came immediately on Rayann's stomach.

This is an example of how a man can make an asshole of himself in bed. But then, so what? Isn't that what sex is anyway? Sex is making a fool of yourself, exposing yourself as an asshole. That's why sex is so intimate. Making mistakes is one of the most revealing and intimate moments of sexual communication.

We men have shut ourselves off from information about our bodies through both shame and Superman notions about ourselves. Every man is expected to be Clark Kent in clothes during the day, and Superman naked in bed. We are the Lone Ranger in sex, rescuing a damsel in distress with our silver bullets.

Men compete over length of time spent in the vagina: "I fucked five hours straight!" Men have tremendous pride over their ability to last long in the act of intercourse. One day a cocksman bragged to us about how much control he had over his ejaculation reflex. "I decide when I come, not my penis," he said, almost with a note of contempt for what he called "Roger."

As Richard Pryor says, "Dudes always used to tell that lie, 'I can fuck eight, nine hours, Mac.' You some lyin' motherfuckers. You fuck nine hours, we know where to bury yo' ass on the tenth. 'Cause I like makin' love myself, and I can do about three minutes of serious fucking and then I need eight hours of sleep . . . and a bowl of Wheaties."

His audiences roar in laughter, feeling compassion for Pryor's raw honesty. Such an unusual nonmacho public admission by a well-known Macho Man indicates that a change in masculine honesty may be starting to take place in America today.

Pryor introduced a character in his recent filmed stage tour, Macho Man. Macho Man defends himself against attackers in the street rather than running away. Macho Man can give his woman an orgasm no matter what the odds. Macho Man, however, finds himself in the hospital nursing a broken bone and "It's a lot easier to mend a broken ego than a broken jaw," jokes Pryor. Macho Man is kind of an automatic fool. In a sense, Pryor is satirizing himself, the Macho Man inside Richard Pryor. Every man has a sexual Macho Man inside him. Do we control him or does he run our lives?

Some part of each man believes the Male Sexual Pep Talk:

I am the active one in sex and the woman is passive. I do "it" to her. I get my penis up whenever I want to, and it should stay up as long as I want it to stay up. The penis is the center of sexuality for me and my female partner. My goal is simultaneous orgasm, but I will be satisfied with at least one terrific orgasm each. I could satisfy any woman if I chose to do so. I control my ejaculation. Once in my woman's vagina I will pump and pump until I decide to ejaculate. I can do all this better than almost any other man!

The Male Sexual Credo demands that every man be sexual. Pity the poor man who confesses a lack of interest in sex for whatever reason, from fear to a consuming interest in another activity. The guilt associated with asexuality in this era of sexual promotion is overwhelming.

The potential sexual problems men face today can overwhelm the pleasure they receive from sex. Even worse, sexual worries can prevent men from enjoying a relationship with a woman so the isolation of the individual is increased in the already anomic environment of the 1980s. Sexual hype must give way to honesty and enjoyment of physical, intimate experiences.

Breaking the Conspiracy of Male Sexual Silence

For many years I had sexual secrets which I guarded jealously. These secrets tormented me until I made a discovery: the anguish of sexual secrets evaporates when they are revealed and shared. So let me be one of the first men to publicly break the male conspiracy of sexual silence.

I am sexually anxious. I have not always been able to produce erections when I wanted them. I have ejaculated "prematurely." I've met women that I thought I could not and did not satisfy sexually. I have, at times, performed well in sex and not enjoyed it, because I was working so hard. I have gone through periods of happy and miserable asexuality.

I even hid my penis from women during sex—and that takes acrobatics, believe me! But I couldn't face up to the possibility that when I pulled down my pants, my partner would look at me and scream, "But it's so small!"

The barriers in sexual communication have resulted in sex being a greater source of pain than pleasure for me in my life. I have always been more aware of what I was not getting than what I was getting. And I couldn't talk with other men because I didn't want to be ridiculed or humiliated. I couldn't talk with women because I didn't want to seem less a man.

I went to bed with a woman I had been courting for months. I felt aroused but not erect, but still felt good hugging and kissing, with my finger moving inside her. She leaped on top of me, moving her clitoral area hard against my leg. It felt good to be used sexually. I took it as a compliment, an expression of vulnerability and contact. She came, and we held each other in our arms. Everything was perfect except one thing: my mind.

Deep down in my male psyche was the unconscious voice that said that she was secretly upset because I did not overpower and fuck her. I was not upset, but my fear that she was upset created a doubt within me.

I thought: If I were really a man, I would sweep this woman off her feet and give her the most overwhelming hard fuck she has ever experienced in her life, something to remember me by forever. Even if she says that she does not want it, she will thank me when it's over.

Decades of D.H. Lawrence readers grew up on such psychic milk. Female resistance increases the necessity of the act. *We* know what the female unconscious wants. Germaine Greer points out that "the penis is conceived as a weapon, and its action upon women is understood to be somehow destructive and hurtful. It has become a gun, and in English slang women say when they want their mates to ejaculate, 'Shoot me! Shoot me!'" Deep down within our male dominating psyche we men experience the nagging, nonstop fear that we have let down our manhood by not overpowering a woman and napalming her pussy.

How could I ever be reassured? It's hip these days to reassure men that they need not be domineering beasts. Underneath the hipness, what is she really thinking? Or feeling? Then again, if she is upset, it may only be because she thinks I am upset.

Even if I ask, and she tells me, I will not completely believe her. It's the male fear of female sexual insatiability.

It's a no-win, circular, self-punishment game, attempting to mind-read each other's sexual-psychic unconscious. We become uptight because of what we think she may be thinking. We are afraid that a question might break "the mood."

Is sex intimacy? Some say the two concepts are synonymous, but others point to the paradox of being impersonal in the act of sex. Germaine Greer described that contradiction in consciousness: "We still make love to organs and not people; that so far from realizing that people are never more idiosyncratic, never more totally *there* than when they make love, we are never more incommunicative, never more alone."

Few human activities are so tied up in R. D. Laing's "psychic knots" as is sex. Men and women often make love to each other in separate mental and emotional compartments, not sharing their deepest selves. Alone in the most intimate act.

A Second Look at "Sex Therapy" and Women's Liberation

A well-respected Chicago psychiatrist was at our home one night for dinner, bitterly referring to her last relationship with a man who consistently failed to get erections with her. "He was withholding from me on a very deep level by being impotent," she said, starkly. She took nonerection personally, and interpreted it as a condemnation of herself. She became so angry that they stopped touching each other and eventually slept in different beds in the same room to avoid a crisis every night. Her constant use of the word "impotent" with us barely masked her fury. We realized, ironically, that no male today could get away with calling a woman "frigid" in mixed company. The concept of frigidity is rightly seen as an attack on women. Yet "impotence" thrives.

Only a hater of men would use the word "impotence," just as only a hater of women would use the word "frigidity." The sex therapy establishment, medical doctors, sex magazines, and the church and synagogue use the word. Psychiatrists and therapists are as responsible for this mental cruelty as anyone else. Sexologists from Masters and Johnson on down define a man as "impotent" if he cannot enter a woman with his penis. One wonders why people-helpers would equate "potency" with intercourse, accepting, however unconsciously, centuries of repressive education.

Dr. Helen Singer Kaplan, considered the dean of sex therapists, calls the word impotent "objectionable, not only because it is pejorative, but also because it is inappropriate." But then, like virtually the entire sex therapy community, she goes right ahead and continues to use it over and over again. Sex therapists are not getting us to look at sex differently when they act like doctors, identifying diseases and dispensing medicines and cures. In the case of "impotence," the diagnosis can create the disease.

Michael Carrera, highly-regarded sex educator, agreed with us. "If you could convince sex therapists to stop using those words and concepts," he said, "you'll revolutionize sex therapy in a very positive way."

The sex therapists finally stopped their overuse of the word "impotence" and created a euphemism. But nothing is lost in the translation—in fact, some might prefer to be called "impotent." The word they chose to use and promote was "dysfunctional."

With a word like that, you begin to feel like a washing machine. The words and concepts of "function" and "dysfunction" should immediately be dropped—in all discussions of sex and lovemaking—from the language of psychiatrists, psychologists, sexologists and all other professionals.

Norman King, a movie producer, shared with us his frustration with doctors and sex therapists:

> Go to a doctor and tell him you can't get it up and he says something like, "What do you want, to be like you were when you were eighteen?" Downer talk! And Masters and Johnson are no help to men, because you need a female partner to go through therapy with you. But that's the problem, you're too sexually screwed up to find a partner in the first place! The sex therapists cop out just like the doctors! So men stop fucking and start lying. And people go crazy.
>
> I know an actor who read every article that had ever been written on the subject of impotence and he went to a dozen doctors in two months. Everyone had a different answer. He nearly committed suicide.

That's the delicious male double bind I faced, too—I needed a partner to grow sexually with but I was too anxious to find one. I wanted to improve but I had no one to improve with. A sex therapist told me she wouldn't even see me at $100 an hour because I didn't have a partner.

"But I can't find a partner because I hate myself sexually," I said.

She looked at me blankly, as if to say, "Yes, I understand your dilemma but that's the way it is."

Ironically, while the fast-proliferating sex therapists perpetuate today's crisis in male adequacy with their language and attitudes, it might well be the women's movement—with its deemphasis on the penis and intercourse in sex—which will end up as the final liberators of masculinity, giving men a choice of who they want to be.

We are not sex therapists and this book is not a cookbook of therapeutic techniques. However, we do feel that when people change their expectations of sex, their "problems" often magically disappear. The process is obvious. Our minds create problems for our genitals.

As a veteran of hours with many different sex therapists, from surrogates to straight behavioristic sex therapists, I share much of what I learned. I feel that most sexual difficulties seem complex, but actually have simple solutions once you look at sex differently.

We are not social scientists and this book is not another research contribution in the tradition of Kinsey or Shere Hite, important as those studies were. Our polled and interviewed subjects serve only as guides on a sexual journey.

The book is not a polemic. We talk about the problems of both men and women. We are not trying to make men or women the "bad guys" in a right-wrong social drama. This is an interaction between people in the roles of male and female.

We know that our vision constantly conflicts with our conditioning. Sexually, it seems the more we change, the more we stay the same, forever repeating the patterns of the past.

The purpose of this book is *not* to describe the overall reality of male dominance over women today. Men do have the power, both economic and physical. The abuses of male domination are clear, from rape to wife-beating to unwanted pregnancies to economic oppression.

The domination by men has been detailed in a library of books and articles. There is no need for us to do that in this book. What has not been done is to show how men are oppressed by their own domination. We want to show how male oppression victimizes men. Our goal is to help free women by convincing men (and women) that male freedom lies with female emancipation and shared power.

Our purpose is to help men and women redefine manhood and masculinity, and to assist the millions of individuals who are personally lost in this period of sexual confusion.

THE FEMALE ORGASM UPSETS THE
SEXUAL BALANCE OF POWER

Sexual Technology

As Carol Marks indicates in her unpublished study of sexual symbolism through the centuries, sex has been a metaphor in each culture. The Greeks used water symbols for sex because they lived near the flowing rivers. The Romans idolized the horse and described sex with horselike names. America worships science, the machine, technology, the computer. In America, our sex is technological, with terms like screw, insert, put our tool in the hole, all industrial metaphors. The technical term becomes "coitus." We are judged for our "performance." Sociologist Philip Slater points out that, "The use of an engineering term like 'adequacy' in relation to an act of pleasure exemplifies the American gift for turning everything into a task."

The Sexual Revolution enhanced the technological definition of sex, conditioning all of us to work to achieve pleasurable ends. The technological society does not preach process. It preaches results. Men become technicians in bed with goals, results, ratings, scores and competition. The technological society invades the bedroom with concepts like "dysfunction." The technological society recreates sex in its own thought mode: a series of well-planned steps leading to the "result"—climax of orgasm.

The pressure for pleasure and technologically correct sexual fun advances through the land. Only the asexual is left in the closet, and sexual anxiety hides beneath the covers. "This is after all the 1980s," writes a college sophomore from the University of Pittsburgh, "and if you didn't spend adolescence fucking like bunnies at least you don't let on. Especially at college, where we are all 'enlightened,' and anxiety is repressed and not discussed."

In our sexually obsessive culture, sexual performance is a primary criterion for judging oneself and others. We are all victims of this overemphasis on a limited definition of sex. Raised in overt prohibition, living in a land of male competitiveness and high-pressure sex salesmanship, is it any wonder that many of us feel like sexually driven laboratory rabbits, upset when we can't satisfy either our no-no past or our fantasy future?

The Sexual Revolution took place without a corresponding transformation of sexual consciousness, and therefore it magnified the underlying angst of both men and women. Instead of liberation, we have competition, domination, miscommunication and worship of technique.

The problem with sex today lies in its mythology. So many myths!

They prevent people from relating intimately to one another. These sexual myths feed the Sexual Industry.

The merger of sex with profit has turned sex into an exploitative, expanding consumer market. Sex is used to sell products. Sex surrounds us, a powerful economy of media, recreation, self-improvement, service, and manipulation. And still more and more people feel sexually inadequate and starved for affection and touch.

Sex therapists, despite their use of terms like "impotence" and "dysfunction," are today serving the role of modern medicine men, reversing centuries of parental prohibition by giving repressed men and women permission to enjoy their bodies.

We are sexually transitional people today, children of centuries of orthodox religion's conditioning, living in a world of hedonistic permissiveness. Within every individual in America is the tension between sexual repression and the modern pressure for sexual experimentation and liberation.

The Sexual Cowboy's "Blue Balls"

Over twenty years ago, in the "easy" sexual days of the 1950s, the man was king. A male friend said to us recently, "I'm glad that I got in at least ten good years of chauvinistic fucking before women's liberation." In the fifties it was the man who got off and the woman who submitted. We used to have an expression: "Did you get any bare tit?" Saturday night was the challenge, then Monday morning we bragged to each other how much we got. And Monday night we exaggerated the conquest even more in our minds as we made love to our sheets.

Lenny Bruce said that women don't understand men because if a man does not have a woman around, he'll fuck a tree. If a woman would fuck a tree, you'd say she was a "nymphomaniac." But a tree-fucking man is normal, strong, powerful. And that all comes, allegedly, from biological need, because we learned the superstition of "blue balls"—if you aroused yourself without ejaculating, your balls might turn blue, and you'd be irritable all day. Let go, eject, you'll feel better. A man needs to ejaculate for his mental health.

Sex was, for men, a process of overcoming and conquering obstacles: from meeting a woman, to striking up a conversation, to seducing and luring her into bed, to getting her clothes off, to getting an erection, entering the vagina, and ejaculating. The obstacle course made sex exciting and dramatic.

The fifties was a time of the automobile and the exploitative orgasm. You saw someone who turned you on and invited her into your car. The scene of sexual education was the dry hump in the back seat. The standard weekend drama: Would she or wouldn't she?

I was in a drive-in movie, or in a park, or wherever I could park my car without getting chased by cops. I wanted her hand on my cock, my hands down her bra and on her boobs, and I wanted to be grabbing her in my arms and kissing her madly.

I would put my arm around her shoulder, waiting for the appropriate response. Does she soften, does she stiffen? I finally figured out the ultimate car-hump test. You try to put your finger in her mouth. If she bites it lightly, she's ready for play. If she rejects it, you're not going to get with your penis what a tongue wouldn't give your finger.

If all signals were go, I would soon be on top of the girl in the front seat, the steering wheel invariably banging me in the head. If I felt relaxed, and figured that she wouldn't lose interest in the switch, I'd suggest we move to the back seat, rushing so not to break the mood. I'd passionately move on top of the girl and then I'd come in my pants in a few seconds of ecstasy.

It was a typical male orgasm. The ejaculation seemed to wash away all my loose nervousness. I was glad that the woman allowed herself to be the backdrop to the release of my pent-up energy.

After coming, I would fight a wave of shame and embarrassment. Sitting up, I'd wipe the sperm away, and guiltily drive away with the girl in my arms. Not a word was said about what just happened. I would try to feel good again. After all, I saw, conquered, and came. Conquest!

Wasn't that what women were for? For instance, some of my college fraternity buddies were once arrested on the complaint of the father of a fourteen-year-old girl who said that they "gang-banged" her at a party. I wouldn't participate in such a conquest, but I would get as much as I could from girls in cars in the 1950s.

Still, I felt in high school that everybody was getting more of "it" than me. I nodded my way through male conversation while listening to the other guys talk about women: "She has great tits . . . What an ass . . . Didja catch those knockers?"

Steve Martin satirizes this approach to women: "Yes, she was witty, she was intelligent. She was born of high station. She spoke and walked proudly. She was the kind who displayed nobility, who showed style and class. But above all, she had the jugs."

If I had objected to the conversation, the other guys would have looked at me with contempt and said, "What's the matter, you don't

like women? You a sissy?" I did everything I could so they would not
think of me as a "sissy."

The Good Girl and the Bad Girl

Since my mother was asexual, the only women I truly respected
were asexual. Naturally I wanted to marry an asexual woman, so that I
could truly respect her. I'd conquer and overwhelm her asexuality for
my own pleasure. I divided women into good and bad; the bad
provided the raw material for your exploitative, impersonal releases.
There was not even the vaguest thought of impotence or premature
ejaculation. Premature to what, you would have asked? Men separated
sex from emotion. Sex was getting off.

Traditionally the man's biggest complaint against the female was
her passivity, that she just lies there like a lump or a board. We males
used to ask each other, "Does she move?" In other words, does she
pretend? The man still believed in the Great American Myth, the
simultaneous orgasm. To bolster the myth, the woman often manufac-
tured screams at the precise moment the man was egoistically involved
in his orgasmic voodoo. It was theater—both partners playing their
roles. The better acting the woman did, the faster the man came. Men
believed that all women experienced orgasms through intercourse. The
will to believe, buttressed by the merger of sex with ego, convinced the
fragile success-conscious male that their pleasure meant female pleasure, too.

Dr. Irving London describes what he calls a recurring story he
heard while doing "frigidity" counseling:

> The man of the house would come home, have a couple of
> drinks, eat dinner, plop down in front of the television, drift
> off into a semistuporous state, and be helped to bed by his
> wife. Revived to a half-awake condition by this activity, he
> finds the stamina to roll over on top of his beloved and
> following a few furtive swipes, plunges home for a two-
> minute stint as he falls asleep. She, dejected, depressed,
> frustrated and guilt-ridden, lies in bed asking herself, "What's
> wrong with me? Why can't I climax?"

Purpose of Female Virginity: Men had most women where they were
sexually safe—asexual. No multiple orgasms, no huge sexual demands,

no indiscriminate screwing around, not much sexual experience. Women wanted to be virgins and then one-man women. Asexual women confirmed our Victorian, Judeo-Christian definition of women as passive and of sex as dirty. Sexuality, therefore, depended on our penile whims, and if we screwed around, it was because our ferocious male sexuality could not be contained.

One can easily see why men wanted to keep women virgins. It was easier for men when they could control the women's sexual experience. With an inexperienced woman, conditioned never to talk about sex, there was no possibility of a negative ruling. She had no penises to compare to his. He had no fear of her comparing her performance or looking elsewhere for more satisfaction. With women today, freer to pursue their own sexual impulses, the male fear of sexual embarrassment is increased. Today a woman knows all the facts about how you make love, and the intimate details of your sexual style, and she can easily compare you to other men she has experienced.

The Sexual Revolution Does Not Revolutionize Sex

The Sexual Revolution started in the 1920s, but it burst open in the 1960s. It combatted the historical idea that sex is dirty, thus liberating the body and encouraging the acceptance of sensual-sexual pleasure. However, it was still a revolution designed primarily for men. "Sexual freedom" meant that more women were free for men to fuck. "What's the matter, are you hung up or something?" was the question, with the implied ultimate insult to the woman of being called "uptight."

Many sexual promoters saw the connection between sex and love as a continuation of the Puritan tradition. Therefore the banner of impersonal sex flew high. In its extreme form, a street leaflet during the late sixties in Berkeley said: "Sleep with a stranger tonight." Lester Levinson, the founder of New York's Plato's Retreat, where people pay $50 a couple to join hundreds of others in naked sex in the mattress room of the spa, says, "Sex has nothing to do with love."

Sex often has little to do with liking, either. An anonymous woman from Akron, Ohio, writes, "When I was single, I must have gone through a hundred men. I was often used, meaning I gave in to any guy who said nice things to me, then I'd never see him again because he got what he wanted and was on the prowl for his next lay. And what the man wanted was a wham-bang and it's all over. I love to be dominated, but not to the point of being used and cast aside."

Many men look to sex for a quick ego victory and a fast tension release. If you take away the power, the sexual interest of many men diminishes. The first time, I was excited. Sexual conquest propelled me. In the role of the pursuer, it's the chase that is the most exciting aspect of the sex act. The second time, the mystery would be gone. I might be turned off. Success brings with it a diminution of sexual desire and a rise in sexual self-consciousness.

Historically, the man's orgasm has been the center of the sex act. In the seventies the woman's orgasm became the main event, and we moved from the tyranny of the male orgasm to the tyranny of the female orgasm.

The Cowboy Meets the Clitoris

One sexual play of the 1970s and 1980s:

He is not dysfunctional.
She is.
She becomes orgasmic.
He becomes dysfunctional.

The Male Sexual Revolution inevitably led to the discovery of the clitoral orgasm. More and more women began discovering that they could enjoy sex by changing the script. "I don't want my partner to dominate me," says one woman. "We are partners." Another adds, "I hate the old image of the passive woman. I definitely am not her."

By the late sixties women had begun writing articles, published first in the underground press, telling each other how to have orgasms through masturbation. The implication was: Since he won't or doesn't know how to satisfy you, learn from your sisters. Books became weapons in the Female Sexual Revolution. *Fear of Flying* depersonalized men, advocated sexual self-interest, and promoted female erotic pleasure. *The Hite Report* claimed that masturbation was more effective than sex with a man. Penis envy? Remember Freud's theory? All of a sudden men began comparing orgasms with women and discovered clitoris envy. As one man explained his image of the new woman, "I come once. The clitoris can come and come one time right after another. I never even know when a woman is through with her orgasms for the night."

The old theater, where the man fucked for his ego and the woman pretended involvement, shut down when women stopped acting (feigning orgasm), and started wanting the real thing.

Women's consciousness burst out inside many a relationship in the 1970s, creating new expectations, and a new series of failed performances, self-condemnations, and guilt. Donna and her husband had been married for six years when in 1973 "he asked me one night where my clitoris was. I didn't have the foggiest idea. I had yet to have an orgasm, but I thought as long as he was satisfied, it didn't matter. By the time he killed himself, I had become convinced I was a lousy sex partner." The no-win cycle of self-reproach continues, despoiling the marital bed.

I had sex for years never knowing physiologically how a woman came. I kept thinking that something mysterious went on inside the vagina. The more you moved, the more you set off a process—that I couldn't understand—that resulted in heavy breathing, shaking, and sometimes, finally orgasm. When the man came, the woman must come too. Sexual magic! If she didn't, something was wrong with her. If the woman came, however, I claimed the credit. I was a damn good fucker.

The clitoris had been in all the textbooks. But nobody paid much attention to it until the women's movement organized politically around the orgasm, saying, "Now wait a minute, let's look at the clitoris." Women began writing about their own bodies, workshops appeared, and the clitoris moved to center stage. Many men, like myself, did not even know where it was. I may have known about it intellectually, but emotionally I never realized its hierarchical position in a woman's body: a little nob about a quarter-inch in diameter, like a miniscule penis under a hood about one-and-a-half inches or so *above* the vagina on the *outside* of the vaginal lips. The central source of female sexual pleasure! It hit with a blow to the male sexual ego that women were not getting orgasms directly through penile intercourse, but through physical contact with the clitoris.

The clitoris, in fact, is a little penis. It is, the biologists tell us, a "homologue" of the male penis. But with such power! Men heard, "The smallest clitoris has more staying power and more explosive ecstasy potential than the largest penis!"

Tony has just completed a five-week course for men on female sexuality. Such a course would have been unheard of ten years ago when men thought they knew everything they needed to know about female response. But Tony came out of the course with a modern myth; the New Male Fear regarding female orgasm and *female* blue balls.

We were having an intimate discussion about the challenges men now face in the sexual bed. I observed that women can have satisfactory sex without orgasm while men still need to orgasm "to feel like a man."

Tony said, "Yes, but women are in pain when they don't come. There is a flow of blood to the genital area and if there is no orgasm release for the woman, she will feel uptight and tense for the rest of the day."

It's the female version of the male blue balls. For centuries we men have been saying about ourselves: if we don't ejaculate, we feel tense. The circle is now reversed. Now it is generally accepted that nothing biologically harmful happens to men if they don't have orgasms. But the myth is out that women are physically upset if they are aroused without orgasmic release. Some women use this new orgasm conceit to force men to give them orgasms exactly as we men used our blue balls—or compulsion to orgasm—to manipulate women.

The topsy-turvy change of the past six years is illustrated by the current male jealousy over female sexual potential. Men may not admit it, but they are in a collective depression today over the orgasms of women. Women have supposedly gone from being nonorgasmic to being *super*orgasmic within the past ten years. Today's sexual mythology is that a woman's orgasmic capacity is limited only by her exhaustion level. Compare that to a man's fifteen-second special. The mythical woman goes on and on in levels and flows of increasing pleasure, ripples and ripples, waves and waves, in one series of orgasms after another.

The modern sexual educators perpetuate the new female image that drives men crazy. Listen to the world's most widely-read sexologist, Dr. David Reuben, on the subject: "Every woman in this world has more sexual potential packed into her pelvis than a corral full of wild stallions. Females are designed, equipped, and destined to have as many as forty orgasms an hour, three times a night, seven nights a week, fifty-two weeks a year. Fortunately, for the men of America, even though they have it, most women don't flaunt it."

Reuben's description sets up a paper tiger—a threat that only "a real man" would be able to confront and conquer! John Wayne would have had to be on his toes for a "corral full of wild stallions"!

Feminist writers also began describing women as sexually "insatiable." Listen to Mary Jane Sherfey: ". . . the more orgasms a woman has, the stronger they become; the more orgasms she has, the more she *can* have. To all intents and purposes, *the human female is sexually insatiable in the presence of the highest degrees of sexual stimulation."*

Unleashing female sexuality was like unleashing a Pandora's box of uncertainty for men. Can a man satisfy a woman with his penis? How many orgasms should I "give" her? When does her orgasm end? Women were becoming like men and getting into sex as sex. Before, women were supposed to link sex only with love, which naturally limited female sexual expression.

We have gone in a few short years from the image of male sexual superiority to female sexual superiority. Little wonder these days so many men are suffering from sexual inferiority complexes, though not yet admitting it. Gore Vidal says, "The tyranny of female orgasm is really going to drive male heterosexuality to the wall."

Men Take Their Briefcases to Bed

It's gotten so that a man today feels that he must *earn* his own orgasm. One man wrote, "Usually I use my fingers and tongue all over her for about an hour before we *fully* start to work on me. This way I feel (hope) that she's had at least one orgasm so I can enjoy my own with a clear conscience."

Can you imagine taking your briefcase to the sandbox? Many women complain about this mechanical attitude of men. Suzie feels she is in bed with a penis attached to a machine, as Jim with technological mastery goes through the various stages from seduction to climax. Jim describes his functionality most vividly: "I work and work, and if I bring the woman to the Big O, then I get my reward: my orgasm." The reward follows the job well done.

The sexually advancing woman takes the initiative away from the man, and implies that she is making a demand for a sexual performance. Men feel that they have got to do more to be a man. Sex becomes an even more competitive technological exercise—a job. Rollo May characterizes this approach as a "kind of neopuritanism akin to that which our Puritan ancestors worked to achieve maximum business profits." No wonder sexual apathy has spread among men. Sex should be relaxed fun—or unfuck it!

Men are so much into successfully providing orgasms for women these days that some men report they are not disappointed when women act like traditional men and fall off to sleep after orgasm. "If my wife melts into a pool of pleasure in the middle of sex and falls sound asleep before I ejaculate, that's fine with me," writes a thirty-one-year-old ex-anti-war activist. "The feeling of being able to give so much pleasure is totally satisfying. I don't feel cheated."

Men have even begun talking and thinking like traditional women. "Basically, I think it's a good experience when women use me sexually," wrote a New Hampshire man.

I'm too Big a Man to Ask: Men seem to feel that to ask a woman, 'Are you satisfied?' is a betrayal of masculinity, because to be a man is to "know." Men are scared because, in spite of the changes—the "revolution"—we are supposed to be in charge, to be on top of every situation. That's how we were raised. To ask too many questions is to admit weakness. So we either convince ourselves that we know or we fall asleep confused and wondering.

The challenge: Should I ask her? Will my question be seen as an expectation or demand? Will it be an implied judgment? Will I put her on the spot? Will I sound like a child? Shouldn't I know?

Men are divided into two groups. One group is made up of those who claim to be sexual psychics, the accomplished mind readers, or more accurately, body-readers. These are the men who think they can tell the woman if she has had an orgasm.

The second group consists of men like the one who wrote us saying, "I never know if the woman I am with has climaxed."

Since women have been fooling the male ego for centuries about their orgasms, how can a man be absolutely certain today when a woman has enjoyed a climax? Ever mysterious, the woman may orgasm, but the man can never be sure if she wants to come again and again, or if that's just a myth, or if she's doing it to make him feel good, or to fulfill some expectation of what *she thinks* she's supposed to be capable of sexually.

"It's tough," confided Richard Pryor to journalist David Felton of *Rolling Stone,* "tough to ask a woman if she came. But it's also tough going to sleep without knowing." Pryor later told *Rolling Stone* interviewer Felton that it was the absolute truth that "I really only learned a year and a half ago that women didn't always have orgasms."

When play becomes work, fun changes to effort. As one man says, "It can be work trying to get my orgasm together at the same time with hers and make it magnificent. It may be work trying to get my woman to orgasm. For me, therefore, it becomes much better touching, feeling. And if I come—well, that's wonderful—but the important thing is that we really feel close together, and we're both really relaxed. I hate sex when it feels the least bit like work."

Overconcern with female orgasm creates insecurity in a man in sex. One woman describes the process, "During the sex act they seem very preoccupied, watching me intently to see if I'm enjoying it. They're too worried to get carried away themselves. They're nervous and distracted. They'll question me afterwards to make sure they're good lovers, or as good as other men."

Rollo May, in *Love and Will*, calls the "excessive concern for 'satisfying' the partner . . . an expression, however perverted, of a sound and basic element in the sexual act: the pleasure and experience of self-affirmation in being able to *give* to the partner."

May agrees that giving a woman an orgasm is considered an indispensible determinant of manhood:

> The man is often deeply graeful toward the woman who lets herself be gratified by him—lets him give her an orgasm, to use the phrase that is often the symbol for this experience. . . . Many a male cannot feel his own identity either as a man or as a person in our culture until he is able to gratify a woman.
>
> Now the problem is not the desire and need to satisfy the partner as such, but the fact that this need is interpreted by the persons in the sexual act only in a technical sense—giving physical sensation. What is omitted . . . is the experience of giving feelings, sharing fantasies, offering the inner psychic richness that normally takes a little time. . . .

The New Female "Performance Anxiety"

Ironically, orgasm, an experience of great pleasure, creates great agony in its absence. Men create confusion with the sexual lie that they must take responsibility for the woman's orgasm. Men guilt-trip themselves when she does not climax, and then blame themselves when they don't come.

The pressure of having to orgasm actually prevents people from taking the steps toward overcoming inhibitions and developing orgasmic sexual potential. The pleasure bed becomes the blame bed.

One man describes his frustration in a common male-female interaction in today's sexual battlefield:

> Lately I have become obsessed with being sure I have done all that I can to pleasure my partner, before I'll allow my own orgasm to take place. If she doesn't orgasm, I'd like to

know why, if she's willing to tell me. I have one very good friend who still has not had an orgasm with me, and we are working on it together. She and I took off her panties, and I started kissing her all over, and eventually ended up going down on her. I did this for over forty minutes and there were times she seemed to come close to orgasm, but she never let down and had one. Finally I had to take a break, and at that point she started to cry. We talked it over and she said she just couldn't orgasm. I felt awful.

As a woman from Toledo writes, "If the woman doesn't come in multiples, most men take it one of two ways. Either 'What's wrong with her that she can't come in multiples?' or 'What's wrong with me that I can't make her come in multiples?' But always the assumption that something is wrong, with one or the other. Well, maybe not literally *always*, but *damned often*. I wish men would leave me alone. I am not a multiclimax person. One good one. That's it."

Women are not fooled by the new male altruism for female sexual pleasure. They know that the "sensitive man" is still primarily concerned with his own self-image of masculinity in bed. The problem is summed up by J. H. of Rome, New York, who says, "A man who is more concerned with whether I 'came' is only thinking of himself—whether *he* had what it takes! And that's *using* me again." It's the old male sexual competition in a new guise, with the continuing search for female approval.

Male concern with female pleasure hasn't yet led to a more loving, intimate sex. Instead, the result has been confusion, miscommunication, and naked bodies relating to one another as images. Woman after woman wrote us that they wish men would stop pressuring them for orgasms. It's a new way for man to say, "Wasn't I good?" creating a male pride that, in fact, belies deep male insecurity. And to maintain male power: "I'm still in charge."

The desire and need to satisfy the partner becomes compulsive. Men make manhood a series of rules. The orgasm becomes the central focus. Men think in terms of goals, successes, victories, points, scores. And orgasms can be measured, while feelings cannot.

The male ego need to produce orgasms for women ends up in female "performance anxiety" as women feel they must "perform" to protect the man's dramatic ego. Her orgasm is part of his theatrical production. This new theatrical requirement doesn't take women far from where they were feigning simultaneous orgasms in the fifties and sixties. Women can get angry because his "need" to give her an orgasm results in her feeling that she must produce in sex to make him feel good. Who are we doing it for anyway? Is he doing it because *he* thinks that *she* expects it? It's the sexual Prison of Expectations, each person doing it for the other (without checking), and forgetting their own interests.

A woman writes, "I don't want him to 'try' to make me come. It's fine with me if he chooses to stop moving to postpone his own orgasm but if I feel he's got something invested in my coming, forget it! I will likely feel tense and not come."

I recall one female partner who became very exasperated with my "results-watching." She once stopped sex and said, "I never want you to think of my orgasm any more. You're putting too much pressure on me. You can do to me what feels good but never expect my orgasm. Promise me that."

"My biggest experience with male sexual anxiety is the man's belief a woman must come—every time he makes love to her," writes a Florida woman. "That was made convincingly evident to me when, within 48 hours of each other, my lover said, 'You *must* come every time with me,' and my husband told me, 'I take it as a personal insult if you don't come every time we make love.'"

The 1970s talk of multiorgasms struck terror in the hearts of men—and women. Myths of sex being easy for the woman become oppressive not only for the man who must match or deliver them, but also for women who now have a standard against which they can compare themselves and compete. A macho female mythology is no better than a male one. Thus women are starting to do to women what we men have been doing to each other for centuries: perpetuate a view of "inadequacy."

Is There Sex for Men after the Women's Movement?

When the women's movement first broke through, I felt threatened to the core of my being. I was baffled. You're conditioned for one thing in male-female roles, and then suddenly all the rules and expectations are changed on you. Sexual relationships have gone through a complete topsy-turvy revolution since the late 1950s. I was one of those men who supported female orgasm politically. Outside I said the right things; inside I felt scared. After all, there was the bitterness of women after all these years. Once released, what then?

In most areas of his life, Tom is a "liberated man." His live-with is a powerful career woman, and he relates very well to women both in his work and socially. He feels strongly that women should be economically, emotionally, and intellectually equal. "But when you bring that into the bedroom, it ought to work, but it doesn't." Tom equates sex with tennis. One person is the server and one receives the ball.

Tom finds it hard to separate sex and domination. He enjoys being "king of the mountain" during sex, and he finds that women like him in that role, too. The height of his experience with female submission was in the sixties when he lived in South Vietnam. He'd fuck one or maybe two women a night. And the relationship was always one of his total power over the woman. For instance, he'd tell a woman to meet him at the coffee shop at 6:00, "not 6:15." And even if he'd arrive at 10:00, she'd be there, quietly waiting, hands folded, not even reading a book to pass the time.

When he got back to America in 1970, he went into sexual shock. He says, "It was like being hit across the face with a board." On one of his first dates he reached across the table of the coffee shop to pick up the bill, and the woman threw a fit. "What do you think you're doing. You're going to pay the bill, and then you'll think I owe you something. Male chauvinist pig!"

Tom says that he found women generally kind of "butch, strident and aggressive." And he just couldn't figure out how to get them into bed. "I didn't get laid for two years. I began to realize even more that I thought of women as objects. My goal was to get a woman naked and into bed—that was my conquest."

Tom went into therapy for two years, and finally started loosening up. One of the first women he became involved with was a beautiful artist living in Sausalito. Sex was a big part of their relationship, and she wanted him to please her sexually. Tom describes her as having all the power: "Eat me now, then kiss my toes." And he felt that underneath all the orders was a sense that if he didn't follow them, then he "wouldn't be as good as Fred," or he would show himself to be "a real male chauvinist pig."

"Not only was she covertly getting off on ordering me around, but she was setting it up so that both she and ultimately I would be denied any sense of pleasure."

One night, though, they had really good sex. "She was a pretty uptight lady, and she would usually moan in monaural sound, and there she was moaning in stereophonic." The next morning, he was just waking up and put his arm around her, kissing her on the cheek. She came back "with such ice in her voice and spit out, 'You make love *at* me, not *to* me!' " He was so angry that she took back the vulnerability and closeness of the night before, that he wanted to break her jaw, snap her neck, and throw her out the window. Instead, he just got up, still completely nude, picked up his clothes and left. As he went down the loft stairs, he passed several of the other tenants as he was pulling on his pants and shirt. And that was it between him and the artist.

Today Tom is in a committed relationship. But he still has not found a workable alternative to "king of the mountain" sex. He says, "I guess what it comes down to is I'd like two Mexican hookers, or I'll settle for a good-night hug." So his love affair with his very equal live-with means he has a lot of good-night hugs, and very little sex.

The movie has changed in the middle for men like Tom. The actors and actresses must discard automatic behaviors. Gone is the swash-buckling, aggressive, conquesting, thrusting man who is *doing it to* the passive, pursued, asexual, *done to* woman. Here is a new woman—assertive, aggressive, even a bit conquesting herself.

One would think that male egos would feel stroked as women started, slowly, subtly, to pursue men. But then women began calling men on the phone and saying, "I like you and want to see you." Now watch men run! Watch man, the hunter, develop a knot in his throat!

Male excitement may be psychologically tied to the pursuit. Can man give up that role?

It's one thing when the man decides the when and how of sex. It's another when the woman asks or demands. One woman says, "I don't believe in the old myth that the guy always has to take the first step. Yet then many men feel they're being called on to perform." A female at Bradley University told us, "So many men get scared when I tell them I like sex."

The challenge for women is how to assert themselves in a nonaggressive manner, unlike the way so many millions of men have been making the first move for centuries: Grab, take, seize, conquer. (Ah, male asexuality would be universal if women treated men sexually the way men have been treating women for centuries.)

A Seattle woman writes, "Although I hear men say they like a woman to be aggressive, I think most men still need to be the aggressors." And a twenty-one-year-old Wooster College student adds, "Sex openness these days is definitely a threat to many people, especially men—the 'aggressors.' "

As the definition of women changed sexually, so the definition of men changed. "I always expected men to be very uninhibited," says a woman from Rochester. "Wrong. They're more uptight than I ever was."

As a graduate student from Southern Illinois University wrote, "If a woman wants total control, it puts me off. I still like to feel like a M-A-N during the act of lovemaking." Slater says that's the reason men want women who are "passive, docile, exciting yet undemanding . . . A man, it seems, has difficulty feeling like a man if a woman approaches him as a free, independent, fully sexual being."

For years I was like the millions of men who believed the only answer to the question, "Who's on top?" was "Man on top." Being on the bottom sexually meant being out of control and passive. And I automatically accepted the idea that *passivity in men means weakness.* When I lose control, I lose my I. And when I lose my I, I no longer exist.

One night I took Peggy to bed. I dug her. I got an erection real quick and we were having a great time. Then all of a sudden she began breathing real heavy and she began shouting, and she leaped on top of me, threw me over, and began heaving her body on mine in a near frenzy. I held on for dear life. I understood, for the first time, what it must feel like to be a woman underneath a man. I worried that I was going to be hurt, that my eye might be put out by a fast-moving finger or elbow. Overcome by Peggy's energy, I lost my erection, and my interest.

Women have become more demanding sexually. And in some cases, insensitive. Listen to this woman who wrote us: "After so many years of disappointments and failures in the sex department, I have actually begun taking the aggressive lead. I am now telling the man what I want. And I want it now. If he does not comply with my sexual wishes, I'll ask him to go home or I'll get up, get dressed and start watching TV, the sexual turn-off."

A thirty-six-year-old male college teacher from Chicago reports a similar experience. "The only sexual fear I have is that a woman will become too dominant sexually for me to handle," he writes. "Many women now demand sexual satisfaction and are explicit about what they want. One woman said that I didn't screw her hard enough. Another said I take too long to climax."

The new Sexually Assertive Woman likes to be on top, at least some of the time. And she can sometimes have little interest in what used to be called "foreplay," but wants to get right down to the genitals and orgasm, just like some men do. The modern woman, after some perfunctory kisses, jumps on top of the man *before* he is sexually aroused. And thus the slower man gets rushed, or must restrain an overenthusiastic woman.

The rigid male-female sex roles have loosened. As women learn to play with a traditionally masculine approach to sex, men necessarily learn to experience the traditionally female approach.

The Female Liberation of Masturbation

Women found themselves at a crossroads in the early 1960s. All around them they heard the songs and screams of the Sexual Revolution. "Come to bed! Get your fresh, hot orgasms now! Right here!" Yet many weren't getting their orgasms. They were getting all the pressure, with few of the goodies. So they decided to throw tradition and Freud to the winds and discover their own solution by going to the source: their own bodies.

Out of despair with men as the providers of orgasm, the modern woman's masturbation revolt began in San Francisco in the late sixties and early seventies. Its Joan of Arc was Betty Dodson, who brought women together to examine, collectively, their own vaginas and clitorises. Its Florence Nightingale was Lonnie Barback, who began consciousness-raising groups for nonorgasmic women; their homework practice was masturbation, and the success rate was phenomenal. The revolution in masturbation became complete when Shere Hite pronounced that masturbation statistically produced orgasm more easily than sex with a man.

The chains of centuries of religious prejudice against masturbation began shaking, as women began sharing orgasm secrets with each other, advising each other on the best ways to orgasm, reinforcing each other's desire for pleasure, discovering their true erogenous zones, and finally breaking free from male power and control with the statement of liberation: "I know how to give myself an orgasm."

Masturbation fought a wicked battle against the forces of sex-is-dirty. For both Jews and Christians masturbation was a sin punishable at times with death. Self-abuse was reported to cause insanity, murder, heart attacks, homosexuality, child molesting and acne.

The ban on masturbation is a crucial aspect of the ideology of sex-as-reproduction. Prohibiting women from touching themselves was an effective form of male control of the female sexual drive. Men then had total power to give or deny sexual pleasure to women. For a woman, it was sinful to feel sexual desire without a male focus or male initiative.

Religion controlled sexual expression. Many people were afraid to masturbate because, after all, "God is watching," while others went ahead anyway, figuring that God is too busy to worry about one more person engaged in self-satisfaction.

When the priests lost control, the psychiatrists took over. Their God was Freud. To guard the new Torah of Science, they had to admit that nothing physically harmful happened to a man or woman who partook. However, the Freudians were more subtle. They suggested that if one became fixated on masturbation, he or she might never advance to more mature forms of sexual expression. Masturbation was something to be avoided. It was "immature."

Ah, the rumors about masturbation. Throughout the fifties and early sixties masturbation was for me the Big Secret. I admitted to a classmate in a gym class in the seventh grade in 1951 that I liked to masturbate. He looked at me, shocked, and began scolding. "If you do that, you're in trouble. My daddy told me you can wear your dick out if you masturbate."

The last thing I wanted was for my penis to wear out! What if it were all worn out by the time I was twenty-one? All the nonmasturbators would be walking around with fresh, new penises, while mine would be secondhand and beaten. For the next five years I masturbated in terror that my penis might collapse from overuse, and in total silence so that my mother would not hear and punish me.

The female political rehabilitation of masturbation took place at the same time the sex therapists were looking for practical solutions to lack of sexual pleasure. Masters and Johnson stuck to their couple formula, and ignored masturbation as a sex therapy technique. At the same time, the 1970s experienced a revolution in mental health care. The medical profession lost its control of the national psyche, and the key words of the day became: self-healing, preventive medicine, positive health, self-responsibility. The idea was that each person was responsible for his or her own health. New schools of psychotherapy sprouted up all over. The number of therapists leaped. Body healing, nutrition, acupuncture, chiropractic became growth industries in a time of recession. Sex therapists became the most expensive therapists in the country. Awareness weekends and workshops emerged as a new educational system in the country. Therapy became the new American form of confession, and each person was responsible for his or her own mind and body. As one observer remarked, "Mental health is the new religion in America." And with the revolution, the old gods were dead, the dragons slain. Whatever worked, worked. And masturbation, as a sexual teaching tool, worked.

Finally, the psychiatric community took a new position on masturbation, as exemplified by a meeting in February 1978 when the sex therapists of the Northeast gathered in New York for their annual convention. One of the main papers concerned masturbation. It was delivered by a bearded sexology professor from Boston University, Dr. Jay Kuten. He gave a stirring, inspirational paper on behalf of masturbation. He praised self-love as the clearest and final break of independence from parents—the discovery of your own source of pleasure. He said that it was a perfect act for staying healthy, staying in shape, and giving yourself "pleasure in moments of relationship withdrawal." He advised partners to masturbate in front of each other as the best self-help sexual education. During the question-and-answer session, a bald Freudian psychiatrist began to berate Kuten. He said masturbation "reveals the extent of retarded behavior" by the practitioner.

"No, no, that's not true," responded Kuten. "In the past at these conventions too many speakers have been defensive about masturbation. I'm not going to be defensive." Kuten took his seat to a round of spontaneous applause.

Dr. Helen Kaplan was next at the microphone. Smiling, she said, "The Eastern Association of Sex Therapists is in favor of masturbation. All opposed raise your hand." No one did and everyone laughed. Thus, the "shocking" feminist position on masturbation, a mere ten years after it was first voiced, gained official support from the leading experts on sexual health.

Freud Turns Over in His Grave

Masturbation is respectable for the first time in history. In one interview, a man sipped his coffee and told us, "Sex is not worth it. I put so much out; I get so little back. I'm giving up relationships. I satisfy myself." Woody Allen said in *Annie Hall*, "Don't put down masturbation. It's sex with someone I love." Alice Cooper told a national magazine that he preferred masturbation to intercourse. And Lily Tomlin asked the critical question, "Sex is such a personal thing. Why do we think of sharing it with another person?"

Perhaps ironically, beyond self-satisfaction, the significance of the modern rehabilitation of masturbation is its role in teaching men and women how to make love together. Self-stimulation has become the major teaching tool for women to learn how to become orgasmic. Masturbation also has become the number one communication and teaching technique between partners. And self-touching has become a dynamic part of lovemaking itself in the late seventies and the eighties.

While women made masturbation a political issue and discovered their sexual joy in its pleasure, men were back at the old grind, masturbating quickly and quietly and having fun, yet feeling weird about it all. Women say informally among themselves: men are quick and terrible in bed. Women ask: Why are men such lousy lovers? One answer: Watch how they masturbate.

Habits learned and practiced during masturbation become the habits people take into partner sex. Men are shy about their self-pleasure. They do it quickly. How many men will prepare for themselves an hour-long hot bath?

Men are goal-oriented, functional and paranoid about "wasting time." They are creators, builders, producers—they have no time for the process of pleasure. It feels childish and self-indulgent to many men to "play with themselves" for any length of time.

Listen to some men talk about masturbation.

"I didn't masturbate until I was nineteen," writes Carl from Columbus, "although close male friends in high school encouraged me to. One night I screwed my mattress and I laughed and then cried. I felt frustrated, lonely and unloved."

Anonymous from California writes, "Feeling very fearful of the vulnerability of again committing myself to the possibility of rejection, I gave up partner sex in late 1969," he wrote. "I continued masturbating, although feeling very guilty about it."

Masturbation can become an embarrassment to a sense of one's manhood. The hidden implication a man fears from other men is, "Hm. Can't make it with a woman, huh?" Even if the other guy doesn't say it, some neurotic part of himself will. He's failed by the very act of giving himself pleasure. Masturbation is considered a putdown in casual conversation. "Are we just jerking off?" is a common question to indicate the wasting of time in any field.

The self-permission to masturbate has freed women from the control the men had over female sexual pleasure. Now men can learn from women the many uses of masturbation and free themselves. Masturbation has become a tool in the national process of sexual reeducation.

3

MEN AND WOMEN CHANGE
POSITIONS (OR DO THEY?)

Shootout in the Bedroom

In the war today between men and women over sexual roles, sex is the fragile battleground where bodies collide. The 1960s was the Decade of the Sexual Man, and the 1970s was the Decade of the Sexual Woman. (Will the 1980s be the decade of both?) In the middle of the 1970s, men and women began exchanging positions and attitudes. Men discovered process and women liberated orgasms. Men searched for their feelings while women began learning technique.

"*You* are able to dissociate your feelings from sex. *You* are able to get into sex as a purely physical activity. *I* need you to tell me that you love me for me to enjoy the physical aspects of sex." Who said that? A woman? Or a man?

A hint: the year is 1979. A woman? Wrong. A man. The year is the key, because we are experiencing a subtle yet fascinating reversal in male-female relations.

With these reversals, however temporary, of male-female sexual games, men have begun experiencing some traditional female dilemmas. The result is that sometimes it's now men who "endure" sex. I've heard myself tell women, "Not tonight, honey, I'm too tired." And now we have the occasional bed scenes of the process-oriented woman goaling to orgasm while the goal-oriented man is shouting, "Process! Process!"

Economics affects sex. Modern American men are facing a unique—yet positive—sexual dilemma. Historically men go to bed with women who are financially dependent on them. The man is protected sexually by his wife's financial dependence. Financial control becomes sexual control.

Today, in the modern industrial world, for the first time on a large scale in human history, women are achieving the power of financial independence, and that situation makes men anxious in bed, too.

Yet inside "liberated" woman may live another woman: the little girl who was conditioned to believe in being overwhelmed by a powerful man-daddy.

My experience with a woman I'll call Rosalie taught me that the New Woman of the eighties is often the passive little girl of the fifties on the inside. My experience with her temporarily destroyed my self-confidence.

In lunging after Rosalie, did I know what I was doing? I was going after a powerful trial lawyer, an activist in human potential, a proponent of sexual freedom and experimentation, an advocate of

65

female independence, and a public opponent of marriage. I leaped after her at a time in my life when I wanted to get married and develop an emotional connection, while she wanted to make up for lost sexual time, experiment and grow.

Rosalie was a tall, dynamic, attention-getting woman, her charisma aided by dark red hair thick with curls and blue eyes. She had her own home, a sports car, and a male secretary. I met her in the early seventies in San Diego when the entire community was involved in personal therapeutic self-improvement, with a particular emphasis on the body. I was captivated by her power.

I should have been suspicious of the fact that I lived in the house she owned, and although I was paying rent, she could have kicked me out at any moment. She considered her time more valuable than mine. I wanted her more than she wanted me. I pursued her, but I couldn't conquer her.

Rosalie and I were unintentional victims of a place and time when the Sexual Revolution combined with the Human Potential Movement. That mix created the ideology that a healthy human being had a responsibility to make pleasure the goal of his life and to rid himself of all his sexual hang-ups as soon as possible. Life's new challenges included open marriage, bisexuality, multiorgasms, group sex and uninhibited sexuality. Sexual expression was the key to mental health. During this period, some heterosexual men berated themselves because they were not engaged in homosexual experiences. In fact, some heterosexuals snuck into the closet and feigned bixexuality.

I remember one particular conversation with my friend Mel, whose usual daily breakfast chatter centered on the repressive Puritan barriers he had overcome the previous nights with the female bodies he encountered in dance classes, bookstores and on the streets.

"You know," I said, "I'm too hung up to have a homosexual experience. That's my problem. If I could do that, I'd be healthier and freer sexually."

"You're right," Mel affirmed. "Men who have had gay experiences are better lovers than straight men. Women are very impressed if you tell them that you've made love with a man. I must do it—soon."

"So go do it."

"I can't," said Mel. "I'm too hung up."

Rosalie wanted to give me three women for my birthday. Each would enter my bed and collectively pleasure me. Visions of performance paranoia overwhelmed me—I refused the gift. Yet in this world of sex in America, I felt guilty because I was turning down an offer of sexual pleasure!

Rosalie wanted me to experiment sexually. She encouraged me to develop a wandering penis. Yet I was "in love" with her; all her bedroom speeches about "breaking the chains of sexual repression" simply enhanced the poison of jealousy within me. When I walked into a party, I wouldn't see people. I'd see penises of various sizes (all bigger than mine!) attached to bodies. I'd be introduced to some new man and the first thing I'd think was, Can his penis take Rosalie away from me? In the Olympic competition between penises, with Rosalie as a judge, I knew there would *always* be another cock down the line which could jump more broads and vault more poles than mine.

Freud talked about penis envy. Well, I had penis hatred.

I blamed my penis—in retrospect, quite unfairly—for not ending Rosalie's search for more and different sexual pleasure. Meanwhile, I believed her philosophy that the goal of life was experience, that sexual commitment was a hang-up, and that I should rove and roam. I kept imagining that all the women I met were challenges to my masculinity. I felt every woman was, like Rosalie, daring me: "Come on, are you a man? Fuck me, pleasure me, show me you're a man. Let's go." I believed the Male Pep Talk—*a man should be able to make love to any woman at any time.* The result was, ironically, asexuality and a lack of intimacy, for I avoided close emotional contact with women for fear that I might be sexually challenged.

And sexual jealousy roared within me like a wild animal. I shivered in fear when I felt that "my" woman was interested sexually in another man. I felt that my honor required that I sexually possess and control any woman I was involved with. My jealousy flowed out of my male madness, control and competitiveness. And when it flowed, my emotions overwhelmed my sanity.

My only consolation was that I was not alone. In a time of the disposable relationship, competition had replaced tradition in the choices of lovemaking, and jealousy flourished, arising out of deep male fears. As a woman wrote to our survey, "After I began sleeping with other men, he became very anxious, and often made negative comments about those men, focusing on their abilities to perform sexually or the size of their sexual organs."

I felt, however wrongly, that all the women I was meeting wanted me to play the role of the honky big-dick strongman. Sometimes a part of me wondered if maybe I was projecting that expectation onto them from my own man-made madness.

Rosalie, though, actualized my worst fears about the Ever-Ready Female. I feared she wanted an orgasm every night. If she didn't receive the Big O from me, she'd be quietly resentful the next day. I was performing a nightly service. So here we have an example of the modern male-female switch. By historical myth it's the horny man who wants sex and the woman who wants loving, emotional contact. But I kept telling Rosalie that I needed her to tell me how much she loved me. I wanted more hugging, kissing, cuddling.

I went to bed to conquer Rosalie's pussy with my penis, tongue or finger—to succeed. Rosalie's praise or orgasm justified my efforts. As a man, I felt comfortable with goal-oriented behavior in the bedroom. Sex became work for me. I not only worked during the day, I also worked in bed naked at night. The success was worth it, but anything to avoid a—Ouch!—bad review.

I kept telling Rosalie how much I loved her. Finally, exasperated with such romantic talk, she blurted out, "Jerry, I wish you would stop telling me you love me with your mouth and tell me more down there." She pointed to my penis.

My penis finally rebelled under the pressure. In bed with Rosalie, my mind and my penis turned sexual activity into a battlefield:

>*My penis:* I don't want to get turned on here. This bed is not safe for me.
>
>*My mind:* Shut up! Perform! Don't let me down! You're robbing me of my manhood! A lot's riding on you! You're humiliating me in front of Rosalie! Shitty, useless thing!

I had set myself up to be the victim of a powerful woman who wanted sexual service, who put herself ahead of me, who gave women's liberation, and sexual affirmative action in the face of centuries of female sexual denial, as the impeccable excuse for it all. But somehow I found it a contradiction that Rosalie still demanded my hard penis to pleasure her and satisfy her womanhood. She wanted both to be equal and to be sexually overcome and conquered.

As Richard Pryor put it, "And some women are chauvinistic as men now, don't get me wrong. Some women go, 'Ah, my God, it's so good! Please don't. No more! Please, stop.' You say, 'Can you wait until I put it in?'"

The ironies and contradictions in bed overwhelmed me. I fancied myself a liberated man yet here I was ferociously blaming myself for not being powerfully macho with Rosalie. And she fancied herself a liberated woman, yet here she was acting like a disappointed, dependent female in bed, crying over my lack of "performance."

We thought ourselves adventurous and liberated, yet here we were victims trapped by powerful myths of the way sexuality should be. One night, after another clumsy round of unsatisfactory sex, laden with heavy images and expectations, we cried in each other's arms, casualties of the war against John Wayne.

We sat in a health food restaurant in the Village. Rosalie told me calmly of her desire to see other men during our visit to New York. I internally rebelled, wondering how her seeing other men sexually was going to affect our ability to nurture—or at least, save—the relationship. Yet these were the hot days of Open Marriage, and it was more "in" to experiment sexually than to try to make male-female bonding work. Rosalie was insistent. "This trip?" I asked in shock. "On this particular trip you need to have an open relationship? Give me a break!"

"I don't want to set any limits on myself," said Rosalie.

I began reasoning, "Our relationship can never grow if you always hold out the threat of another sexual relationship."

Rosalie had stored-up anger. She was fuming. We began to make the issues of other men and her commitment the footballs between us as we began arguing.

"You never get turned on anyway. Your penis doesn't really want me. You're impotent."

I almost lunged at her. I think I would have strangled her if we weren't in a restaurant. I felt so awful, I wanted to die.

A table full of people next to us turned to look. I stood up and fled. I ran down the street, crying.

You survive. Always. I finally burst the chains of my own masochism. I stopped apologizing for Rosalie and got in touch with my anger. All of my male friends were already either advising me to break Rosalie's jaw or leave her forever. One friend said he would break my jaw if I continued to see Rosalie!

I had made Rosalie mommy. Until I overthrew inside myself the need for a mommy, I'd always be dependent emotionally on a woman's word. "Learn to mother yourself," advised a female therapist during this period. "Nourish yourself." Everyone was telling me to take my authority, become my own parent, and learn that self-love comes from within, not as a gift from another person.

I never saw Rosalie again.

We had conveniently served each other as parts of a circular sadomasochistic relationship. I became a handy scapegoat for all her anger at men, her unresolved anger toward her father and husbands, all of whom, she felt, mistreated her. She served to process my guilt, too: She would pay me back for all those quick fucks, all that sex-as-masturbation, the psychological rape of women. Rosalie and I needed each other during the particular historical period of the mid-seventies, she to sexually punish me, I to feel victimized. My victimhood would justify all my past offenses, and give me the new power of the underdog: *To see women as oppressors, too.*

Contradictions Within Contradictions

The Myth of the Sexually Liberated Woman: Women are becoming more assertive. Yet impulses toward passivity and dependence still reign. Women are in conflict, sending men double messages. A Detroit auto mechanic wrote: "Most of the women I've been with have remarked favorably about my soft, sensual ways with them, but I still get vibes that they want (and expect) rough, asshole, macho treatment. I've had a woman say to me, 'I wish you were more aggressive and told me what to do. I don't know what you want!' And then she added, 'I remember these two guys, they could make love for two hours straight!'"

The adoption of male competitiveness and goal-oriented, judgmental behavior by women reflects the contradictions within women in this period of change. "I really feel for men who do not see themselves in terms of the typical male sex role," writes one woman. "It's hard to make the initial moves too. The women's movement is definitely leading men to come to terms with their role as well. It's funny though, emotionally I want a self-assured, experienced man! I want a man to be in charge in spite of myself."

And many men fear that they will be rejected for being too gentle. "My greatest fear," said one salesman, "is having my initiatives mocked as too slow, or not aggressive enough. It's a bind to have your gentleness rejected, when so many women are discussing how they're oppressed by overaggressive and presumptuous men."

A seventeen-year-old Canadian truck driver wrote, "The new women's consciousness hasn't affected my sex life one bit because all the women I meet are passive chicks waiting for me to take the initiative."

Men are usually expected to make the first move. "I have *never* made the first move on any man. They always make the first move on me, every single one of them," says a New York model.

The macho reaction of some women reflects an insecurity based on current contradictions. Within each woman is a battleground, a struggle between past and future, between Puritanism and sexual abandon, between her self-acceptance and her desire to be confirmed in her womanhood by a man.

When I first read *Fear of Flying*, I got momentarily threatened by its concept of the "zipless fuck." Even though I knew that one of my main sexual turn-ons is to mentally undress women on the streets of New York, in airports and in restaurants, I didn't want to be seen by women as a sex object, especially one who must also be a performance machine. I resented the objectification of sex, and the isolation of emotions and feelings from sexual activity. Journalist Rose Wetzsteon wrote, "It scares the shit out of us that women are fully as capable as men of feeling a biological, impersonal sexuality, utterly autonomous, completely unconnected to their feelings about a specific man."

A male friend recently told us of the pain he felt in his gut when his close female friend continued to see a guy that she had no personal or friendship relationship with. She didn't even like waking up with him the next morning. All she liked to do was fuck him. He had a huge, long penis, and lasted for hours. "It hurt me when she left our friendship to go spend time with his penis," he said. "I know it's stupid but I still feel bad about it." Women, he argued, helped create "the competition between cocks." His voice trailed off as he said, "Wouldn't you like to be able to last forever so that you could please any woman?"

Women used to shun each other at parties and compete for the attention and time of men. Today women talk to each other. And female locker-room talk is sometimes as rough as male macho stories. Women can say to each other, "He's a good lay. Don't miss him."

"My girlfriends and I usually rate guys on a scale of one to ten on sex. We talk about it. Usually after you see a guy, your girlfriend asks you for his score," says a woman from Pennsylvania.

As women stopped being objects, they sometimes began seeing men as objects. It used to be that men looked at women and thought, "Does she fuck?" Now it's just as likely that women look at men and say, "Does *he* fuck?" We've gone from, "Will she?" to "Can he?"

The performing man gets an assist from a new bed partner—the performing woman. "The times I run into trouble are when I am pretending to be the big, heavy, perfect, multiorgasmic woman," writes one woman. "I find that puts men on the defensive, just as their macho trips do me. I mean, we are in bed together to perform (who is watching, anyway, to perform *for?!*), or are we there because we like and care about each other, and want to feel good?"

Hal's Penis Defeats Jerry's Penis, 1–0

My first marriage lasted five years. I thought it would last forever. We made magic together. We looked at the world as our playtoy and ran through the world like innocent children. We were pals, buddies, lovers and partners.

We were almost too happy in our adventurous life to give much time or attention to sex, so we counted on spontaneity, which got us nowhere. I furtively read a few sexual how-to books on the side, but I never found their knowledge expanding my expertise, or moving me past inaction. We communicated freely and openly in many areas of our life, but when it came to sex we counted completely on mental telepathy. We both had a number of myths about sex. And I felt worse—even, horribly, suicidal—when I thought about it, because as the man, I knew that we both felt that I should be leading, directing, producing and controlling the entire sexual play! Yet I was passive, feeling self-conscious about my penis.

I knew, however, that my wife, whom I'll call Debbie, had to tiptoe around me—my ego was too sensitive and my temper too quick. Little surprise when one day it happened. She came home one day and told me. The one sentence that hit me like a ton of bricks. "I am leaving you for another man," she said, looking at the floor. "While you were away, I spent the night with Hal. I spent time with him. I love him and plan to live with him."

I felt the heavens cave in on me. I became a helpless, mad, crazy six-year-old falling to my knees to beg her to take the words back. I couldn't eat. I couldn't sleep. I walked the streets like a dead man. Then one day, in a murderous rage, I threw a fit. I tore down from the wall all the pictures she had artfully arranged. My madness was giving reason to her sexual betrayal. I had only myself to blame, because I myself had promoted sexual freedom for our marriage. And now I was eating it.

Oddly enough, our sex had begun to improve during the brief period before the break-up. She even once looked at my penis and said, "Hey, I think it's growing." It was. My erections were getting bigger. They were making a last-ditch effort at a lost cause.

The Chase: What I had taken for granted was now being taken away from me. All my possessive and competitive juices were mobilized. I became an obsessive, focusing on the many mornings, lunches, movies, walks, kisses, conversations, significant moments and good times we shared together. Would life be worth living without these moments? I wondered.

To make matters worse, this was 1970; the outbreak of the women's liberation movement after the sixties, and all the forces outside our marriage coalesced to tell her to leave me. Women were abandoning their men on political and social grounds. But Debbie had left me for another man— Ouch, what a pain in my gut! That I couldn't stomach. Everytime I got depressed, I rushed to a bar and drank two Irish coffees, a solution to sadness that Phil Ochs, one of my close friends, taught me.

I was insane. A temporary insanity, I hoped, caused by sexual rejection. But the thoughts kept growing inside my mind: "Some other man's penis is bigger and better than my penis. Hal's penis had defeated and humiliated my penis. Debbie wants Hal's penis rather than mine."

Yes, women were getting their act together; they were becoming sisters, but what about us men? What man would give this pain to me? What man would steal "my woman" from me when we were living together? What worm would steal my life from me? What price would brotherhood take?

I thought to myself that it would be a positive result of sister liberation if we brothers got together and stopped killing each other with our competition for women, but alas, fat chance: *The cock rules.* Hal had moved in on me while I was away and helpless, and had taken Debbie without so much as a brotherly grunt. And you know what? Hal himself wasn't such a bad guy. I liked him. But I detested and hated him and dreamed of cutting him up into a thousand little pieces—when I wasn't seeing his penis carrying Debbie out of our apartment.

I was a casualty of the Million-Year Penis Wars. My woman—my possession—had just been stolen from me by the charm of another male. I felt demoralized, depressed, and then furious, angry. What we men do to each other with our male sexual competition. I felt other men laughing at me. I had a totally macho reaction.

Sex, historically, especially in macho cultures, is a matter of honor to a man, and a cuckolded man symbolically grows humiliating horns. I had to fight off conditioned mental pictures of "sexual honor," and accept Debbie's decision as that of a free, independent being, which said nothing of my value as a human being. But it was tough. I tortured myself with compulsive thoughts of sexual rejection.

I remember the advice of a book salesman I met during this period of sexual rejection. "If your chick leaves you, go out that day and get laid. Prove to yourself that you can still do it, that you are desired. Don't let some dame take away your masculinity. There's always pussy around. More than enough."

I couldn't do it, however. I went from sexual disaster movie to sexual disaster movie until I settled on an easy solution: asexuality. I went for nine months without any naked physical contact with another person. My male friends nurtured me well during this period—we men are learning to mother each other—yet we never questioned the male sexual idiocies that were causing my personal havoc.

And then one day, from the pit of my stomach, came the realization that it was completely appropriate that Debbie and I separate, because we were growing in completely opposite directions, both valid, which no longer could be merged into a common goal. My feelings of rejection were tied to my sense of competition, not to the relationship. I agreed with Albert Ellis who said, about similar situations, that the appropriate response is sadness, not feelings of rejection. Debbie had actually done me a favor. She had seen the future before me. I stopped feeling sorry for myself. My depression lifted.

It was, after all, only my male madness that identified my gonads with my total human worth. And made her the source of my self-esteem.

Men Make Women the Judges of Their Manhood

Fear of rejection by a woman can emotionally paralyze a man. "My biggest fear in relationships with women," writes a twenty-four-year-old California graduate student, "is a strong fear of rejection, that she might say something derogatory about me at a bad time. I really dig talking to women. I love the feel of a woman's body against mine, both with clothes on and off. But I'm very afraid of women."

Men imagine the Sexual Doomsday. As a Pittsburgh bus driver wrote, "The one thing I fear the worst is to have sex with a woman, be right in the middle of intercourse, and have her get up and walk away out of disgust or anger about something I did or didn't do. The worst thing a woman could say that might hurt me sexually is that I was a selfish asshole. Thank God nothing like that has ever happened, but I still have a fear of this happening for some reason. I feel I'm a damned good lover."

The sex-war wounds dig deep in a man's heart and determine his fears for future relationships. "I am afraid that someday, maybe starting today, she is going to change her mind about liking to fuck with me, *which my ex-wife did,*" worries one man.

Male sexual habits—emphasis on performance, reliance on results, and a competitive mode of looking at one another—set men up for the ever-present threat of rejection. And that makes men especially vulnerable to the people they select as judges: the important women in their lives—or sometimes, a female ship passing in the night. Men compete among themselves, and install women in the role of sexual judge.

As Helen Mayer Hacker wrote, "The ability to perform the sexual act has been a criterion of man's evaluation of himself from time immemorial." After sex, or the next morning, men look at women with those three questions in their eyes: "How good was I? Was I real good? Or just a little good?"

There are a lot of things that a woman could say about a man's driving skill, or his creative talent, but if a woman says, "You just don't fill me up," or "You don't satisfy me as much as Paul," the man's mind will go crazy and he'll begin thinking, "Jesus, did the last ten women think that and not tell me?" A woman can knock out a man's ego for months with just one slight on his sexual ability.

A twenty-five-year-old woman in the army, constantly surrounded by "horny men," says, "Men are vulnerable and a lot like little boys. A little negative comment that slips out can really upset a man and he'll dwell on it forever. Inside that male macho exterior is a heart that can easily break."

An engineer from the Midwest agrees, "Sexually speaking, a woman can destroy a man's ego, if she puts him to the test . . . if she makes a contest or an endurance marathon out of sexual liaison," writes L.K.R. of Edwardsville, Illinois. "I do not wish to be a mere member of a woman's vast diary of experiences. I want to feel as if I were something special to the woman I am making love to."

When asked about any aspect of their sexual life, most men quickly begin quoting women, rather than themselves, as their authority sources. "I'd be real hurt if a woman said that I wasn't stimulating or exciting in bed," writes Art from Kansas. "Or that I was selfish or cruel to them. Or worse, that I reminded them of some other guy."

Like many men, I had a morbid fear of women discussing my sexual prowess, maybe because I knew how crudely men discussed the sexual behavior of women. And men can be so completely destroyed by sexual comparisons by women. Dick, twenty-eight, went to bed with a forty-year-old black woman with three children. "I had a few very good sessions with her until she expressed her wonder why 'black guys can do it so much longer than white guys.' It hasn't been the same since."

Women reveal the nervousness of many men. J.T., an eighteen-year-old woman from Hicksville, New York, said, "Most men I know ask me hinting or outright how they compare to my other men. About half of them say they can't perform at their best until I encourage them and let them know that they are good enough or equal to my other lovers."

Millions of men have similar worries. They can learn from each other, though, and they would feel better if they knew that most men go through similar rejection nightmares, and that they do it to themselves in a form of self-torture.

Penis Wars

A comedian joked on the "Tonight Show" that, in the days of rubbers, boys used to carry them around to impress other boys, rather than to use them with girls. Jules Feiffer suggests in a *Playboy* interview of 1971 that males "were trained to think about women as conveniences, receptacles, appendages and adjuncts, but never to think of them in the same terms in which they think of their buddies. . . . There is first a sense of relating to sex in a social way rather than a sexual way. It has to do with rivalry and envy, with competition with the other fellows, more than it has to do with women."

Feiffer relates what he calls

> . . . one of my favorite [cartoons]. There's this guy who says to his friend, "I've quit going out," and his friend asks him what's bothering him. The guy describes what happened the night before. He's sitting home alone, the telephone rings and this great sexy voice says that he doesn't know her, but she's a friend of a friend, she just landed at the airport, and she doesn't know anybody in town, and can she come over and see him. He knows she's going to be awful-looking, but she shows up an hour later and she's the greatest-looking girl he's ever met, with the most extraordinary body he's ever seen. They sit and they drink and they talk for hours. She's got the most fascinating mind he's ever known and they've read the

same books and they like the same music. They just fit together like nothing else that's ever happened to him.

They come together in the most gentle way and they make the most perfect love. It's the best, the most exciting, the most wonderful moment he's ever experienced in all his life, and he says to his friend, "All through this, do you know what I was thinking?" His friend asks, "What?" And he answers, "Wait'll I tell the fellas!"

Men are conquerors and they do not discuss their defeats. Men promote a male positive-thinking philosophy as their sex pose. They become individual baseball teams playing against each other for the greatest fucks in the land. That's why men can't communicate with each other about sex. Because they're playing ball. They inflate, multiply, enliven. They flex their penises to each other; they flaunt. If you've got it, flaunt it, the saying goes, and so they flaunt it whether or not they've got it.

Men are constantly making other men feel inadequate. The bragging that men do to each other about their sexual prowess ends up makin all men feel secretly insecure. Since they always tend to exaggerate, they can never live up to either their fantasy, or another's reality (fantasy). Men live in the Land of Sexual Inferiority. As John Atkins reports in *Sex in Literature*, "Most modern Erotica and all pornography is bragging. . . . A man will brag about his own imaginary performances and then persuade himself that the performances of other men in fact equal his own absurd claims."

As a standard sex joke goes, "Boasting Sam, one of the worst braggarts who ever bent a bar rail, was loudly lamenting that his doctor had ordered him to give up half of his sex life. 'Which half are you going to give up?' asked a weary listener. 'Talking about it or thinking about it?'"

How many times in my life have I been in conversations when a man began to describe in vivid detail how he fucked a girl so hard that she screamed when he came?

I was eighteen. My friend Alex and I were talking about chicks. He was describing in vivid detail how he had "fucked her so hard that his pecker almost fell off." He asked me how I felt when women screamed at the top of their lungs during sex. Story upon story of male sexual conquest heaped upon my ringing ears.

And I sat there in agony, no stories to tell, no adventures to relate, no ears to ring. Alex and I were good friends; I wanted so badly to rip down my pants and scream at him, "Don't you see, don't you see how small my cock is! I can't do any of those things you're talking about."

I was on the verge of pleading with Alex, eight years my senior, what to do with my hidden plague? Yet I couldn't bring myself to do it. What if he laughed in my face? What if he told me that my cock *was* small? What if he kept a wry grin on his face all the time whenever he thought of me because no matter what I did in my life to compete with him, in the end there was no contest.

Alex could relax because, well, after all, you've seen the size of Jerry's cock, now, haven't you? And so I lay in bed restlessly and the last words I heard were Alex's: "Jesus, I'd like to fuck the redhead with those gigantic boobs."

The (Shh!) Male Virgin

Male virgins are especially sensitive in the locker room about what other men think of them because they may believe the statement, as expressed in Kurt Vonnegut's *Breakfast of Champions*, that you can tell "by the angle of the dangle if the meat's been beat." The male virgin is on the hot seat. He pretends to be Mr. Macho while secretly condemning himself. Sex therapists were shocked to discover the amazing number of men in their thirties, forties and fifties who have never had intercourse. Yet a 1970 study of college youth found that, "A senior who is still a virgin in the liberal subculture of our campus, has failed to live up to his own and his peers' ideal of masculinity."

And you would never know from some of the external behavior of the virgin himself. Because of the male myth that men must always be in charge sexually, male virgins try to fool women. Pat from Hicksville, New York, wrote us about one such scared soul.

> He was a well-educated engineer who constantly spoke about his sexual escapades and love of sex. After seven dates he had not even touched me. On the eighth date I made an advance at him. After two hours of foreplay I realized that something was wrong. He said, "Please don't tell anyone about this 'cause I've never been with a woman before." I was stunned that this twenty-five-year-old man who constantly talked about his sexual prowess was a virgin.

I was a virgin all through the Sexual Revolution and into my late twenties. It was my deep, dark secret; if anyone had discovered it, I would have considered suicide. I wore a macho mask of experience; I acted nonchalant about sex, but all the time I had no idea how to put my whatsit into her whatat. I was completely unfamiliar with female genitalia, and I had picked up and generalized my mother's distaste for her own.

Women in the 1950s and early 1960s seemed to be even more ignorant than me about sex, and they did nothing to help me. Bragging was the main form of sexual communication and education between men. So I could turn to no one for assistance, except instinct. And frankly, instinct let me down.

Finally one woman grabbed my penis and stuck it in. Whew! She had no idea how significant what she had just done was to me. For all she knew, she might have been in bed with the Sexual Conquerer. Never did she learn that she had just made history by transforming an old virgin!

Competition Invades the Nonmacho World

Tender men now compete to be the "tenderest man on the block" and sensitive men struggle for the Sensitivity Prize. Dan, a sensitive yet competitive Oregon salesman, writes, "Compared with other men, I think I am more gentle, more concerned, and more turned on by the whole woman. I care about my sexual partner. I am probably not as physical as most men but I can stay hard for three or four hours even after one and sometimes two ejaculations."

Men now compete for the honors of being the most "noncompetitive." Even this irrationality makes sense because, as Joseph Pleck says in *Men and Masculinity*, "In almost everything we do, male culture encourages us to compare ourselves with other men, and to see them as a standard showing what we should be able to do." And Dan continues, "I'd like to think that I'm much better than most men in bed, simply because I've gotten so much into my own sensuality. Sensitivity and openness are two of my better qualities. I feel I am better read and experienced pleasuring women than most men my age."

Yet, sensitive and insensitive, we compete in a vacuum. We

compete against mythical men and mythical events. Few, if any, heterosexual men know how other men make love. As Dan goes on to say, "Comparison with other men is hard to evaluate since very few men have told me, a man, what they really do in bed." And Dan adds, in a rare moment of doubt, "But I have never discussed sex openly and honestly with another man without all the usual lies and macho bullshit. I can't really say for sure one way or the other."

The Limits of Male Friendship: A thirty-nine-year-old married, wealthy man from the Southwest writes, "My mind is vibrating with sexual thoughts much of the time, but I keep them pretty much to myself. I *never* entered into a bull session with my male peers because I was afraid to expose my lack of experience to their scrutiny and never even had a close male friend to whom I could talk about my sex life."

Men learn about this most crucial area of human relations, sex, on the street corner, where, as one man put it, "Everyone pretends they know and then tells you something wrong." Men systematically cut themselves off from each other. "I don't know how other men do in bed," writes a nineteen-year-old from an upper middle-class family in Ohio. "I mean, everybody tells how they do, but really, who knows?"

Men constantly create even greater and greater challenges for themselves. Sensitive lovers want to be loved for themselves, not for their abilities or their money or their position or their power. They constantly pry, "Does she love me?"

Sources of possible anxiety run deep. For example, fame. Fame became for me a flasher-into-bed, an aphrodisiac for women, but at the same time *my enemy* once I got vulnerable. Does she love me or my fame? A twenty-four-year-old bookstore clerk from White Plains, New York, put it this way: "My sexual fears and anxieties revolve around women not wanting to make love with me as a human, but because I'm a black man."

Good Sex, No Feeling!

One of the biggest complaints by women is that men try too hard in sex. A twenty-six-year-old woman from Palm Beach, Florida, put it this way: "Men are involved *at* the act, instead of *in* the act. A woman has got to know how to gracefully end an encounter if the man is trying too hard." As Julie from Colorado says, "I wish men only knew that there isn't a penalty for mistakes or failures in love."

Lorraine is a woman who says that she has spent too much of her life underneath performance machines. "I keep wanting to stop in the middle," she says, "and say, 'Hold on. What are you thinking, what are you feeling?'"

"Men are still so hung up on being performers rather than *real* human beings with real *human* fears," advised one woman. "If more men could realize that women are turned off by this type of behavior, everyone would be a lot better off."

I was petting once in bed. My partner stopped me midway, before I got my clothes off. "What are you doing? Why aren't you in touch with me? I'm not turned on."

A leading sex therapist, Bernie Apfelbaum, suggests that when sex is more mechanical than emotional, partners ought to try some outrageous communication games. He suggests that couples with mechanical proficiency who lack emotional satisfaction stop right in the middle of intercourse, preferably at the peak, lovingly separate—and immediately begin talking about the experience.

"The point is," writes Apfelbaum in a letter to the authors, "that people need to learn how to stop whenever sex gets compulsive. Things often get very compulsive as soon as people get a little turned on. That's when people need to stop and share the anxiety about whether they'll make it. Breaking contact is essential to getting in touch with what is going on."

Apfelbaum, who gained national attention because of his work with single men and surrogates, says that many men come to him "who have no difficulty getting erections. They get an erection before they get to bed. In fact, some premature ejaculators have automatic erections."

Some men we interviewed who admitted to premature ejaculation complained that they lacked feeling in sex. They had no erection difficulty—but a feeling deficiency. Better to shut off emotions completely than to be faced with the possibility of "not functioning"!

The purpose of sex is pleasure, fun, intimacy and communication, yet men are so dependent on proving something in bed—their manhood or their sexuality or their strength—that they sometimes become technical and nonintimate in this most naked of human experiences. And thus the sexual experience is flat.

A woman from Alaska sympathizes with men. "Failure to perform is an especially terrible thing to a man due to society's standards of the image they feel they must maintain. I've felt inadequate myself at times and it really is a terrible state. Men feel they have let me down."

Men too serious in sex? "And men do worry," says a twenty-three-year-old Atlanta woman from a Catholic family. "They are always expected to be ready, to always be prepared to perform to everyone's expectations. It is not really so—no man is Superman, as no woman is Wonder Woman. If we just give each other a chance, there could be a lot more loving and a lot less pretense for both sexes."

Sex today is often a way of attempting to establish intimacy, but that attempted intimacy fails because sex has become more and more a performance geared to impress. The pressure becomes enormous on the performance-oriented man who now demands female orgasm to prove his masculinity. Masters and Johnson point out that it is men themselves who set up the situation, seeing sex as a "personal achievement test with specific performance goals" rather than an "authentic expression."

For men, orgasms are the equivalent of dollars. Man's role is clear: Compete! Make money! Give orgasms!

The best definition of the experience of sex as performance we found was in Alexander Lowen's *Love and Sex*. "The concept of performance," he wrote, "distinguishes public actions from private ones. The sexual act is a performance if it is used more to impress one's partner than to express an inner feeling."

Men think of themselves as performers in so many possible acts: Am I willing to eat her? How uninhibited am I? Can I keep it up and use it when needed? Am I gentle enough? Hard enough? How am I comparing in all these areas with other men? And what's my overall grade?

Michael Rossman, the Berkeley sex therapist, writes that the "social reality of being male in our society" may be the source of male sexual problems. He identifies the common social qualities of the men he's seen:

> young men, students in a school which conditioned them intensively to perform in terms of goals, tests and expecta-tions; to defer their gratifications and repress their emotions; and be unaware of their bodies. They were being groomed to occupy positions of power and control, to be managers and experts, and not to confess their ignorances and uncertainties; and all this reinforced the stereotype myth that required them to be able to have the expertise, take the initiative, and control the action in sexual transactions.

Sex is a contradictory area of activity for men because so much else of a man's life is a performance, in which he is judged, compared, rated, and then rewarded with money or its equivalent, or punished with its lack. To survive, men must learn to perform successfully, to enact specific behaviors to achieve a goal. Why should sex be different?

Of course, many well-done performances do feel good, including a well-done sexual performance. The sex act treated as precisely and delicately as a Japanese tea ceremony is a performance. Even the sucking by the mouth of the vaginal area becomes a performance. If men do it poorly, they satisfy no one, no matter what their feelings. The question is to what extent is it a performance? What is a man's intention? What is he feeling? How conscious is he? Who is he communicating with, and for what purpose? What is the connection of sexual performance to intimacy with another? Good sex can include performance, when chosen. However, men have overrated the performance aspect of sex, and therefore devalued the feeling underbelly, the real communication—the intimate sexuality.

"I have noticed that most men have performance anxieties, especially in the beginning of a relationship. When a man realizes that nothing turns me off more than a preconceived programmed sexual scenario, he generally relaxes," writes a thirty-two-year-old anonymous woman from Pasadena, California.

It is ironic that some of the best sexual performers receive no satisfaction from sex. There are millions of men who perform adequately, whose erections come automatically and whose style is impeccable, but who do not enjoy sex. The feeling is not there. It feels mechanical.

What they want is deep communication and close connection; what they get is perfect form. What they want from sex is the communication of vulnerability, what they get is "successful" sex. They want romance and love; they get a physical experience.

Some men report a lack of desire or feeling. Their self-expression is rigid. They suffer inhibitions of intimacy. They do sex the way a carpenter builds a bookshelf, adjusting to the new sexual female by learning *how* (the American practical, scientific way) to satisfy her beyond comparison.

Male competition and performance is a perfect setup for lack of desire. What *she* thinks becomes more important than what *he* feels. It leads to a lack of enjoyment with successful performance. "When foreplay is finally initiated," writes a Canadian woman, "the male may sometimes be clumsy, *not* involved with his own pleasure and often oversolicitous in his lovemaking. Somehow I get the feeling that he is not as involved in the playing of the story as he is with his thoughts of tomorrow's reviews."

Rollo May makes this analysis of the performing man in *Love and Will:*

The more one must demonstrate his potency, the more he treats sexual intercourse—this most intimate and personal of

all acts—as a performance to be judged by exterior requirements, the more he then views himself as a machine to be
turned on, adjusted, and steered, and the less feeling he has
for either himself or his partner; and the less feeling, the more
he loses genuine appetite and ability.

Masters and Johnson recommend that men focus on sexual
pleasure and feeling, and forget erections, but being scientists interested in classification and measurement, they see the proof of sexual
pleasure in the existence of the erection. Sex therapy overstresses the
functional, the results—while good sex goes beyond "results" to
feelings. Few, if any, sex researchers have studied the relation of
effective functioning to positive feelings. Apfelbaum says in an unpublished paper, "Everybody knows that people can perform sexually,
have erections and orgasms, and not enjoy it at all. . . . Everything in
their (Masters and Johnson) book is about sexual arousal on a purely
physical level . . . this made sense in their medical framework."

How many men silently identified with the character Jack Nichol-
son played in *Carnal Knowledge*—the superstud who ended up so cut off
from his feelings and sense of joy that only the narrowest sexual script
could arouse him in any way? He had progressed from a hot seducer-
conqueror to a forty-year-old man displaying his old girlfriend's
pictures like trophies on the wall and, in order to feel sexually excited,
needing to play out a totally choreographed master-slave relationship
with a prostitute.

A woman from Rome, New York, explains her experience of this
phenomenon: "For one man I know, promiscuity equals anxiety.
Rather than withdrawal, it is an unfulfilled desire to score in order to
prove masculinity. Which, in the long run, is really proving inadequacy. The inability to experience fulfillment simply leads to addiction.
Orgasm leads to the desire for more and better. Truthfully, can it be
satisfaction then? When sex is compulsive, it is not free and it is not
satisfying."

"American men are driving themselves toward limpness in the
seventies and eighties," according to a man we'll call George, who
quotes women as his authorities. "Every woman tells me in the
morning, 'It's different with you, I haven't been fucked with such skill
and intensity in years.'" He sat back and closed his eyes briefly before
continuing. "For me, fucking represents everything from searching for
the mother, to feeling physical companionship, to doing something
masculine so well that I can brag about it in the country club, to losing
yourself in a woman. I want to be hard, as hard as I can be, as soon as I
can be. I especially like to stop in the middle of fucking for a long time

to demonstrate how much control I have. I sometimes get hostile just to fuck her harder. Sometimes I like to hit her head, very gently, across the headboard of the bed as we are coming. But, I mean very gently.

"I can give a woman fifteen orgasms an hour, but you've got to make sure that she doesn't think that you expect it, or she'll tighten up. So many women these days are suffering from constricted cunts, a form of vaginal atrophy caused by men who won't be men, who won't complete the sexual performance, and buddy, it is a performance. If you don't accept that, how can you perform well?

"Blame it on the energy crisis, living in a country dying of no leadership, lack of will, of no self-confidence, an overconsumptive, nonproductive society, the death of Puritan guilt and the birth of an uncomfortable hedonism, or the loss of our masculinity in Vietnam, but damn it, American men are choosing impotence. I can understand it. They are afraid of rejection by the woman. They even use getting drunk as an excuse. Anxiety sets in and renders them impotent. It takes a strong man to say 'Here it is baby. Take it.' If you're lame and the woman leaves you the next day, you can blame it on your cock, not yourself. If I give it hard to her, and she leaves me, well she's leaving me. So many men want to be limp because they can't stand to be rejected by a woman. If the woman accepts you limp, you are in control. Then she really wants you, not your penis, or fucking ability. You really feel loved. And you can make your penis hard whenever you want to. The pressure is off to keep performing. I understand why American, and probably even European, and maybe all men in the world, these days want to be limp.

"Have you heard about the kundalini orgasm? You get hard as a rock, enter and don't move. You look into each other's eyes for fifteen minutes to an hour, without any movement. You stay hard as a rod. Breathe together. Then at a precise moment you make. one fast movement of your penis. Give it the best thrust you can, with total intensity and concentration, and it's unforgettable. You and the woman come together in unbelievable orgasm.

"But really I prefer good, old-fashioned, powerful fucking. Time. Patience. Commitment. You've got to tune into each other. Make her feel comfortable. I have a wandering lust. I'm a junkie and women are my heroin."

This sexual summa cum laude demonstrates how challenging sex is to many men. Instead of loving communication, it can be a test of will and control, an exercise of power and potency. Sex of this kind can be satisfying, just as mountain climbing or wrestling can be, but it lacks ease and a sense of trust. It lacks the emotional honesty necessary for intimacy.

NOT FOR MEN ONLY

Men Are Sexually More Vulnerable Than Women

A tough businessman said to me at lunch one day, "Women want me to be mean. They don't like me when I get soft and sweet." He leaned over his hamburger when he heard we were writing a book on male sexuality and whispered, "Most men, you know, are scared shitless of sex."

Men are much more sexually vulnerable than women. Male genitals hang out; men can't easily fake orgasm; if they don't get an erection, they can't hide it or fulfill the male function of reproduction. Therefore it is not surprising that men have invented the superstructure of male chauvinism to hide their basic vulnerability. "A lady could fuck me and not want me," says a Pittsburgh salesman. "I'm the guy who needs the hard-on."

A woman, on the other hand, can accommodate a man's penis inside her vagina without being turned on. Vaseline or any other lubricant will wet the vaginal highway and provide smooth entrance for the penis. A woman can conceive a baby without being sexually excited or having an orgasm. A woman can fake sexual electricity to make the man's ego feel good and to end sex quickly. Women have been doing it for centuries. Man's bank balance is there for all to see.

A friend of ours once watched his wife make love to a mutual friend for two hours. He did it to free himself of "possession toward my wife and jealousy, and to break through sexually." After the session he said to his wife, "You looked like you were having more fun with him than you've had in a long time."

"Are you serious?" she replied. "I never even got turned on. You don't know how to read me sexually after all these years?"

No technical symbols, like an erection, are *required* for a woman to be lovingly there. A woman from Atlanta, Georgia, shares her understanding for the male situation: "You might say I have a compassion for men with problems because at one time I could not orgasm. I would fake it because I wanted the man to feel he really turned me on. A man can't fake it like a woman can. He may even be loving the foreplay without an erection but he'll still find it hard to relax for fear of how the woman feels."

"With a woman there's no visible proof she's nervous. It shows up for me by not being able to come. If I were a man, there's a good chance I couldn't make it happen either," writes a New Mexico woman.

A male friend told us that his ex-wife admitted to him, in a rare moment of male-female sexual noncombat, "I guess if I were a man I could probably count on getting an erection maybe thirty percent of the time. But I kept that realization a secret from you."

Erica Jong hit the screw on the head when she said,

> . . . the older you got, the clearer it became that men were basically terrified of women. Some secretly, some openly. What could be more poignant than a liberated woman eye to eye with a limp prick? All history's greatest issues paled by comparison with these two quintessential objects: the eternal woman and the eternal limp prick. . . .
>
> That was the basic inequality which could never be righted: not that the male had a wonderful added attraction called a penis, but that the female had a wonderful all-weather cunt. Neither storm nor sleet, nor dark of night could faze it. It was always there, always ready. Quite terrifying, when you think about it. No wonder men hated women. No wonder they invented the myth of female inadequacy.

The fact that biologically a man cannot lie encourages men to be closed-mouthed with each other, and to exaggerate in order to hide the vulnerability of being a man. When you're so vulnerable, you've got to build a big fence around you so that no one can get at your "soft spot." Finally, men lose vulnerability with themselves, and forget that they are really terrified.

"Your Mind Is Willing but Your Body Isn't"

Few men will volunteer—or even admit—that they have trouble getting or staying erect.

"I never have that problem" is the automatic response, bringing to mind Jeb Magruder's explanation of Watergate, "From the first moment, there never was any doubt that there would be a cover-up." Men claim no problems but on some level every man has a fear of impotence. Hemingway's Jake of *The Sun Also Rises* is one of the most famous characters in literature with genital problems. Norman Kiell, in *The Varieties of Sexual Experience*, writes that, "In choosing impotence as a principal plot device, Hemingway was betraying one of the most fundamental and pervasive fears he, and most men, have: the fear of losing one's manhood, which carries with it the fear of either never having had it or never fully attaining it."

The potent man can be running away from impotence, the way the violent man is running away from cowardice and fear. No wonder, for as Sam Keen, a *Psychology Today* editor, writes, "The worst thing that can happen to us in this life is for a man to be impotent and a woman to be frigid. The religion of sexuality says that the highest thing of value is sex, and in sex the goal is orgasm."

Dr. Shel Feldman, author of *The Virile Man*, says, "I've found that every potent man has an impotent guy inside him somewhere. But if the impotent guy inside you is confronted it's a giant step toward becoming even more potent. Yet almost everyone I see measures themselves down deep mainly by one extreme when it comes to sexual performance. The wrong extreme. . . . In sex we use standards which, if we applied them to other areas of our lives, would qualify us for the nuthouse."

No statistics exist—or actually can exist—on erectile insecurity in America today. The subject has been too delicate for discussion among male friends. Where is the man who will tell another man that he didn't deliver? It takes courage even to reveal erection stage fright to your therapist or physician.

But virtually every man—and woman—has personally experienced at least one horror movie about the inability of a male to, as one man put it, "deliver the sexual goods." Listen to one Macho Man's recollection to us: "The first time it ever happened, I was horrified! Terrified! Humiliated! I was thirty years old in Lisbon, Portugal, with an absolutely gorgeous girl about twenty-three or twenty-four. I wanted her like hell! She thought I didn't like her and became very upset with herself and me, compounding the situation! It was the first time my cock had ever failed me in my time of need!"

How can a man describe to a woman the agony he feels and how that suffering is increased by *his* interpretation of *her* reaction! Peter, one of the men we interviewed, wrote in his journal: "She reached for my cock and it was limp. I could feel her body pulsating with fear. Even though we all put on a false front, we always blame ourselves when something doesn't go our way. Elizabeth's face revealed horror. She panted for penetration from me. I wanted to do it—but I was limp as a dishrag, and getting limper by the moment. I felt like dying. I felt completely worthless as a human being."

Few men can imagine sex without an erection. Most men automatically—and falsely—identify their sexual arousal completely with their penis's alertness. The game is determined by the final score. The goals justify the process. As Jim, an electronics engineer, points out, sex is incomplete without the erection leading to orgasm. Jim says, "I can't really enjoy sex fully without an erection and an orgasm—at least one. But after my orgasm I can certainly enjoy sex without another."

"Men lie about sex," says Norman King, a fifty-four-year-old advertising and marketing multimillionaire. "You want to know the truth? Nobody is fucking any more. I am not talking about fucking at home. I am talking about men who can't fuck their wives or their secretaries."

King thinks the pressure has come from the New Sexual Woman, which increases male desperation. "It used to be dinner, then a movie, then home to fuck. Today the dinner and movie are no longer necessary. Women expect to fuck before dinner. And fucking is always a test for the man. The penis does not lie. The erection is the moment of truth."

King, like many men, envies women: "All they have to do is open their legs, and enjoy it or not enjoy it. Nobody knows. But men, we are public. If you don't get it up, it's horrible. And the moment it doesn't happen once, it's death, because you're going to start worrying it's going to happen again, and your worrying is going to stop your erections. So you forget about sex and start making money!"

King finally realized that there were millions of dollars to be made on the erection. He sent a questionnaire to a thousand Wall Street businessmen, and the response rate was 30%. He sent the same questionnaire to a list of blue collar workers and the response was "even better. Enormous. Men are desperate. They have nowhere to go for help." King's idea, in the development stage, is to start a series of Male Potency Clinics, like McDonald's hamburger stands, all across the U.S.A. to dispense biofeedback techniques, erotic movies, high-powered vitamins, feel-good shots and sexual educational lectures to men chasing their failing erections. "And," he adds, "every man at some time in his life is going to have some difficulty with his erection. You watch. It gets harder as you get older."

As a teenager, the mere visual sight or flicker of fantasy of the female shape might result in the A.E. (Automatic Erection), the way the mouth begins to salivate at the smell of food. Eventually men discover that they must physically stimulate their genitals to create and maintain what was once automatic. Many men get scared when they lose the A.E. and require physical touch and mental play to keep it. What once came automatically now takes time.

It's often the pressures for performance that block the performance by allowing anxiety to ambush sexual concentration. Then a man wrongly begins scolding his penis, and blitzkrieging his self-concept of masculinity, when it's the pressure to please that is often the problem in the first place. Especially if a man is in bed with a beautiful woman. "I've been impotent with five luscious and ravishing women," writes a twenty-one-year-old from Florida. "The more beautiful they are, the more pressure I feel to make it."

The Politics of Potency

What some therapists call "nonreadiness" is often a protest. It is noncooperation. It is the penis saying, "I will not play with you." My penis cannot create the conditions for its life, but it does have veto power. As Sam Keen puts it, "Impotence and frigidity are revolutions in the body politic. Your body is trying to tell you something. It's making a statement to you. Often frigidity is the way of resistance to tyranny and fascism. Sexual tyranny and fascism is when your head is telling you, 'Okay, buddy, this is what you're going to do. There's one right way and there's one wrong way.' Respect impotence, and respect frigidity. Don't cure it, find out what it is saying."

That's when the politics of potency comes in. To what extent is "impotence" a disguised rebellion at the sexual demands of women? Or withdrawal at the loss of male power over women? To what extent is impotence the result of the competitive performance demands with which men hype each other? To what extent is "impotence" the penis's demand for self-respect and autonomy?

Men often believe the worst about themselves. In some African tribes an "impotent" man is an outcast. Other men stay away from him for fear of "catching" the disease. However, in some male chauvinist cultures, men are actually very sympathetic to other men. They do not have the therapeutic self-examination tradition which assigns self-responsibility (and therefore a possible inkling of blame) to the man. In those cultures, as in the tradition of the Berbers of Northern Africa, the men support each other because they blame the woman. A nonfunctioning man is considered by historical myth to be the victim of a woman who puts a curse on him by writing his name on a piece of paper, putting the paper on the blade of a knife, shutting the knife and burying it. Only when the paper is destroyed can the man regain his virility.

In the West, the myths about "impotence," until recently, concluded that the nonerect man suffered from a deep psychological maladjustment. Everything from unresolved oedipal complexes, to latent homosexuality, to castration anxieties were scare concepts marched out by psychiatrists to haunt men. Dr. Helen Kaplan refers to the man who ingested six drinks and then invented a freudian-sounding horror story to analyze his lack of hardness, forgetting the most obvious cause—that, as Shakespeare said, a little alcohol may whet the desire, but too much blocks the performance.

Another psychiatrist, Dr. Arnold Lazarus, tells the story of a nineteen-year-old-man who sincerely believed that his penis was endangered by the vagina's violent spasms and contractions. "The chief psychiatrist accordingly referred to 'deep-seated castration anxieties'. . . . Yet, when one of the doctors simply corrected the lad's misconception and offered him factual information bolstered by the force of his own prestige, the problem was instantly resolved."

For some men, the moment of entrance provides the greatest challenge. In Indian folklore a common male myth is that the vagina has teeth! A famous scientist once hoaxed the psychiatric community for fifty years. He invented a case study of a man who got his cock stuck inside a woman's cunt and, like the canine, just couldn't get out. He lost his penis. This paper was published and quoted in scientific papers until the hoax was revealed. Only among people who on some level held this fear could such an absurd claim have been believed for so long.

"Your Mind Is Willing but Your Body Isn't"

You probably know her name. A top reigning Hollywood sex symbol and TV superstar. We met in an Italian restaurant in Beverly Hills where I was having dinner with the publisher of a West Coast magazine. She was sitting alone at a table not far away. At first I thought she was waiting for somebody. Then it became surprisingly apparent she was having dinner alone.

"I often come by here for dinner alone," she told us twenty minutes later, after the publisher invited her to sit with us. Up close she seemed smaller in stature than she appeared on TV. And I was happy to see a slight mustache, because it humanized her, making me realize that she wasn't perfect. We talked enthusiastically about the differences between New York and Los Angeles. We both agreed that the L.A. sun cannot match New York soul. We talked about every subject in the world except the one I was slowly becoming most interested in: sex.

Finally, I invited her and the publisher to drop by a George Carlin concert I had planned to attend. The publisher begged off. Surprisingly, she accepted. And then it began, the unfolding of an unbelievably good dream—that turns into a nightmare!

We held hands during the concert, and I considered that a sign of good things to come. After the concert, in the car in the parking lot, I boldly put my arm around her in a testing move and she softened and moved toward me. I drove out of the lot one-handed, and kissed her at the first red light. In two miles I very forwardly put *her* hand on my penis and it was hard. I felt myself getting hotter and hotter as I drove through the streets. Unable to wait a minute longer, I pulled over to the side of Melrose and we began to make out in a driveway off the street.

For me at that time, there was no greater sexual pleasure than to dry hump with my clothes on. My penis size is hidden, I am erect and I can exercise perfect sexual control. I feel at the peak of pleasure. We kissed long, slow, delicious kisses. We hugged. I rubbed my hand over her tits and her whole body and we rolled over and over in the car in true fifties-style sex. Another car approached. She suggested we go to her house.

It was breathtaking, comfortable, filled with books. The dope we smoked was some of the best I've ever savored. The champagne was Dom Perignon, and there were even pharmaceutical Quaaludes. We were kissing wildly while drinking, smoking, talking. I asked her questions in what she laughingly referred to as the Jerry Rubin Premarriage Interview, while we took breaths between kisses. "Do you have a lover? Are you interested in a relationship? Do you ever smoke cigarettes?" By three A.M., when this beautiful lady and I fell back onto her bed, I was happy, high and hot, and I hoped I'd be able to keep it up. Within three minutes we were naked.

But what moments earlier had been pure sexual abandon now became a sexual test, a performance. Now the point was to get hard and stick it in. And keep it in. And if I didn't, I'd be a selfish man who believes in quickies for myself. The sheets were soon drenched with my sweat. When I finally managed to get erect I tried to insert my cock inside her but every time it came close to the entrance of the vagina my erection softened. I finally entered.

The strangest feeling of all is when you are hot and strong, and slowly, you feel yourself losing your erection inside her pussy. Hurry, hurry! You flash through your motion picture mind all the fantasies that you can to save that failing erection! You wonder: Does she know? Can she tell? Can she feel it?

"You're hard, but you're not really hard, do you know what I mean?" is the way one man put it in a men's consciousness group. Everyone in the room nodded.

Once the penis starts its downward slope, it starts getting soggier and soggier. Pretty soon you know you are as soft as a pancake. And it all happens inside. You're confused. Embarrassed.

I lost my erection.

My flaccid penis didn't seem to faze her, although I figured that as a sex symbol she would expect all her men to have automatic, self-regenerating erections. Patiently, she said, "Here, leave it to me," and she took my cock into her mouth. I almost pushed her head away; I hate to have my cock sucked when it's not hard, like someone trying a last-ditch attempt at mouth-to-mouth resuscitation, slurping at my small member. And then I worried, how much time do I have to get it up before she gets disgusted? And what can you say when she fails and she's been working an embarrassingly long time on a limp dick? "Don't worry about it, it's my problem." Whatever you say sounds stupid.

After a while I said nothing, but gently nudged her head away from my groin and tried to move her into my favorite position in hopes that would aid me in getting hard. I guess we all have our favorite positions that stimulate us the most direct way. Mine is to lay on top of the woman with her legs closed and move up and down in a dry-hump style, bringing back the memories of those bad 1950s drive-in dry fucks. I moved on top of her in this manner, but to no avail as far as my penis was concerned. I was too nervous, I was blocking, I couldn't relax. I was trying too hard.

The more I tried, the more I tensed and immobilized my body's muscles. As a man I've been taught that in times of crises or doubt you must *do* something. So I kept doing, pushing, trying. Yet having an erection is a matter of allowing, not pressuring. All my trying just proved the truth of Fritz Perls's gestalt slogan that "Trying is Lying." At last, the dream woman's impatience overcame her. She pushed my cock aside and said, "Your mind is willing but your body isn't."

It was as if she had plunged a nine-inch sharp knife into my stomach, and blood began pouring out over the sheets. I felt like saying something. My mouth was open, but nothing came out. All I felt was a hollowness in my gut. There I was, naked in her bed, my manhood ripped to shreds, lying there like a helpless child. If I had been a real man at the time, I would have cried. I wanted the floor to open up and swallow me whole.

Your mind is willing but your body isn't. The words rang in my ears. I tried to understand them. How could my mind be willing if my body wasn't? Didn't my mind tell my body what to do? Maybe my body was willing but my mind wasn't. Was she angry because I had promised her implicitly a sexual adventure that neither my mind nor body was willing to deliver? I had failed as the male, as the provider.

She was fast asleep, and I was lying there, abandoned, feeling like a fool, a knave, a fraud. No matter how badly I felt, the irony of the situation did not escape me. Had she ever looked at the sleeping back of a man? Did she desert me in my time of need because of accumulated anger at scores of men who had sexually deserted her? Here I was alternating between making excuses for her and feeling that she had searingly castrated and humiliated me. It is hard to describe the pain of sexual humiliation—the pain that rips to the core of a man.

Pain! The pain of being a man who is in bed with a woman but not feeling like a man. The pain of not knowing how the other person feels, or for that matter, how you feel. The pain of finding the bedroom a test rather than a pleasure bed. Losing and failing.

I couldn't face her in the morning. I sneaked out of her bed and quickly got dressed and disappeared in the middle of the night like a criminal. I left hating her for her cruel honesty. But mostly, I hated my cock for not coming through when I needed it.

I woke up in my own bed, dulled. The only way I could get out of bed was when I thought about how much work I had to do. Work, my only salvation. And I dragged myself through the day, unable to shake the shroud of the previous evening's experience.

The Dutiful Erection

The experts on male sexual anxiety are the gynecologists, who hear it from the women. Catherine told her gynecologist, "I've just about given up on relationships. I'm discouraged. I've seen so many men in the past year. More than half of them couldn't get or keep it up. Those that could couldn't care about pleasing me. The big effort was usually: Can they keep their erection? What's wrong with men these days with their erections? I'd give anything to meet a decent, nice man who enjoyed sex, could get erections and cared about pleasing me too."

It's difficult to aways produce an erection to please the woman, what one writer calls a "dutiful erection." (To which his girlfriend responds, "I never want to see one of those.") Ironically, men discover that the desperate need to prove potency is itself a major cause of "impotence." It puts pressure on the performance, creates a potentially catastrophic attitude, places the partner in the role of judge, and makes each sex experience an event.

And in the past ten years, American men have been instructed to do just that: "manufacture" on-demand erections for the "consumer" woman. Reading Dr. David Reuben is like receiving direct educational training in impotence. "In a sense, when it comes to sex," writes Reuben, "man is the manufacturer and woman is the consumer. His job is to (1) manufacture a rigid and erect penis, (2) deliver it to the consumer in good condition, (3) help her to install the product, (4) remain on the premises long enough to be sure it provides her with satisfactory service." He concludes, "Every woman is programmed to have an orgasm *virtually every time she has intercourse.*"

Who puts the greatest pressure on the penis? Without a doubt, men. But even if men could turn their demands into preferences, they'd still find women who require erections for their own reasons. One man wrote to us, "Erection is important to me during sex because women are taught this myth that males should always have one when they're in bed with you. I find it impossible to reeducate most women concerning this."

Inside every strong woman lives a male chauvinist who wants to be overwhelmed by a strong erection. Many women are still looking for that Big Cock in the Sky; they want us to convince them that they are women. Many macho men insist that women want them to be chauvinistic, and they have a point.

True to traditional sexual roles, some women won't let themselves receive pleasure until the man's pleasure instrument first shows itself. One woman says, "His erection *is* important to me. Without it, what good is it? It sounds funny, but it's true! I for one am highly (and I mean *highly),* stimulated by the sight of a nice hard-on! It's a big factor in my stimulation in the sex act."

A woman wants to be desired, and the penis is a male desiring instrument. It is a symbol whose meaning is "you're sexy." Betsy, a waitress from Topeka, said, "If I was trying to arouse a man and he didn't get an erection, I'd feel very disappointed—mainly in myself—and I would tend to wonder more what is wrong with me rather than him. (Am I not appealing enough, etc.)"

Women can feel hurt and rejected when the man does not produce an erection. A twenty-one-year-old woman from Tulsa, Oklahoma, reveals her self-blame: "Sometimes (most often) it makes me feel it is my fault—I'm not doing the right things. I'm not stimulating enough when he thinks about me, or he's thinking about someone else, and the realization it's me and not her defeats them."

"If a man doesn't have an erection while I am trying to turn him on, I get mad at myself," writes a woman from Arkansas. "It's important to me that a man have an erection during sex. It makes *me* feel important and attractive."

Even when they know better, women admit that insecurity turns to self-hate. "I'm giving him head," writes one woman, "and he can't get it up. I feel very bad for two reasons—one, he evidently doesn't feel relaxed with me or just doesn't like the way I'm doing it; two, I feel like a failure, a repulsive creep who can't make him feel a thing."

Many women identify their own sexuality entirely with the man's erection. If he didn't rise and stay risen, something clearly was *wrong* with *them.*

When self-blame takes over, can self-hate be far behind? And isn't the next thing to strike out defensively against your partner? Listen to one woman's lament: "I would totally flip out if I couldn't arouse a man sexually enough for him to have a semi-erection," one woman writes.

High in a Manhattan highrise the conversation turned to sex. The six guests were celebrating one friend's birthday, and the champagne was flowing. We decided to become provocative, and ventured the view that it's better if women come first, because for men, one orgasm often ends sex for the night. (Kinsey said that 92% of all men did not go beyond a first orgasm.) The other men reacted ferociously. "Not true!" "I come many times in one night!" We had no idea who was telling the truth and who was lying that night since we know that in sex, lying is virtually expected.

We asked the other women at the table how crucial a hard penis was to them in sex. Louise spoke up. She was an actress known for a long string of wooed, loved, deserted and resentful men. "I guess I'm traditional and old-fashioned," she said, "but I like hard and big penises. I know it's not hip to admit it, but that's how I feel."

Later we began talking privately with Louise about erections. "If I'm naked with a guy and he doesn't have an erection, I want to know why. I expect immediate arousal. I've always assumed that a man gets erect like an uncontrolled reflex, like batting your eye," said Louise.

We softly corrected some of Louise's misconceptions about male arousal and the erection, especially the vulnerability of the male response system to a sneak attack by the submarine of anxiety. She said, "I guess women are as ignorant of male sexuality as men are about women." She kept shaking her head.

We finally realized that women need as much education about male sexuality as men need about themselves and about female sexuality. Information, plus new attitudes, will create a transformation in sexual pleasure. After all, men brainwashed women in the first place to male expectations in sex. Men equate sex with orgasm through intercourse. In order to orgasm, men (usually) require erections. Women know that men demand orgasm and erections; therefore women expect erections. And when it doesn't happen, women tend to personalize its nonhappening. And then question their own attractiveness, which lets loose psychic madness.

There are, however, some women who are not upset by a no-show erection. Dr. Apfelbaum suggests that many women don't care whether or not a man's penis is hard. A soft penis may be communicating interference, but a hard penis may imply that the man is turned on—when he isn't. He's got an ever-ready, spontaneous, automatic erection, but *he* may not even be there. He may have become a penis that is performing.

Another sex therapist confidentially told us, "A few years ago I was seeing a woman and I felt very turned on, and didn't get an erection. The woman liked it, because she said that the last man that she had sex with was a man with a nonstop, dominating erection. She felt used by him in sex. She missed sensitivity and feeling from him."

Indeed, some of the women who answered our questionnaire said that they didn't expect or need erections. One woman, M. K. of Cleveland, wrote us, saying, "Most of the time, his erection is not essential. The way he groans, sighs, moves his hips and body turns me on much more than nothing but a stiff old penis. How dull. I look at it as nothing more than an extending barometer of itself."

Most men, however, still think that all the woman is waiting for is his erection—the center of sex. The opposite is often true. Donna from San Jose says, "I think it's a sad sight to see an erection right at the beginning of sex, because that means he's all in a hurry to relieve himself." Apfelbaum calls it "the premature erection." Another said, "I like it when a guy gets into bed with me with a limp cock. I know he's there not just to get his rocks off, but to enjoy me and the whole process of lovemaking."

Women might learn not to take a no-show erection personally when they realize that it is often a compliment to them. One man personally shared with us his experience that, whenever he couldn't have intercourse, it was because he liked the woman and wanted a relationship with her. The liking produced tension and a desire to please. "If I didn't want a longer relationship with the woman, I would have no difficulty," he said. "That's one of the things I noticed about my sexual impulse. If I like the woman, I often become anxious."

Huge Trees, Tiny Twigs

Men's problems: "First of all, there are *big* problems and *small* problems," joked Gilda Radner on a "Men's Problems" TV show spoof on "Saturday Night Live." Many men are petrified that their penises are either too small or too big, too thin or too crooked.

At my college speeches, I sometimes ask the men in the room to publicly reveal the size of their penis, erect and nonerect. If they want, they can pass. We gave a workshop at Princeton University for the 1979 conference of the Association of Humanistic Psychology. Two hundred people, including sex therapists, psychologists, family counselors, growth seekers, men's movement leaders and other activists in the people-helping-people network across America gathered in a room, not knowing what to expect, and soon they found themselves in one of the most intimate conversations about the situation of men and women in bed today.

Early in the workshop, we asked the men to stand and reveal the size of their penises, in the flaccid and erect state. A nervous and excited titter shook the room. I said, "I'll start, so people will feel comfortable, because I've got a small penis."

Before I had a chance to give my measurements, though, a woman raised her hand, saying, "That's ridiculous. Who measures their penises, anyway?"

A distinguished-looking middle-aged man from the other side of the room replied, "I do. A friend of mine, a woman doctor, thinks all men are born with a ruler in their hands. Fully erect, I'm one-sixteenth over six inches. I felt good about that because I've been reading *Penthouse* and they say six inches is the magic length." (Boos and laughter from around the room.)

"A normal nonerection is approximately one-and-a-quarter to one-and-a-half inches." After a pause for effect he continued: "And a nonerecetion after a cold shower is approximately half an inch." The room burst out in appreciative laughter as he continued, "You must realize by now that I'm an analyzer."

Another man said, "Hey, the real sophisticates in the comparison game measure things like angle of the dangle. And they measure not only the speed to full erection, but the rate of acceleration."

"I must be abnormal," said one man, "because I can't get mine that small. I used to think my penis was small. I remember when I was eight or nine years old and I'd go into public urinals and look out of curiosity, and of course make a comparison, and once I felt that I was a dwarf. Little did I know at the time that this guy was built like a horse and was exceptionally large. Yes, I absolutely did measure my penis and I still remember reading the articles in the magazines where you can send away for penis enlargers. I deliberated whether or not I wanted to do that. Would they work? Or would they cause damage?"

In our workshop a man asked, "I've always had this concern: how do you measure the curve?"

"Use a tape measure, not a ruler," responded another man.

"Most important is this," said another. "I thought I was small until I learned that you don't measure from the top, you measure from underneath."

Finally, the competition in the room became, "Who could be honest in revealing their smallness?" One man finally warned people not to all seek "the gentleman's 'C.' How come nobody will stand up and reveal anything if it's over six inches?"

At the end of the workshop, a short man in a turtleneck sweater called us aside and said, "I didn't have the balls to say this during the workshop because I don't want to go around advertising that I have a big cock. But the reality is that women tell me, 'Hey, I enjoy your big cock.' I've got several women that go out with me because I have a big cock. We have great sex. They like the penetration, the depth. They like to be filled up completely by a masculine person. And I love to perform for them. Because of my penis, I tell you, I get a lot of return engagements."

So even in a room full of sexual humanists, the feeling of sexual competition and the big penis ethos has not died out—just gone underground.

But the absurdity of the sexual competition is undermined when honest and open discussion begins. Men compare themselves to other men in sex because it's a secret competition. And the competition reinforces the nonintimate aspects of sex. Would the comparison of our penises and orgasms continue if we made them public?

The winners in the cock fight quote women as the judges. A disc jockey from Alaska reveals himself most symbolically: "How do I compare my cock? On the basis of what 'she' says: vastly superior, definitely in the top two percent for several reasons—seven-and-a-half inches, two-inch diameter, like most wrists; staying power when desired; and most of all a caring, give-a-damn, loving attitude."

He continues, "Among the 'she' people: a former Vegas call girl who'd visit me (free) repeatedly and said that I gave better head and she achieved a faster and more powerful climax than with all previous lovers, including lesbians and other bi women; another callgirl who'd knock on my neighboring window on her off nights—again free; and another woman who, after five different afternoons of making love and/or fucking, she gave me $1100—no strings—apparently 'cause she was happy; and this final illustration was a top photographers' model who could have anyone!"

A few pages later, the disc jockey comes back to the subject of number one: "Actually he's pretty scarred up and perhaps could even be called ugly on close inspection, scars from chicks with sharp teeth, from sand (when fucking on a damned beach, which I'll *never* do again), abrasions from too much friction/hair, going too long—five-and-a-half hours one time. . . ."

Bart, another sweepstakes winner, says,

I love it! I'm proud of it! If I had my "druthers" I'd like it to be a little thicker and at least a half inch longer, but I must emphasize that I am in no way unhappy with it! These good feelings about my penis come from women. I'm sure if their reactions to it were not consistently good, mine would not be good. My limp cock measures three to four inches in length. I would prefer that in its relaxed state, it hung five to six inches in length. Erect it measures seven-and-a-half inches from pubic bone to tip and is about six inches in circumference (depending on where you measure). No woman has ever complained to me about its size. The preference for more thickness and a little bit more length is mine and mine alone!

I would not like to have more than eight or eight-and-a-half inches in length because I have hit bottom in many women and they have told me I have all they can take. This makes me believe that to have nine or ten inches could cause problems when attempting to fuck a goodly percentage of the female population.

Only a few men are satisfied with the size of their organs. Size has become such an obsession that in the past fifteen years, during the outbreak of the competitive Sexual Revolution, more than three thousand United States patents have been secured for instruments to attach to the penis-tool to make it bigger. Ah, the American obsession with technology to solve any human problem! Some of these devices are advertised in the national sex magazines as "Enlarge Your Penis" aids.

Caveman wall pictures emphasize the large erection. The earliest stone carvings include men with erections. Greek vases show men with huge erections. Our erotic literature throughout the ages is replete with examples of the opinion that "the male organ . . . is the foundation of sexual pleasure and that women's pleasure depends entirely upon male equipment and performance. Crudely, the bigger the better."

In many cultures, and during Shakespearean times in our own civilization, the "exhibitionist" codpiece, adorning and augmenting the penis, was worn. It may be making a comeback even today, if Eldridge Cleaver's new codpiece-pants business succeeds.

Since Japanese culture says small is beautiful, and honors the power of the tiny, we wondered if the Japanese extend their attitude toward computers and transistors to the penis. "Look at Japanese pornography," says the author of a history of the penis, Mark Strage. "The penis is as large as a man's arm in Japanese erotic art. Only in liberated America is the idea widespread that size does not matter. And I think we only do lip service to that idea."

A big penis means Big Business. With women, however, we believe that Small is Beautiful. As Germaine Greer says, "The best thing a cunt can be is small and unobtrusive . . . no woman wants to find out that she has a twat like a horse collar." Mark Strage explains, "If the fit's not right, you can say that the hole was too big."

Human beings tend to break themselves into pieces and in consumer, advertising-heavy America, compare their pieces with each other. With the men, the most elemental male competition is over penis size, while for women it is often breast size.

Men, however, are the true experts at detaching and objectifying. The *Playboy* sex pollsters ask men: Are you a breast or a leg man? Do you prefer the asses or the tits? What shapes do you like? Men have been cutting up and comparing women's bodies for years. Little surprise they were doing the same to themselves, and focusing on their primary weapon—the penis, their instrument of reproduction and pleasure.

Even Anthony Pietropinto, coauthor of *Beyond the Male Myth*, which whitewashed men in response to *The Hite Report*, says that many men "regard their genitals as detached objects, independent of their thoughts and emotions, and their sexual partners become the equally detached targets of their genitals." Most men we interviewed totally identified their sexual turn-on with their penis. In sex, most men think they are their penis. Period.

Men are usually more concerned about the size of their genitals than they are about any other part of their body. And it is a secret concern. One woman, ironically, suggests that men wear signs on their chest giving the size—erect and nonerect—of their penises. "That way we can settle the competition for the best places in the male pecking order and get on to important work," she says. "I don't know what the hell men are competing about, anyway."

Venable Herndon, author and Hollywood screenwriter, wrote in *Ms.* Magazine that he first recognized that "men are deprived of a knowledge of their own bodies, perhaps even more severely than women" when two men and two women, strangers to each other, began undressing in the Esalen baths. "I had imagined that the men would have a hard time pretending that they were not looking at the women. Wrong! When we stripped, the men had a hard time not looking at each other."

Herndon says that he never saw his father's penis, limp or hard, and therefore imagined it to be a "monstrous engine, a veritable battering ram. After all, he had five wives, many affairs, and a whole bunch of one-night stands."

I snatched a few looks at my father's cock once in the shower and it seemed like a huge tree compared to my tiny twig. I never saw my father's penis hard. I feel occasionally depressed when I go into a men's room. There they are—big cocks, long enough to be carried by hand while urinating. My penis always seems much smaller, and that hurts.

Why did my penis look so small? Could it be that everyone's cock looks small to himself? Could it be an optical illusion like looking at your penis in a strange mirror?

The tension of men naked with each other can be overwhelming. You and a male friend go into the john together and find yourself at urinals next to each other. You have never seen your close friend's weapon. And you can never just turn and look. You can't examine or you might be accused of "homosexual tendencies." Watch men trying *not* to look at the length, width and shape of other men's genitals.

Why the ban against looking at each other's genitals? Why the veil of secrecy, which perpetuates the mystery and the competition? Here, too, men can learn from women. Artist Betsy Dodson created masturbation classes for women in which the women lovingly examine each other's vaginas and clitorises with the rule of the game being, "Every woman's pussy is perfect. Every woman's pussy is beautiful."

I took a sensuality class at Esalen that broke through my genital-secrecy barriers. Sue, the massage teacher, suggested that all fourteen people strip naked. They were some old, fat people in the workshop, and I figured if they'd do it, I certainly would. We each took turns walking around the room in the raw. We examined each other's penises. We massaged each other's genitals, with no aim other than touch. I had never before seen men's penises that clearly, for no purpose other than pure observation.

I realized a penis is a penis is a penis. All are beautiful. Men need to reduce the importance and embarrassment attached to the male genitals. And certainly, in sexual situations, the penis should only add to the intimacy between partners, not distance them from each other with judgment and shame.

The Female Judge Strikes Again

The sexually hip view these days is that size does not matter in terms of sexual satisfaction. This view, perpetuated by sex therapists, is that since a vagina will fit any penis size comfortably—like a tight, elastic glove—size is irrelevant. Wrong. Size probably does not physiologically matter. But thoughts are as real as physical measurements. And the idea that women do not care about penis size is wishful thinking on the part of many men. Many women have bought the American bigger-is-better philosophy. A lot of female judges out there prefer gigantic male tools. The fact is that women are often as macho as men when it comes to penis size, as we've seen in some of our questionnaires.

One of the most poignant examples of this was revealed by Ernest Hemingway in a meeting with his close friend F. Scott Fitzgerald, who called him up one day in Paris in 1943 and invited him for lunch at Michaud's. Hemingway later wrote, "He said that he had something very important to ask me that meant more than anything in the world to him and that I must answer absolutely truly." Hemingway had no idea what it was. Hemingway later wrote that Fitzgerald's distrust of his answer virtually destroyed the warmth between these two friends.

Fitzgerald ate through the whole lunch without even hinting at the big secret. "I kept waiting for it to come, the thing that I had to tell the absolute truth about; but he would not bring it up until the end of the meal, as though we were having a business lunch," recalls Hemingway.

"You know I never slept with anyone except Zelda," said Fitzgerald.

"No, I didn't."

"I thought I had told you."

"No. You told me a lot of things but not that."

"That is what I have to ask you about."

"Good. Go on."

"Zelda said that the way I was built I could never make any woman happy and that was what upset her originally. She said it was a matter of measurements. I have never felt the same since she said that and I have to know truly."

Hemingway suggested that he and Fitzgerald go to the bathroom. They did. They returned to the table, and Hemingway said, "You're perfectly fine. You are okay. There's nothing wrong with you. You look at yourself from above and you look foreshortened. Go over to the Louvre and look at the people in the statues and then go home and look at yourself in the mirror in profile."

Fitzgerald disagreed, then said, "But why would she say it?"

Hemingway responded, "To put you out of business. That's the oldest way in the world of putting people out of business. Scott, you asked me to tell you the truth and I can tell you a lot more but this is the absolute truth and all you need."

Fitzgerald still doubted. The two men went to the Louvre to look at the statues and the sizes from profile. What a humiliation this must have been for Fitzgerald, to ask the literary symbol of machismo if his equipment qualified him for masculinity. No matter how much Hemingway reassured him, he suspected Hemingway of politeness. Finally Hemingway elaborated, "It is not basically a question of the size in repose. It is the size that it becomes. It is also a question of angle." Hemingway "explained to him about using a pillow and a few other things that might be useful for him to know." Finally Hemingway lashed out at Fitzgerald's dependence on Zelda's judgment.

"Forget what Zelda said. Zelda is crazy. There's nothing wrong with you. Just have confidence and do what the girl wants. Zelda just wants to destroy you."

Fitzgerald lamely defended her. "You don't know anything about Zelda."

Fitzgerald left hurt and doubtful, fearing that Hemingway had not given him an honest answer. Fitzgerald grew angrier as time went on about Hemingway's answer. Finally Fitzgerald began to brood on Hemingway's duplicity. What Fitzgerald had said "meant more than anything in the world" to him was the size and measurements of his genitals.

A man's entire ego can rest on his two-to-nine inches. And a woman can flatten the ego of a puff-chested man with a simple comparative comment on the size, thickness and appearance of his penis. Poof. One comment and your ego is down for the count. This authority gives women power over men, and can be a basis for revenge. In *Combat in the Erogenous Zone*, Ingrid Bengis becomes afraid that her lover is losing interest in her. Because of this, she begins to feel empty when he is inside of her. She consciously precipitates a crisis in his life.

> I realize . . . I don't want him to reach anything inside of me if he doesn't love me. After we stop he asks how it was for me . . . I answer very quietly, as if providing neutral facts. "Not so good," I say, "I must have stretched out inside. You just don't fill me up any more." I can feel the pause before he answers. The rush of self-doubt that goes racing through him. I feel myself suddenly very powerful . . . I have the power to destroy his sense of himself just the way he destroys me. And I want to do it. "I don't want to hurt you," I say. "But I have to tell the truth" . . . The next night he can't get an erection. I'm glad but also ashamed. The thought passes through that I am a castrating bitch. The thought makes me want to cry. But I think, "Well, it serves you right," and force myself to go to sleep.

There are a lot of Zeldas out there. Some women may not even know that they are. Listen to these women who wrote us:

> With regards to penis size I must say that I enjoy the fact that my present prince is generously endowed. Candidly, I am demanding. Besides a full complement of mental, emotional, spiritual, intellectual characteristics and values, I also require a man who is physically endowed. I like moderately large to very large men.

> Unfortunately the size of a man's penis very much matters to me, and a large penis is much more satisfactory, or has the potential to be in my case. However, if I were to go to bed with a man who has a small penis, I would not let him know of my disappointment. I'm sure, as articles that I've read indicate, that penis size doesn't matter to many women. One reason that penis size matters to me is that I would rather climax from vaginal penetration than clitoral stimulation.

> The size of a man's penis counts. I used to think the opposite but I have altered my views on that. The size alone can excite me.

Some women prefer a large penis because of the visual effects—and because it makes them feel feminine:

> I cannot deny that I have opinions concerning penis size and erection! There is a tendency for a shorter penis to come out of the vagina, particularly in moments of heightened excitement which can be for me a little disconcerting, breaking the momentum and rhythm of the sexual act sometimes at a crucial moment. Adjustment in technique or position can generally minimize such difficulties. A fatter penis seems to provide greater stimulation, but this isn't necessarily important as manual and oral stimulation can be used as well. But I love to look at a big penis! It brings out the woman in me!

Some women can be quite specific in their desires. A sixteen-year-old San Francisco girl writes, "The size penis I would prefer would be approximately seven-and-a-half to eight inches long and very thick. The size and looks of the penis have a lot to do with the extent to which two persons can enjoy sex."

Men with extremely large penises can occasionally find themselves with a problem as well. A thirty-year-old actress writes, "I like average-size cocks. A little bitsy cock is a bummer cause I like to feel it against my cervix. But a big cock is a bummer too cause then it will hurt me. A large penis plunging into a not-so-large vagina is painful. I don't enjoy such pain."

Sex researchers argue that the size of a man's penis bears no relationship to the size or weight of the man. But a macho book, *The New Sexual Etiquette,* edited by Patricia Holt, published in 1977 as a response to the "fact that 94% of all men are lousy lovers," tells women where to look to find out. The book, purporting to reveal the real opinions about sex of hundreds of San Francisco women, offers small solace for the man concerned about the potential limitation of his penis. *The New Sexual Etiquette* suggests to women that they look at a man's fingers carefully before going to bed with him, because if his fingers are long, he has a big schlong.

Women checking out men's hands the way we men check out their breasts and asses? *The New Sexual Etiquette* states boldly, "The size and length of a man's penis *does* have a measurable effect on the woman's enjoyment of the sex act. It is astonishing how many otherwise knowledgeable sex experts believe just the opposite—or at least say so when counseling men. The fact is that if the woman is sexually active with many men, she will note immediately—and yes, compare—the size and length of her partner's penis as soon as he enters. How could she not? . . . the physical attributes of the entering visitor are registered as minutely in her mind as her own physical attributes are and have been registered in his."

But Other Women . . .

Many other women sincerely do not care about penis size. They have done market research and concluded, in the words of a woman from Santa Barbara, "Size doesn't matter." She says, "I have been with a man with a small penis—about four inches long, very thin—and a man with a large penis—about eight to nine inches and quite wide—and I rate those two men the best lovers I've ever had."

Susan from Colorado found sex very frustrating with her husband who "size-wize, was very large. I never measured him but it must have been at least nine or nine-and-a-half inches. He was very experienced. I figured something was wrong with me—I never had an orgasm." Then Susan went to bed and had her first orgasm. "He had only three inches! It was fantastic!" She adds, "I know size doesn't mean a thing—I hope you can convince the male population."

The victims in the Penis Contest are men. They can always find someone bigger to feel inferior to and someone smaller to give them a feeling of superiority. But where is the intimacy? Sex is more than the penis. And the penis is more than its measurements.

Deborah, a twenty-seven-year-old New Yorker, wonders, "What makes men so paranoid about the size of their penis?" She was in bed with Harold when he asked her, "What do you think of my penis?" Deborah thought it was average, but she didn't want to say that. "It's attached to your body," she said. "I then went on to describe *all* of his body to him. Among other attributes he had a beautiful ass and I described it in glowing terms. He was very self-conscious at first, but I was able to relax him in bed simply by talking with him. That is the secret, isn't it? If I had any sexual advice for men or women it would be, talk it out."

Another woman says, "As I get older, I find that I can also get a lot of pleasure from even fairly thin penises, which I never thought possible before. The particular thin one I am thinking of belongs to a man I love very much. That is the difference, I think."

An Essential Prop of Manhood?

Sexual competition and the New Woman have resulted in a new male preoccupation—the desire to last longer during intercourse. Standard prefeminism quick sex is still common, but female anger and male shame about it have increased. Susan, a waitress from Philadelphia, expresses her modern anger at old sex:

Why do so many men have a "How quick can I get there?" attitude toward sex? A man has no idea of how cold it feels for a woman to just lie there and spread her legs without any type of foreplay while he drives his cock into her (usually without any lubrication) and asks her the classic question—"Did you come?"—five strokes later! . . . This guy came in thirty seconds, and then he practically accused me of frigidity because I hadn't come already. I suppose it was a cover-up for his own feelings of inadequacy, but even understanding it, I didn't want to put up with it.

Historically, rapid male sexual response has been considered a good thing, an evolutionary survival mechanism. Man the hunter prided himself on his ability to ejaculate and disappear. It meant he would not be attacked during this period of vulnerability. Kinsey applauded premature ejaculation: "Far from being abnormal the human male who is quick in his sexual response is quite normal among the mammals, and usual in his own species. . . . It would be difficult to find another situation in which an individual who was quick and intense in his responses was labeled anything but superior, and that in most instances is exactly what the rapidly ejaculating male probably is, *however inconvenient and unfortunate his qualities may be from the standpoint of the wife in the relationship."*

Premature ejaculation actually used to be popular among women. As a matter of fact, premature ejaculation was a tactic used by women conspiratorially along with men to end sex—fast. Men have historically been encouraged to come quickly by disinterested wives and profit-oriented prostitutes. For the latter, the quicker the turnover, the more money she makes; for wives, boredom with fucking is one of the primary causes of the widespread female feigning of orgasm. The idea is: if he thinks I'm coming, he'll come; he'll feel like a man.

Nowadays women do not want sex over with quickly; they want

longer sex. What was once a satisfactory form of sex has now become a "problem" that men have to change. The definitions of manhood have changed, from rapid ejaculation and hunting activities, to the new Mt. Everest of Manhood—giving your woman an orgasm. The durability of erection—and the postponement of male orgasm—has been defined today by men and women as essential props of manhood. Since it's generally accepted that women take longer than men, the male drive to last longer—and be known as a long fucker—is the goal of all the "heavy hitters," and the fantasy of all the Woody Allens.

It's become the country's newest indoor sport. The man and woman are throbbing away, rolling into ecstasy, with vibrating pelvic movements. What is the man thinking? He's doing everything he can— from thinking of the ball scores, to all the work he's got to do, to pretending he's with a very unattractive woman (reverse fantasy)—to reduce his sexual excitement so that he doesn't lose control over his penis and then fiercely come, and simultaneously feel like a total asshole.

The charge of "premature ejaculator" can destroy a man. He feels "selfish"—the worst you can say about a man's in-bed behavior. "One man," says a New Orleans secretary, "is so depressed he cannot look me straight in the eye or even talk to me." Women quickly learn their power. "I've had men climax and not even be in me yet," writes a woman, twenty-five, from Rhode Island. "A woman feels powerful laying there with sperm on her leg." She adds, "Finally you try to tell him you don't care, that it's okay and he's still a man to you."

Men fear female fury. The man cowers in bed in the hopes that he won't spill his seed too fast and look like a fool. And hear this kind of reaction from his partner: "I consider a man with premature ejaculation a failure in bed." Writes another woman, "He is selfish and out of control, a big zero. It's most maddening to be left in an extremely excited state looking at a snoring man's back. It takes me a long time to become unstimulated. I'm so involved with my feelings I can't really take the time to worry about him, which causes guilt and just adds to my turmoil. If I happen to like the guy, I'll give him a second chance. If he does not perform the second time, out he goes; I don't even want to see him anymore."

Trying to define "premature" ejaculation is like asking a Zen question: How premature is premature and from whose point of view? Masters and Johnson say that a man ejaculates prematurely when his erection does not bring his woman to orgasm at least 50% of the time. But what if the woman required thirty minutes or more of thrusting to come? Would my ejaculation in the twenty-fifth minute be considered premature? Or what if she didn't climax from intercourse? Despite all the evidence that they themselves gathered and popularized, Masters and Johnson still cling to an intercourse-dominated view of sexuality. Their definition of premature ejaculation can only make men and women feel inadequate.

Three Responses to Premature Ejaculation

The First Response: I'm sorry! The premature ejaculator's favorite orgasm battle cry is "I'm coming, I'm sorry." Apologize, apologize, apologize, that's all they do, say the women. "He played with me a couple of minutes, then inserted, and not even a thrust and he came. As did the apologies—again. The guy usually feels so bad. He really tries to make up for it. I *hate* that! That really is uncomfortable for me. Just hold me—words aren't necessary," writes one woman.

The Second Response: I'll change! I'll try harder! In order to avoid the sexual untouchable label of "premature ejaculator," many men flip to the other side and become mechanical pleasers, obsessed with their partner's orgasm, never considering their own "selfish" desires.

The Third Response: Good-bye! I still recall, all too vividly, the night I was driving home from a party in a college town in Pennsylvania with Amy, the ex-wife of one of my ex-shrinks. I began to desire her sexually. I was getting hot behind the driver's seat. We pulled over and began necking madly. She said, "Come over to my house."

We leaped right into bed, clothes off, and went right to it. She first cautioned me that I must not plan on sleeping over. "If the kids see you in the morning, it's not good. It's not good education for them to see a different man in their mommy's bed every morning."

She took my burning cock and slipped it into her oceanlike pussy. I knew that one thrust and I'd be a goner.

By this time I knew that I could do nothing. So I held tightly to her and gave myself over to my orgasm. The climax, quick and furious, was shattering. I felt like I was swimming underwater in ecstasy for seconds. When I came back to earth and consciousness, I began to pump. Pump, pump, pump—I was pumping against that inevitable postorgasm going down of the penis, pumping to inspire her to sudden orgasm before my pump wilted. No go. I wilted and she hadn't come. I couldn't stay in her in such a battered state.

Amy looked me in the eye. "You men are lucky," she said. "You can come whenever you want. It takes us women much longer."

I was even too embarrassed to consider eating her at that moment, which would have rescued the day. Instead, I was out of the house within minutes, a quickie in more ways than one. I felt two feet tall.

5

RELATIONSHIP TRAINING: BECOME
THE RIGHT PERSON

Oh So Healthy

Body consciousness invaded the 1970s. Health became a national and personal passion. People began taking control of their blood sugar and their cholesterol. Nutrition, exercise, therapy, self-awareness and vitamins became subjects of daily neighborhood conversation. I began to jog years before the streets became unsafe for pedestrians. In one day I could be found jogging, doing yoga, being rolfed, downing fifty vitamins, learning massage, experiencing acupuncture, bioenergetics, Reichian therapy. In two years I attempted to reeducate my body. I once drank so much carrot juice that my medical doctor found that my legs had turned orange. I was reflecting the national trend of people to take responsibility for their bodies and health, to stay young, to age gracefully, without the aches and pains of our parents and grand-parents.

I sang the political slogans of the 1970s: "You are your body! Your body is you!"

I thought that if I could gain control of my physical and mental health, I would be ready for a relationship with a woman. Ironically, I was so busy jogging, eating health foods, taking vitamins, and getting rolfed and massaged that I ended up with no time—or energy—left for sex!

It's like D.B. from Vancouver who wrote us, "I went on a health food kick once for over a year. Eating vitamins, kelp, Vitamin E, ginseng (a bit), going to a health spa every two days—but I never seemed to get an opportunity for sex during all that time."

What my search taught me was a new appreciation for the self-care of my body. It's ironic that, in our object-oriented society, many people take better care of their cars than they do of their bodies. I learned from my health search to eat light, exercise, and emphasize positive health—or disease prevention—rather than medical war against symptoms.

I began to develop a new relationship with my body. Historically I had been no different than most men, using—rather than experienc-ing—my body. I ate junk food and pushed my body for external ends—forced exercise, pressured work, performance tests. Now it was time to revise my relationship with my body. And serve and listen to it.

I enrolled in a three-hour massage class for three times a week. There I was naked with twenty-two other people for eleven hours a week—to get a certificate as a qualified massage-giver. The California syndrome had successfully captured me.

In massage class I learned that it's harder receiving than giving pleasure—or a massage. It was that old male work orientation. It is hard for me to do something as an end in itself. I need a result, a paycheck, a reward, something to denote the end. To touch for the sheer joy of touching is insufficient. My mind is too busy avoiding boredom when I am touching. Give my mind something to do. Keep it busy.

The man *giving* pleasure is in control. The male in me always needed to be in control. I identified the female side with softness and weakness. As a man, I had a horrible time with passivity, which I saw as unmasculine. Being passive implies being out of control and I, as a man, fear losing control. When I lose control, I lose my I. And when I lose my I, I no longer exist. I am dead.

My first defense against pain was my skin. Don't touch me! said its sensitivity. My legs are especially sensitive. My crotch and ass area brings me to giggles. Being squeamish and ticklish in these areas, I protected myself against imagined pain.

Why couldn't my mind ever take a vacation? Why did it always have to be busy?

I dropped out of class before getting my massage degree. But for the moment I was through trying to control the world and I was allowing the "feminine" side to take control of me.

I then joined another all-day massage group. We all undressed and stood naked with each other. We formed a circle, strangers all. Armed with a towel and massage oil, we took turns massaging each other, including the genitals. The rules were to keep your attention off sexual imagery, and to make the experience as sensual as possible. Having my genitals touched without an erection felt good. A soft penis has many feelings. There was no pressure for me to get hard or to feel sexual stirrings. I learned that men knew how to massage just as warmly as women. If I didn't open my eyes, I would not be able to discern the sex from the touch.

I spent a few years in desperate search for the wisdom of my body. For eleven months, once a week, I would drive across San Francisco to the office of a white-haired Reichian therapist, undress, lie naked on his bed, and breathe for forty-five minutes, while he deepened and corrected my shallow, tight breathing.

I breathed to feel the experience of orgasm, to allow surges of pleasure to reach all parts of my body, to let my energy run amuck. I realized how much I had held myself back from pleasure. I even used to hold my breath during orgasm! Rather than letting go and feeling.

I got rolfed twenty-two times. The rolfer uses his fingers, fists, and elbows to push into the tense parts of your body and create life among the pain. It was my pain. I put the tension and fear there. Through rolfing I began to relax submerged parts of my body.

It was a period of intense therapy for me. I went to Berkeley to see a bioenergetics therapist. He pointed out that my energy and breathing was concentrated in the upper part of my chest, which symbolized control and power in the world. He had me breathe directly into my genitals and into my legs, to consciously direct energy into my legs. He recommended pelvis-swinging exercises to develop an easy, relaxed pelvic movement to supplement the driving power of the penis.

Jogging proved to be a sexual stimulant. The breathing of running anticipates the breathing of orgasm. Jogging prepares the heart and breathing for sexual expression.

I graduated from the fifty-hour course sponsored by the Human Sexuality Program at the University of California to train professionals to become sex therapists.

A few years later I attended the four-day conference of American sexual counselors, teachers, educators and therapists in Washington, D.C. I ran into an older man who seemed joyous to resume contact with me. I looked at him, but for the life of me I couldn't place the face.

"Remember me," he said, "I massaged your feet about three years ago at a sex workshop in San Francisco."

Instantly, my feet remembered him.

How to Free Yourself from Your Parents

Every individual in America today experiences the crisis of relationships and the family. The old family is dying, and the new one is struggling to be born. Meanwhile, each generation gets a succeedingly negative view of marriage and relationships. Everyone born post-World War II has learned in some way the antimarriage ethic:

I'm holding out for the best. I need to keep my options open. My freedom is the most important thing. I'm living for the moment—what's best for me now? I better not make a commitment; commitments mean trouble. I'm saving myself for tomorrow. And meanwhile, I must avoid the pangs of daily, ordinary rejection.

Many of our parents did not pass on a good view of marriage and relationships. We saw tradition and fear tape together relationships that never should have stayed together. But they stayed together, at least until the children were reared. Marriage was, after all, largely an economic and social arrangement, with the self-interest of the partners taking second place. The postwar changes of birth control, recreational sex, feminism and a growing "me" individualism in American society changed the relationship balance. Divorce geometrically burst onto the scene, and social chaos and personal emotional suffering exploded accordingly.

We are today faced with so many alternatives that we cannot choose. We have one foot stuck in the past and one toe in the future. We are transitional people, suffering the conflicts of double messages. We need to take the best from the past as we create our own future. Yet however modern we seem, we find ourselves mechanically repeating the fears and insecurities of the past. Unconscious repressions and limitations are passed on from generation to generation with parents serving as channels. Are we that different, after all, from our parents and grandparents?

To create the form of the yet-unborn family dynamic we must free ourselves from the concepts, practices and messages of our parents' generation, so that we can live in the present and get what we want—sex with intimacy and friendship; a relationship based on loving support, sex-role freedom and shared power.

To the extent that you can free yourself from psychic—and largely unconscious—control by your parents, reversing a pattern when you catch it, you find yourself less and less making the women in your life *your mother* and the men *your father.*

This can be especially important for the children and teenagers who faced special problems in the sixties and seventies, when the number of divorces quadrupled to such an extent that we now live in a society where to be a single-parent child is normal. Or to have a different last name than your live-in parents. Early divorce, like a bad early sexual experience, can scar a child, and perpetuate fears that persist for years. The result is something that both men and women notice today: the fear of family and commitment, the desire to rebel against parents by avoiding marriage, and the avoidance of children. A fear of relationships—which is almost a social disease in divorce and broken-home-torn America today—can be confronted by honestly coming to terms with our childhood conditioning.

We Learn Our Parents' Relationship and Often Repeat It in Our Lives: Childhood memories and patterns can last a lifetime unless they are brought to the conscious and confronted. I listen to all the voices inside my head, lecturing me how to feel about relationships, sex and male and female roles, and I realize that many of these voices do not belong to me—My mother and father, although dead, are still alive inside me!

At the age of thirty-three I realized that I was repeating my parents' patterns in every one of my relationships. I brought my parents into bed with me every time I had sex. And they kept saying, "Don't do that. Don't enjoy that!" And, internalizing my mother's sexual rejection of my father, I feared women and rejected them first.

I entered an intensive thirteen-week parental deprogramming program, originally called Fischer-Hoffman Psychic Therapy, now called the Hoffman Quadrinity Process, during which I discovered for the first time how similar I was to the dead parents inside me. Making the patterns conscious is the first step toward internal liberation. The following Parental Exorcism—an intensive deprogramming freedom-from-parents process based on blame and then forgiveness—comes from a series of experiences I had in the therapy capital of the world, San Francisco, during the early seventies when I found myself rejecting women to confirm my mother's rejection of my father.

1) *Blame your parents:* After identifying the patterns, you must free yourself from guilt by seeing where you got these patterns—from your parents and from society's programming. You are innocent. You learned them as a child. Your society gave you these fears, doubts and negative expectations. You have chosen to keep and reinforce them, but you did not invent them. I cooled out much of my hostility to women at the age of thirty-five when I screamed at my "mother" for all she taught me. I released myself from fear of men when I accused my "father" of instilling fear in me. I did not have to do any of these blame processes with my real parents, because I was not dealing with them, but with the parents inside me.

Every mother has to deal with her son's budding erection. Today's resexualized women feel more at home with its arrival, yet they all become surprised on some level. As Sherry, a first-time thirty-nine-year-old mother, said, "I was told when pregnant to expect a lot of things, but I was still surprised when my son Andy's penis trippled in size and became hard as a rock. He seems to take it for granted, but he's only seven months old."

Unfortunately, unlike Andy, I was one of the pre-Sexual Revolution babies raised by a woman who felt like a stranger to her own sexuality. She taught me *not* to see my penis as a source of pleasure, but to hide it, and feel guilty about its potential power. She taught me her discomfort with her own body, which became a problem when I began dating. I was supposed to provide pleasure to a woman, yet I had internalized a dislike for her female body. I was five years old, fondling my genitals. It felt good, a part of the body that yielded pleasure with direct touch. I ran naked into the living room where my grandmother sat. I did an impromptu streak in front of her. My mother, horrified, chased me back into the bedroom and scolded me, "Don't you ever go naked in front of your grandmother again! And stop touching yourself down there!"

Yet it's men who pressure women to turn off their child's sexual pleasure. Men deprived my mother of her power, independence and sexuality. Her domineering father taught her to repress her body. And so she passed on to me, her first-born male, the anti-female sexual teaching that she learned from male society. Had there been an active women's consciousness to support her in the forties and fifties, she might have rescued her sexuality and right to pleasure.

Men hurt themselves when they teach little girls to be ashamed of their bodies. Female hatred of sex eventually punishes men. The little girls grow up to be mothers, depriving men of their pleasure.

Men put work over pleasure. My father rarely shared his vulnerability with me. His anger was the expression of his insecurity, the externalization of his inner pain. Growing up, I adopted his solution to uncertainty: work hard in the outside world, forget the inner. Shortly before he died at forty-nine of his fourth heart attack in two years, he lay in an oxygen tank in a hospital and began crying. He spoke of my mother, who had died nine months earlier of cancer.

"Mother wouldn't sleep with me," he sobbed. "She was afraid that her father downstairs would hear and get angry." He began crying uncontrollably. My father had suffered years of sexual psychic torture without uttering a peep of pain. He always seemed so in charge. And underneath it all were all those tears.

2) *Describe on paper your mother and father's relationship:* Include their sex life or lack of it, their sex roles and psychological interaction, as accurately as you can. List on another paper all their conscious and nonverbal messages to you as a child. And then take a third piece of paper and describe as objectively as possible your own relationship history, your patterns, your sex life. Then compare your life with theirs and their instructions to you and don't be surprised if you are either adopting your parents' patterns directly—or indirectly—by trying to do exactly the opposite!

3) *Forgive your parents:* After freeing yourself of blame by *totally* blaming your parents, see them both as six-year-old children learning the sex role messages they dumped on you. I saw how my mother, as a little girl, was programmed, and I felt compassion for her. I saw my

father as a little vulnerable child. My parents were only the channels for society's negative messages passed on from generation to generation. We are all living off the fears of the past, driven into us by our childhood conditioning.

There's an insidious backlash to blame. Blaming your parents for your relationship difficulties perpetuates childhood helplessness. The attitude of blame means that we are giving others responsibility for our behavior. Blame of others is masked blame of self. When we free our parents of blame, we free ourselves from blame—the first step toward self-acceptance.

The Parental Exorcism Process becomes complete with affirmation writing:

4) *Make a list* of all the messages and habits you choose for your life, like: It is okay for me to enjoy sexual pleasure. It is okay for me to make a commitment and develop a relationship with a woman (or man) that works. It is okay for me to love and be loved completely and unconditionally. Then repeat them again and again—in writing, verbally, in your thoughts.

Freed from the unconscious negative messages of the past, we are able to be reborn, and to begin to create with others, relationships that bring out the love buried within us.

My negative sexual expectations were:
1. Let's get it over with.
2. It won't be fun.
3. I have got to perform for you.
4. I don't want to do it.
5. Hurry up, it will be over soon.
6. I just want to get tension release.
7. I'm scared of your body.
8. You won't like my body/cock.
9. You don't taste good down there.
10. You may not like me.

My reprogramming is:
1. Let's enjoy it for a long time.
2. It is going to be fun.
3. I have to do nothing for you.
4. I want to do it.
5. Relax, it will last as long as you want it to.
6. I want to experience total joy.
7. I'm excited by your body.
8. You are going to love my body/cock.

9. You taste great down there.
10. You will like me!

I finally realized that it is a waste of time looking back into the past to dig for causes, reasons, crucial events, and childhood beliefs. The search for the past can go on forever and be a new form of avoidance in the present. I had done some important work in clearing up my attachment to the past, and now I was going to concentrate on change in the present. I wanted a relationship that worked. I knew there were two secrets to having the right relationship:

• Be the right person.
• Choose the right person.

How to Free Yourself from a Bad Relationship

Bob is a typical male of the 1980s. He can't develop a relationship with a woman that lasts longer than three weeks. A two-month fling is considered long-term in his mind. The average interaction is a weekend. Whenever we discuss love and romance, his eyes twinkle over Helen, the one woman he lived with for six years, who one day woke up, decided that he had been oppressing her with his "maleness," and left him. Bob is still waiting for Helen to return. The chances are nil, since Helen has long since joined a women's collective, and now dates men in their early twenties. He calls her up every six months to receive his standard rejection notice. As long as Bob waits for Helen, there's no room in his heart or mind for anybody else. Yet he keeps waiting, hoping that she'll see the light, forgive him and restore the past that is no more.

Bob is like millions of men and women who break up in this era of musical beds and consecutive monogamy. The dead relationship often lives inside us, physically preventing new emotional growth. We nurse our pain, addicted to the patterns which the old relationship represented. Millions of people remain in relationships that don't satisfy because we don't know how to escape from them. We're so petrified of aloneness that any relationship, however bad, is better than no relationship!

I learned that in freeing myself from a bad relationship, I was, in fact, fighting a negative part of my personality—the part that did not want relationships to work because I did not "deserve" love. I also blamed myself for choosing the wrong person, wasting time, not making the relationship work, investing so much in something that resulted in so little. Ending a bad relationship is like giving up a poor business investment: you've got to cut your losses; stop sending good money after bad.

The Emotional Exorcism Process cures you from addiction by freeing you from blame. Self-blame keeps you in the circular masochism of the relationship. As a student from Southern Illinois University wrote us, "If you run into a selfish person or an overly aggressive female or male or whatever, forget it. Don't carry a grudge or become upset. Write it off as experience. Move on."

There are five essential steps for ending a relationship that is difficult to end.

1) *Stop seeing the person:* The first step is the hardest. The decision to end the relationship and to avoid a hidden agenda of tactics to bring him (or her) back. To end the relationship, you must decide to end it completely—give up all hope (or desire) for the relationship to return. Convince yourself that even if he (or she) wanted a reunion, you wouldn't. The deeper the addiction, the harder you've got to be on yourself to end your pain and to create the room for a new relationship, one that gives you what you want.

I was so addicted to my pain that I wanted to continue my emotional rollercoaster, continuing to see Rosalie, looking for clues to reunion. Anything that would give me a chance to hope again. Finally I realized the basic truth—all contact perpetuates the patterns I am trying to exorcise, and merely postpones the time of true separation.

2) *Suppress and repress the person's name every time it comes into your mind:* Your mind is not always your friend. Your mind constantly brings up subjects and thoughts that don't do *you* any good. Your mind may become obsessed on what you don't and can't have. "The mind," says Swami Satchidananda, "can act like a drunk monkey." Meditation and yoga are ancient methods for learning to control one's own mind, so that we run it, and its anarchy and troublemaking doesn't run us.

3) *Forget the good in the relationship and concentrate only on the bad:* My mind kept torturing my body with all the positive things about her and the relationship. Then I made a list of all Rosalie's negative qualities. I wrote down an anecdote to illustrate each negative quality. Every time my mind brought back a positive memory of her or us together, I took out the gory details and read and reread them.

4) *Feel Your Anger:* Was I angry! I felt used, humiliated, aban-

doned. I felt I had wasted part of my life. And then I realized that my anger was a continuing attachment to Rosalie. Hate was a tie as strong as love. Anger meant that I still wanted something from her. Anger was an abdication of my own responsibility. Break the anger, and you break the final connection—she leaves your consciousness. How break the anger? By an act of will.

5) *Give up your anger:* I saw Rosalie as a five-year-old girl. I saw how she absorbed those qualities, fears and insecurities that gave me such a rough time. I saw that she was a victim of her own conditioning. By letting go of the anger, you complete the Emotional Exorcism.

Finding Intimacy: The Power to Give Up Power

Through the whole period of my psychological reconditioning I knew my purpose—that above everything, I wanted an open, intimate relationship with a woman. Above orgasms, above ego, above money, the one thing that seemed so elusive was intimacy in a successful relationship.

What lies behind the cool male mask? The fear of emotional dependency. The panic of rejection. The insecurity of maintaining one's masculinity. Men collapse in the face of potential sexual abandonment. So many men keep their distance from women. *If I need her, she has this power to hurt me.*

"Why is it so hard to get a man to say, 'I love you'?" asks a woman from Ohio. To many men, love implies need. "There is a terror in sexual intimacy," writes Dr. Irene Kassorla, "because it breaks down all distancing barriers." Intimacy counters the practical relationship rule for many people these days: Don't come too close.

Some men cannot live without female emotional support. In *The Hazards of Being Male,* Herb Goldberg argues that the total dependence of the male child upon a mother figure continues throughout his entire life. He hides it as he ages. That dependency explains why men collapse emotionally more often than women after the break-up of a relationship.

Yet men also protect themselves against the condition of childhood when we were powerless and totally dependent on mother, who knew all of our secrets. She knew, deep down, that we were not Mr. Macho.

Men need and fear the mother in each woman. She can reduce us to emotionally helpless children in an instant.

So we depersonalize women into parts of the body. Male depersonalization of women is legendary. Warren Farrell, men's consciousness pioneer, says male objectification comes from our fear of rejection by women. "It's a lot easier to be rejected by an object than by a real person," he points out.

And so we find many men, in the opinion of women, focused on externals, without an ability to communicate emotionally. Woman after woman complained to our research project that the men they know hide their feelings and resist commitment. Feminists surprise men by saying that what women dislike most about men, sexually and romantically, is not their dominance but their distance—a detachment expressed in emotional passivity.

"Women don't like it when men withhold themselves from a full and complete relationship. That's what I sense in my female partners," writes one man. "They don't really care whether or not I'm good in bed, nor my size, nor orgasms. But where are you, man, in this relationship? How do you respond to me? They want to make sure that I am in the here and now with them in sex, that I am here."

Before you can be intimate with another person, you must first be intimate with yourself. For many years as a "tough male," I was hiding my own sweetness, my own vulnerability, and my own softness behind an armor of defenses protecting my fear of rejection. I agreed with Alexander Lowen that until you love *women*, you cannot love *a woman*. And I also agreed with others who said that until you can love the woman inside you, you cannot fully love yourself, or a woman.

When a man learns to nurture himself, he is on the road to emotional intimacy with another. A therapist gave me that advice one day when she found me drowning in tears and Irish coffees over a lost girlfriend. "Jerry," she said, "you must learn to be your own best mother."

Some men come to sex to reveal their desires to be embraced and enjoy themselves, rather than to perform. Other men, able to suppress their sensitivities, perform sexually with as many women as possible, successfully fulfilling the requirements of masculinity. Some of these are nervous men struggling hard to become great performers. These men often avoid emotional interaction with women. Sex is a performance. They run the risk of having fantastic sex that feels empty the following morning.

For other men, the same performance expectations create fear. They shy away from intimate relationships with women, especially sexual, because they fear they may not live up to their own self-image of manhood.

Intimacy begins with words. "The way to fall in love with someone is to share your problems with them," says Dr. Irene Kassorla. Intimacy in sex means touching, the close sharing of souls, the falling away of social roles so that we become children and animals together, in close communication.

Intimacy is frightening, because we are so exposed to hurt. You can fool yourself, but it's awfully hard to consistently fool another person. Intimacy is a mirror. If two people see each other—and not images or roles—the intimate relating will allow the greatest rush of self-discovery. Image-relating is not intimacy. To be intimate, you must be able to see through the other person, and still accept him or her. The one person you cannot fool with illusions is your mate if your relationship is intimate, and not made up of images, fantasy, or a conspiracy of silence.

At the crux of Intimate Sex lies dependency. The dependent state means a loss of power and control. As children, we were dependent; as adults, we try to hide our dependency. Only the man willing to be rejected can experience intimacy, which allows no defenses.

Ironically, the powerful man must be willing to give up his power and control to experience intimacy. The most powerful state then becomes the intimate, dependent, "powerless" sexual state, in which the man is as dependent as a child. True intimacy comes with sharing yourself, revealing feelings, relaxing your defenses, losing control, giving up power.

Meeting Ms. Right

My first relationship, in which I had dominated, ended when my female supporter shocked me one day by leaving me for someone nine years younger. My second relationship, in which I had been dominated by the woman, ended with me fleeing a restaurant with her shouting, "Impotent! Impotent!" I then had a flurry of one-night to one-week stands that ended with varying degrees of dissatisfaction. Mostly, I joined the New Sexual Army of partnerless singles as I made love to my sheets every night.

Despite—or maybe because of—all the new sexual opportunities, like millions of men and women, I considered myself unmatable, unable to get what I wanted. Wrong. I was getting what I wanted. I really didn't want relationships to work—and I made certain that they didn't.

The sexual romantic crisis of the lonely adult is a national epidemic. People are driven by the overwhelming passion for intimacy yet they are stopped cold by fear. Fear of caring too much and becoming too vulnerable, and then being ridiculed or rejected.

I lived for two years in a two-room bachelor apartment in San Francisco's North Beach. I drank cappucino every day at the Trieste and trained for a relationship the way some people train to be lawyers. I had changed my mind about commitment and relationship. Long a foe of marriage as an institution, I decided that I wanted to get married. I wanted a relationship based on commitment because it was more fun and more fulfilling than musical beds. A deep relationship based on growth and risk is more exciting—ultimately more involving—than a series of unrelated encounters and interactions. In truth, all my therapy was aimed at that one purpose—to find a life partner.

Oddly enough, I had become a new kind of victim—a victim of the tolerant, sexually free sixties and seventies, when it became okay—if not preferable—not to marry and not to start a family. Commitment became unhip.

In fact, I myself was once a crusader against the family, striking out at its undemocratic and isolationist nature. I considered myself oppressed by a society that paired up. But I was tired of the S.R.—the Short Relationship—with all its pulls and dissatisfactions. I found myself spending time dreaming and planning my escape from singlehood. I would join the elite—the world of couples.

Somehow I despaired of ever making a relationship work in Los Angeles and the Bay Area of Berkeley and San Francisco. A more relaxed attitude toward casual sex pervades the air—affairs are "no big thing," as one man put it. Warren Farrell called it "divorce training"— the pressure by feminists, growth leaders, social radicals and lifestyle experimenters to "be yourself," to listen to your own needs first and remember, there's always someone else around the corner. Relationships are dropped like yesterday's laundry.

I moved to New York and decided to take a practical, goal-oriented plan to launching a relationship and making it sail. I'd go to four parties a night, collect fifteen phone numbers, and systematically begin calling women up! I realized that finding a wife is like finding a job or an apartment: you decide what you want, go where the likely prospects are hanging out, and go through rejection after rejection, wrong choice after wrong choice, until you find the one of many appropriate for you. Finding a life partner is a logical, disciplined exercise, but the odd thing is like with everything else, you've got to expect the unexpected. The last place I expected to find "her" was my friend's party. In fact, I had jammed in four parties that night and sandwiched this one in the middle. All I expected was some hot political conversation and talk about the "good old days" by beautiful male souls who considered themselves retired in their late thirties. I even brought a date from an earlier party to this one.

But there she was, standing alone in the corner. Instantly I was attracted. So beautiful! Yet two inches taller than me. Could I accept a girlfriend taller than me? Would she want a smaller man? Maybe she'd like to get married tonight . . .

All these reveries went on inside the privacy of my own head as I approached her. She was the type of woman who usually rejected me, so to protect myself I often rejected them first through shyness, distance, aloofness. It feels better to reject them than to be rejected. Even after all that California therapy, I watched my mind produce all the reasons why she should not be interested in little ol' me.

"Oh, Jerry Rubin," she said, "you know my father, George Leonard." Indeed I did. A philosopher on the West Coast. I immediately concluded that as the daughter of a brilliant intellectual, she must be brilliant too, and my interest skyrocketed, because what I wanted most of all was a woman who combined beauty and brains with softness. I talked so fast I almost tripped over my words. I tried to angle a way to ask her out to lunch, but her boyfriend soon came over, breathing heavily, driving me away. I moved, sadly, defeated, to the other side of the room.

Two hours later I started to leave the party and looked for Mimi to say good-bye. But, alas, she was sitting on the couch staring into the eyes of her boyfriend with absolute Southern devotion. Her eyes were literally eating him up. My date saw me staring at Mimi. She said, "Would you want a woman to look at you like that?" expecting me to give the traditional feminist response, "Nah, it looks as if they're too dependent on each other." Instead, I looked at her and said, "Yes, that's exactly what I want."

For the next two months I went from unhappy date to lonely party looking for a woman with whom I could combine friendship with love. The search seemed hopeless. I was getting tired of calling women up and being disappointed even though I found myself on the rejecting end more than the rejected. Then a break! I heard through the grapevine that Mimi was no longer "involved." She was working as a marketing executive for a large advertising company. I called her up and we made a Saturday night date. I arrived carrying flowers.

After becoming convinced through fifteen minutes of cross-examination that Mimi did not mind "in the abstract" dating a man shorter than her, I said, midway through the evening, "Mimi, I have something to ask you, but I'm too embarrassed to do it."

"You're going to ask me to live with you," she said, laughing.

"No, not exactly, but close," I said. "I'm going to ask you to marry me."

Mimi refused. She was right. At that moment we were images relating to one another. As the evening ended, we began embracing and kissing, I felt a huge erection breaking through my pants. My entire body was afire. Suddenly, Mimi moved away and said, "Now, wait a minute. Let's get to know each other first." I felt relieved: my sexual excitement waned. I sent her red roses the next day for her birthday.

The next few days I called all my friends and told them that I was in love. They all had the same advice. A female journalist from Australia said, "Go slow, Jerry; don't seem too interested or you'll scare her away." A public relations man ending a three-year marriage said, "Don't rush the natural process." Stew, my long-time male soul-mate, said, knowing me all too well, "Now, Jerry, slow down, don't go for a one-round knockout. The best relationships are won in the fifteenth round."

Mimi and I dated, like your ordinary suburban couple, every Saturday night for two months. I tried to go slow, but it was hard, and twice my pushing resulted in our breaking up. Then we got together again.

Mimi and I started sex slowly. She led me and I led her. We had sex as one part of a growing, loving relationship in which we wanted to make each other happy. After four months of dating, we decided to take our relationship to another level—a trial living-together arrangement. We lived together a year, and then began to discuss marriage. Finally, when talk of marriage became real, I got cold feet. Mimi wanted to get married and I was scared. Scared of alimony, scared of being trapped, scared of repeating my parents' patterns, scared. I recalled my parents' unhappy marriage and took to heart the message of a friend: "The best way to destroy a good relationship is to get married."

A female cartoonist said to me at a party, "Getting married is an act of tremendous courage these days." I decided to transcend my fears. We got married; nothing that I feared has yet materialized. Instead, married for the first time at the age of forty, I feel born anew.

The rebirth of romance renewed my life!

Sharing Your Sexual Secrets

There is a gentleman's agreement among men—all the more powerful because unstated—not to talk about sex in an intimate way. The phobia of homosexuality keeps men from getting close to one another. If I get intimate conversationally, the next thing might be a hand on the knee.

Stew and I have been friends for years. One night in the early seventies, walking the streets of the West Village in New York, we were discussing the feminist pressure of the time for men to become closer. Stew said, "What I really like about you, Jerry, is your mind." I suddenly felt like a disembodied mind walking down the street. But I also felt reassured. Had Stew said, "What I really like about you, Jerry, is your body," I would have made a fifty-yard dash—in my mind, if not with my legs.

Refusing to share our fears or talk about our inner emotional worlds becomes a serious handicap for men. It prevents men from supporting and nurturing one another, and prevents men from ending the implicit pressure their competition puts on one another. Men are afraid to share their fears with each other. Men talk to each other sexually on the level of "Didja hear what happened to me?" or "How was she?" Male friendship is largely based on externals—relating to the outside rather than the inner world.

Michael Lerner, a long-time friend from political activism days, was taking a leisurely drive with me one Sunday afternoon through the hills of Oakland, California. Michael and I, like so many male buddy-friends, had bemoaned our difficulty and hardships in relationships with women, but I had never volunteered my panic underneath our common misery. How could I tell another man that I think my penis is too small? And that I don't think I can satisfy a woman? That I'm not as skillful in sex as other men?

"Listen, Michael, I've met this woman I really like. Her name is Mimi."

"I know," he said, staring distractedly at the scenery. "You mentioned her fifteen times during lunch."

"Yeah, but Michael, I don't think I can satisfy her sexually as well as other men," I said. "My veins are too small to transport blood to my penis." He perked up, and stared at me. "What did you say?" he asked.

I revealed the madness that underlies the male pressure about sex. My fears of the multiple female orgasm. My fears of dying someday of a heart attack during orgasm. All the sexual fears that had been my private, secret devils for years, shared with no one, no girlfriends, no male friends, not even my therapist or medical doctor.

It felt good to pour out all my sexual fears to another man. He listened and then said, "All your fears are total bullshit. Talk about them with Mimi."

Michael and I spent the next seven hours discussing the peculiarities of male sexuality. Through the conversation, I realized the evil of secrets. Sexual secrets can wreck a man's (and woman's) soul. The secrets that we say to ourselves but want no one else to know. And the deeper secrets, the secrets we do not even want ourselves to know.

By sharing my secrets with Michael, I exposed their absurdity and freed myself from the Secret Male Sexual Circle, the spell that we men have mysteriously cast about each other never to reveal our sexual nightmares. The most important thing about the conversation was the fact that we had it. When it ended, I could tell that Michael did not think any less of me. He did not collapse or faint. He did not write me out of his friendship. He heard everything, and nothing changed.

The conversation with Michael broke the ice and enabled me to raise the subject of male sexual fears with Donald, who was often in the company of beautiful women. I shared my sexual doubts with Donald while he listened quietly. Then he spoke up, "Many women prefer small cocks. You should find out what your partner likes. Ask her. It's the simplest way."

"But I really have a small penis. She couldn't like that."

"Hogwash," said Donald. "Your cock can't be any smaller than Paul's, my lover. His is about the size of a baby finger. And I love it! He's very uptight about it, but I'm not. Share your worries with your partner and she'll love you for being so honest and open. The only thing that makes a relationship work is total self-disclosure."

I never knew before that Donald was gay. "I didn't trust you," he said. "Now I do. You've been honest with me, so I can be with you."

I shared myself with other men, and they shared themselves—in a nonmacho, noncompetitive way. I realized that I was not alone. I wasn't so unusual sexually, after all. Talking about sex intimately with two male friends enabled me to raise the issue directly with Mimi. I shared all my sexual fears with her. She listened and smiled.

Michael and Donald were right. It made little difference to Mimi. It only made us closer.

The only thing wrong with sexual secrets is their secrecy. What we hide grows into myth. At one of our workshops, each of the ninety people shared a sexual secret. The room grew mysteriously dark while, in low, mumbled tones, some women shared, "I've never had an

orgasm." Some men shared their fears: "I can't keep an erection"—
"My penis is too small"—"I've never given a woman an orgasm"—
"I've never been in bed with a woman."

Suddenly the room felt lighter. The heaviness was gone. The
seriousness left. Once the secret was out, the "problem" was half-
solved.

ASEXUALITY: THE HOTTEST GAME IN TOWN

The Asexual Revolution

In a world of sex promotion, like modern America, it's become most rebellious not to play. The pressure to engage in sex and the reaction against Victorianism is so great that a nineteen-year-old girl in Ft. Wayne, Indiana, shyly hides her face, and then admits to the shock of her companions, that yes, she still is a virgin.

Asexuals may be the true revolutionaries of our day, objecting to the widespread pressure to take it all off. They are everywhere. Look to the left, to the right, there's an asexual. But most won't admit it. They are as much in the closet as homosexuals have been. And they may be the outcasts of our day too. Listen to the moaning of a twenty-two-year-old anonymous man from St. Louis: "I do not want other people to know about me the fact that I go for months without sexual intercourse."

Asexuals threaten the sexual-promotion establishment. Happy asexuals indicate that sex may not be the royal road to happiness and intimacy. Therefore people respond defensively, insulting asexuals by calling them things like "neuter." One California man says that he recently took a nine-month vow of celibacy for yogic reasons. The widespread rumor throughout his office was that he had become a homosexual.

The ultimate confession of nonmanliness is that you simply have no interest in sex. Barry McCarthy, leader of men's consciousness groups at American University in Washington, agrees that a man is more likely to admit to impotence than to lack of sexual desire. The worst is not being incapable, but not caring.

Men feel they must be cool about sexual noninvolvement. Consider how bad—on some level—the man may feel, not living up to society's image of the "always horny" man, who would "fuck a tree" if necessary.

Famous asexuals are doing men a favor with their promotion of asexuality. Ralph Nader is quietly rebelling against the male rat-pack pressure to define masculinity by the work of the genitals. Nader may be like the men we interviewed who felt that some types of male-female relations reveal a social weakness, in particular the male pursuit, sexual or otherwise, of female approval. It is clear that Nader's libido is completely invested in workaholism, and producing results in the external world, rather than in bed. His life is a revolutionary statement against the American consumer preoccupation with sex.

Andy Warhol is another man who, in a rare expression of

unhipness, is challenging the fashion toward rampant sexuality. Andy is a blatant celibate. He promotes it and justifies it. He says that some people get energy from sex, and others find sex a drain on their energy. Andy says that he finds sex a drain on his energy. In his autobiography, Andy describes the inner soul who doesn't like sex:

> The best love is not-to-think-about-it love. Some people can have sex and really let their minds go blank and fill up with the sex; other people can never let their minds go blank and fill up with the sex, so while they're having the sex they're thinking, "Can this really be me? Am I really doing this? This is very strange. Five minutes ago I wasn't doing this. In a little while I won't be doing it. What would Mom say? How did people ever think of doing this?" So the first type of person . . . is better off. The other type has to find something else to relax with and get lost in.

One surprising fact that came up in our interviews is that the new national pastime of jogging is often "running away" from sex rather than getting prepared for it. Some men point to increased breathing capacity, heartbeat efficiency, and blood flow. But ask the wives. They've been found complaining that their boyfriends and husbands have taken up running and given up sex. One marriage, we heard, even ended when the husband refused to stop running two hours every evening.

One male author admitted to us, "Most men, these days, have a 'Why bother?' attitude toward sex. Women are making it tougher in bed these days, so men have started running." Indeed, around the track, a man can feel like a man. He receives the same physical release he finds from exciting sex—and there's even an orgasm of a kind after awhile in intense running. There's no trouble having to relate to another person.

The author continued, "Lots of men say they felt real good after sex until they found out that what they liked about sex was that it gave them an excuse to do some deep breathing. It felt good but they didn't know why. Then they started running and left it on the road, so to speak."

Sex When You Want It (And Not When You Don't)

Can someone be called asexual if he masturbates? Does asexual mean that someone is free of sexual thoughts? Or is it someone free of sexual actions only? What is the word to describe the person whose only sexual expression is occasional, or even frequent, masturbation? There is no word to describe the person who doesn't have sex with another person but who does masturbate and/or does have sexual feelings and thoughts. This omission in our language covers millions of people and should be a clue to how uncomfortable we are with sexuality *sans* partner.

Is the partnerless man of our age missing anything? To have a sexual release, he can always masturbate. He saves time, because pursuing, courting, and seducing women is very time-consuming and nerve-wracking. If he is a workaholic, he has more time for his favorite pastime.

I hated myself when I wasn't having sex with a partner, because I bought the American Myth—sexuality equals masculinity. When asexual, I felt humiliated, so I pretended to be sexual. I could not talk with other male friends about it for fear of ridicule. I shocked a close buddy once when I confided in him, "I find sex boring." I never should have said that, because he was so genuinely shocked that he kept bringing it up years later. "It amazes me that you find *sex* boring."

The prejudice against asexuality and solo sexuality is too great. Ironically, though, sex without a partner is normal. It's okay to have a life without sex with another. It's also okay not to even masturbate. The pressure *for* sex is too overwhelming. It deprives some people of their autonomy, forcing them to play certain standardized sexual stereotypes.

The only danger of not having a sexual partner is the effect it has on the quality of one's relationships. Those men who are giving up on other-person sex are losing one opportunity to reveal themselves, in naked and vulnerable childlike ways, to another human being. Orgasm may not be an essential requirement for a human being's happiness. But holding and being touched is essential: hugging, feeling close, being in the intimacy of sweat and smell with another person.

Each man and woman needs to find the sexual level appropriate for him or her, free from beliefs of what "a man" and "a woman" should be doing, free from fear, and guilt and pressure.

Men don't have to be sexual. There is no rule that says that if you abstain, you are not masculine, not loving, not giving, not capable of intimacy. Sex has been overpromoted; there's no need for someone to feel guilty because he's not sexually interested or motivated.

It is possible to have a close, physical relationship without sex. If you want, you can have all the benefits of loving, touching, hugging without that always-present requirement of intercourse and orgasm. When asexuality and partnerless sexuality become acceptable, all of us can breathe a sigh of relief and have sex only when we want it.

For years I accepted on faith the myth that all marriages that end fail in bed. Or that the secret to a healthy marriage is a healthy sex life. I therefore mystified bedroom play, making it so important. Whenever you make anything so important, you create the possibility of failure.

Latest sociological research, however, shows just the opposite: that the bedroom is often the symptom of poor relationship communication, not the cause. There is no sexual standard that the couple must adhere to. Each couple sets its own definition of sexual pleasure, and makes it work through honest communication and mutual support.

Sport fucking is usually quite nonintimate, very asexual in its impersonal sexuality. Jules Feiffer calls "social fucking" a substitute for intimacy with a woman. Sex therapists report their experience with happy couples who have no sex whatsoever. Sex works best when it is an extension of friendship.

The New Male Headache

Too many people are miserable because of what's not happening in their lives, because being without a sexual partner is not a choice for them, but a forced alternative. They are sexually alone out of fear.

The Ever-Ready Female is busting up the male act. The historic female asexuality may often have been a cover for male asexuality. The man kept his wife sexually cool so that he would not have to refuse sex. He let her refuse sex for him. Monogamy, ironically, serves as a protector of the male sexual self-image, because the man is already "taken," committed to one woman, and he can therefore have sex rarely with his wife and yet preserve his image of sexual manhood with other women.

But although a growing number of women are actually becoming more sexual, the reality lags far behind the reputation of the sexually liberated lady. The pattern in most of the world persists—the sexual man tempting the asexual woman. She rewards him with her favors. One man, an engineer, outlines the drama in the date culture of America: "I take her out to dinner and if everything goes well, she'll come back to my place after dinner. If she does, it's money well spent. If not, I may have to take her out again. Or we may even get into an argument. Some of these modern women, they like to use sex as a form of control and anger against men. They deliberately deprive you of sex."

Yet what happens when, as millionaire Norman King put it, "She wants to fuck before dinner!" The tables are turning on single men. Men who ooze sexuality through their pores but who are scared shitless of naked contact—men who put their energy in their careers and not their penises—are being lovingly subverted by sympathetic women friends who are no longer embarrassed to put their arm around you, and blow and whisper in their ear, "Let's make love." A chill goes down the spine of the flattered sexual nonseducer.

In the fifties and sixties, when men complained that women were cold, getting a woman to bed was a favorite competitive male sport. Now sex can be a challenge for the man. The New Woman has confronted him with her receptivity, and one solution has been a total male withdrawal from sex.

To protect my asexuality, I had to be especially critical of women. To avoid sex, one needs a fault-finding attitude. I meet a sexy woman at a party and we begin to hang out, get personal, and I know that she knows that I know that soon we may entertain naked thoughts, and so then I begin to notice the many things about her that I do not like: her physical appearance, her height, her attitudes, her cigarette smoking. I even found myself actually getting hostile in the company of a sexually threatening woman.

Woody Allen's first girlfriend in *Annie Hall* accused him of using his impassioned obsession with the Kennedy assassination conspiracy in their bedroom at night to avoid sex. There was a time in my life when I wouldn't go to bed with a woman who believed in capitalism. I changed. Next my prebed political test turned out to be psychological. She had to be reasonably healthy. I'll sleep with her *if* . . . Every person has his own private list of "if's."

At what point do you stop sex? Before meeting a potential lover? Before kissing and touching? Before undressing? Before genital contact? When do you tell yourself STOP?

What requirements do you have before you will become close, intimate and vulnerable with a woman?

The male withdrawal from sex follows (or is unmasked by) the born-again fervor of the female discovery of orgasm, women demanding that men fulfill their provider roles by producing orgasms. More pressure for men! A thirty-one-year-old artist from San Francisco told us, "I can see why men are now becoming more inhibited about making love. Before it was all their doing, women were supposed to know nothing and were virtually ignorant about their own bodies, so men were not expected to please them. Now women expect men to be able to please them."

The Sex Act has been the man's theater, produced and directed by him. And within the demanding woman still lives the passive woman who wants the man "to do it to her." The many personalities of each woman—and man—comes out in the vulnerability of sex.

"The women I work with mostly still seem to want John Wayne types," a Toledo woman wrote. "They enjoy sex more, but they feel it's still a man's responsibility to initiate and carry through—and his burden if it goes wrong."

The man, occasionally, loses interest. The struggle, the conquest, the adventure is gone. All that is left is the experience itself. The awakening interest in sex by women is stymied by the resistant man.

Susan, a waitress, said she was raised to believe in the always-horny man who "turned on" the woman. Then she found her husband letting a year go by without sex. She tried seducing him, but his attention was glued to the television set. Finally Susan gave up. "He would never discuss it," she said. "Finally I accepted his definition of our relationship as nonsexual."

The man who refuses to discuss sex is putting himself in a power position: Accept my reality or else. Silence and emotional detachment become male weapons, used to avoid the dangers of sexual failure and disappointment.

Some men use charm, intelligent conversation, and even wit to keep the subject off sex. Marilyn, a strong, attractive, single, thirty-eight-year-old woman, could not understand why her Washington lawyer friend kept making and breaking dates, started looking at his watch when it became ten at night, always had a few telephone calls to make when it became time for emotional closeness. When it became no longer possible to postpone the inevitable "sexual moment," he finally spoke up, "I think we have more potential as friends. Let's not let sex destroy our friendship." Marilyn felt rejected. But her friend was scared, scared of not telling her how he felt, scared of not admitting to himself how he felt, scared of not admitting to himself that he might not satisfy her completely, scared of not living up to some internalized competitive male image.

Today, scared men can act as sexually coy as women, and women are starting to sound like men in putting down the man: "He is using sex as a weapon for control in the decadent way women did by developing headaches. With him it's a stomach ache. He never makes love with me when I want to and he never initiates the first move. That to me is the great insult a man can pay to a woman. No woman, anymore than a man, wants to beg for sex. What men don't seem to know is a woman can actually hurt inside if she's aroused and wants sex. It's a release of tension and denial is painful."

To what extent does sexual refusal mask an anger (and therefore withdrawal) from women? One woman says, "My guy avoids sex because it means that he has to give." The change in sexual power relations between men and women in the 1960s and 1970s has meant that men have to be on the giving, as well as receiving, end during sex. Is the modern sexual avoidance merely a hip expression of the traditional male fear of giving?

A woman from the Bronx writes,

I am thirty-one, married, black and a mother of three. My husband has been suffering from sexual apathy for about two years now. Perhaps suffering isn't the right word. I'm suffering and he doesn't seem to mind. I've tried to talk to him about it, but he always says it's not a problem for him. We used to have an active and easygoing sex life, maybe four times a week. Now we average once every nine or ten days and for me that's not enough. He says that he is happy with our marriage but that sex isn't really important. Very often after not having sex for nearly two weeks he will ejaculate almost immediately upon penetration. This is very frustrating, but I'm usually so glad for any type of physical contact with him, that I don't complain. In the winter he's too tired, in the summer he's too hot. With him approaching forty I don't think things will be getting much better without some outside help. I don't want to offend his ego, because he gets so angry.

Many of the women who wrote us expressed their anger at male sexual aloofness. After all, male asexuality perpetuates conditioned female guilt about sexual pleasure. "HELP!" screams one woman in a letter to us. "Usually after the first encounter, all men are sexually apathetic. It drives me crazy!"

Like the man, the woman denied sexually feels unloved. "I feel like running to someone else who will tell me how wonderful my sexuality is," says one woman. "I would like to be able to really know, and not just intellectually, that lack of sexual reciprocity on a man's part doesn't mean that I am bad, my sexuality is bad, or that I am unlovable."

One letter writer, though, sympathizes with the male situation today. She writes, "Why on earth should we women start bemoaning male sexual apathy when we women have been parading around such traits as our hard-won battle scars for years? We are one sex. Hopefully men will realize their current victimization."

Until both men and women realize the sexual pressure they put on themselves and each other, though, there will be a lot of fighting replacing the fucking they want or think they want.

"We're fighting rather than fucking!" Dave screamed at Sasha during one of their incredible battles. After verbal abuse they'd push each other, throw things, even punch each other. At the exhausted end of the fight they'd break down and cry, embracing in shame and disgust. "Look what we've done. We've been fighting instead of fucking." As they fought, Dave's inner voice said, "This is the energy that we could be putting into sex! What does this say about me? And our relationship?" Dave realized that they were fighting so intimately in an attempt to make an intense, deep connection between them—in truth, fighting had become their sex.

A scene in Bob Dylan's movie *Renaldo and Clara* dramatizes another reason the scared husband becomes the angry husband. He picks a fight because he feels unmanly. He is not keeping his woman satisfied. Renaldo gets angry at Clara: she's late. "Hurry, hurry," he says, but she knows that something else, not her lateness, is bothering him. He's fuming about something; but doesn't even himself know what. Finally she confronts him; he accuses her of sleeping around. She screams, "You haven't fucked me in three years. I've got to go somewhere for loving. I need more than an arm around my shoulder." Shamed, Renaldo responds, "What's so fucking important about fucking anyway?" Renaldo is angry at Clara because he is angry at himself for not living up to his own sexual standards.

Fear of Failure, Fear of Success

Is it the male competition and performance about sex that makes it so important and therefore something to avoid? If sex were simply a nonjudgmental fun experience, would it create such fear—and panic?

A sensitive man from Whittier, California, offers us an unusual peek into a man's head: "Sexual shyness has kept me from approaching women, and deprived me and them of much joy. It has kept me from responding wholeheartedly to *their* approaches. It has also contributed to impotence. It has kept me in an unbearable tension between attraction and fear, so that at times I would leave parties and go home. Potential partners, I imagine, have felt that they had enough problems without taking on my load, too. Actual partners have been reassuring and kind, but their 'kindness' intensified my inferiority feelings."

And then he adds, revealing the underlying source of his anxiety and tension about sex, "I didn't want kindness. I wanted to be Bull of the Woods."

When sex becomes a test with performance standards, with the possibility of failure, or even a low rating compared to other men, why bother? If men feel they will lose more than they will win in bed, better to stay away. Why risk failure or embarrassment? Sex creates fear and, as time-management analyst Alan Lakein says, fear is the basic cause of avoidance.

Male sexual fear may be the greatest single cause today of nonrelationships between men and women. A computer programmer from Newport, New York, describes how his anxiety creates sexual avoidance, which he then feels guilty about: "I respond coldly or shyly to an approach from an attractive woman. And instantly I ask myself why, but usually too late to correct the impression I've given. I've still never gotten over the fear of rejection so I habitually pass up sexual opportunities and then regret passing them up."

Fear of failure might sometimes mask an even deeper fear: fear of intimacy. Asexuality keeps women at a distance. The sexually cold man is often not cold at all, but wants his independence. Indeed, sexual problems can become a convenient excuse for maintaining one's comfortable emotional distance. Surprise! Sexual problems protect the man. He is not really scared of not performing well—he is using that fear to avoid intimacy. The male image of the fantastic provider-performer, setting up Olympic standards, enables men to create boundaries of emotional distance. From this perspective, "fear of failure" does not exist at all, but is actually a disguised "fear of success."

The noncommunicating, scared sexual man protects himself in advance of his hurt. And the performance requirements also enable the sexually successful man to keep sex a sport and keep his distance. It's as Holden Caufield says at the end of *Catcher in the Rye*, catching the emotional mood of the day, "It's funny. Don't ever tell anybody anything. If you do, you start missing everybody."

Another way to keep one's sexual distance is a common-characteristic of the modern psychological era—intellectualism. We talk so much about ourselves, our sexual lives, our abstract designs and dreams, that we lose touch with our bodies, our physical and emotional expressions. Instead of fucking, we spend time talking about fucking. Instead of experiencing sex, we analyze it. "He subsequently told me that he's unable to handle a sexual relationship," wrote one woman about her new boyfriend, an urban intellectual. "He wants everything on a lofty mental communication level only."

Workaholism As a Substitute for Sex

Money is a big sex game, and dollars are orgasms. Work is one expression of our manhood. Aaron, a writer, sometimes worked so hard at night that he fell asleep at his desk only to wake up the next morning to continue to work harder. Aaron admitted that, deep down, he was using work to forget the absence of a warm physical body in his arms. Some men fear aloneness and time with nothing to do. Thus, for them, obsessive twelve-hour workdays fill the vacuum. And work becomes their sex. (Or are they working for some mythical sexual goddess in their future?)

For men, and now more and more for women, work and sex are becoming intimately related. Success in work can be an energy-giving aphrodisiac. Success creates passion. When you are successful, you feel more positive about yourself, and you radiate a more electric vibration. As one businessman said, "If things are going great at work, my sexual desire increases."

Business failure can dry up sexual interest. A business or financial blow can cause a sexual electrical blowout, as the man begins to question his survival.

Depression cannot be contained to one pocket of the emotions. Depression is a major cause of sexual anxiety. And then sexual anxiety becomes a cause for more depression, and the vicious circle is on. The penis is a sensitive barometer of the state of the organism. On the other hand, dollars and power can prop up the male spine. If sex fails, a man can reclaim his masculinity with work and money. Whereas in sex and intimacy, feelings can take over, in business and power, the man on the make has little need for feelings. Feelings are feminine, a sign of weakness when you are making the "hard decisions" in business.

I know that everytime I've broken up with a woman, I've had a temporary burst of work production—to hide my panic. And for much of my life, work has been my sex. I have been moved by work ego and work fantasies as much if not more than love ego and sex fantasies. I can even find myself naked next to a beautiful woman—and what am I thinking about? Career. Work. I am like Faye Dunaway in *Network*, having an orgasm to dreams of TV super-ratings.

But in most parts of the world, in ways obvious and subtle, if you have money, you can buy the woman or her time—so money still becomes a sexual goal for men. The growing financial independence of women lessens their sexual dependence on men. And may even free men from their own frantic pursuit of money and power through workaholism.

There is a growing reaction of many businessmen in their mature years against the work-is-everything ethic. "Work can be a real drag on your love life," writes one Houston oilman. "I really burn out a lot of energy working, and that's energy I can't recall for sexual pleasure-making later. I'm working fewer hours to allow more time for intimacy and sexuality in my life."

Work can never be a substitute for love and intimacy. When you are working because your goal is love, you will never get true satisfaction from your work. You will work and work, and you may receive money, and more money, and all the power you can handle. But you are still not satisfied because what you really want is a woman you love telling you that she loves you.

Is Asexuality Harmful to Your Health?

Asexuality is only physically harmful when it is fattening. I had a date with Diane and we went to a Mexican restaurant. Tonight was the night; we both knew it. After five dates, tonight was the night we were going to end up in bed. "I knew you were uptight sexually," she shared with me weeks later, "when I saw how you stuffed yourself during dinner." After wading through three enchiladas, two tacos, loads of rice, beans and guacamole, two beers, flan and coffee, I barely made it back to the car, let alone bed. And when it came to be 1:00 A.M. I had the perfect excuse. I meant it when I said, "Honey, I'm so full I'm ready to burst. I'll give you a call in a day or two, okay?" Food becomes a replacement for sex. A hamburger replaces the orgasm.

Although I considered my asexuality both unmasculine and unsexy, I didn't blame myself when I was not involved in either masturbation or intercourse. Doctors agree that no harm comes to the male body if one does not ejaculate. Abstinence from food causes death; abstinence from sleep causes death. Abstinence from sexual release results in automatic release through wet dreams, and maybe even a lot of energy to redirect elsewhere.

The belief in the vital power of orgasm persists in our culture. Wilhelm Reich, in many ways psychological father of the Sexual Revolution, sees the orgasmic release as the letting go of the built-in tensions of the system. Orgasm, said Reich, is the releasing of your body's essential energy; the more powerful the orgasm, the healthier you are.

The yogic spiritual tradition says that sexual energy is a powerful internal force rechanneled throughout the body if not wasted through orgasm. Freud expressed somewhat the same thing in his concept of sublimation. Norman Mailer talks about the contest between his orgasm and two pages of great "orgasmic" fiction.

Many abstaining men feel no internal biological pressure to ejaculate. The only sexual pressure felt then is social and cultural—the "you must" voice within their own heads.

One of the few dangers of asexuality though is that sexual arousal is, after all, a habit. Success breeds success. Positive reinforcement combined with repetition develops positive habits. Disuse leads to disinterest. Asexuality breeds asexuality; sexuality breeds sexuality.

Saul, a New York publishing editor, told us that when he told his therapist that he had not had an orgasm for twenty-eight days, she instructed him to masturbate that very night. As men get older, they must continue to orgasm, or else they will find it harder to have erections. Your blood flow naturally slows somewhat during aging. It's like exercise. You've got to keep doing it to enjoy it.

So asexuality is only harmful for the man over forty who wants to increase his sexual activity in the future. For young men or older men who are satisfied with little or no sex, asexuality is perfectly healthy and is becoming a growing movement in an age of sexual pressure.

THE RUBIN-LEONARD NON-METHOD
FOR FEELING GOOD SEXUALLY

How to Teach Yourself to Become a
Good Lover

The growing women's consciousness in sex—leading to a more self-aware woman who knows what she wants and is unafraid to ask for it—creates new pressure on the man to become an adept lover. And that means: practice. The man is no longer the unquestioned king in bed. He must know what he is doing.

Masturbation proved to be the road whereby females in the past ten years have reclaimed their sexuality. Women used masturbation as a teaching tool to practice the process of *reaching* orgasm. Could masturbation be the same teaching tool for men, only one where there is an opportunity to learn and practice the *postponing* of orgasm? Since masturbation is a mirror to one's sex life, it is a good way to develop patience, sensitivity, softness of touch and caring—to relearn sexual habits and skills.

My goal in masturbation usually was to get hard and quickly reach the goal—orgasm. Sometimes my orgasms were little ones, and other times I came so explosively I had to grab the mattress to control the internal eruption. But I was definitely more interested in the result than the process.

"How can you find a lover as good as your own hands?" asks one woman who has just seen the most exquisite lovemaking film she's ever seen—a woman making love to herself for an hour. "Such sensitivity, patience, love. She dwells on all the hidden places of her body. I learned that we've got to be able to give it to ourselves before we can give it to another."

But a common myth says: You don't masturbate when you have a partner. Are masturbation and partner sex mutually exclusive? On the contrary, sex researchers have found that people who enjoy masturbation tend to enjoy partner sex. People embarrassed about masturbation are usually embarrassed about sex with another.

A sex therapist in San Francisco suggested that I could become a good lover by changing how I masturbate. Her assignment:

Spend an hour a day naked alone in bed. Focus on your entire body, including your genitals. Take the telephone off the hook, and completely avoid all other stimuli. No music. Begin touching yourself erotically without any consideration of time. Be in no hurry to orgasm—you've got a lot of time to come. Keep your mind on sex and touching yourself.

Turn yourself on. With no goal in mind. Gain and lose your erections. Feel your body all over. Channel penile energy throughout your body, and especially through your heart.

The physiological process of erection is the transportation of blood to the erectile tissue of the penis by arteries. Blood is always entering and leaving the penis. An erection takes place when the rate of inflow is greater than the rate of outflow, resulting in the penis becoming rigid.

Erections can originate in two ways. The first is local physical stimulation of the nerves in the penis itself, which sends a message to the arteries and starts the increased blood flow. The second route is through the mind. The mind creates a movie or registers an image which sends a message through the central nervous system to send blood to the penis. Usually one source of sexual excitement leads to the excitation of the other. Touching the genitals produces sexual thoughts, and sexual thoughts produces a desire to have the genitals touched.

Both pathways to erection, the local and the mental, can be done together in a symphony of sexual arousal. The mind by way of smell, imagery, memory, imagination, or a visual delight; the body by touch and massage. They work independently, and they can work together in a symphony of sexual arousal.

Keys to Sexual Desire

Men are in a "desire crisis" in sex today because the rules have changed. The old sex game, the Wild West and the conquesting man impressing the rescued female, has given way to new rules—equal responsibility and mutual interest. The change has left modern man temporarily without a modus vivendi for sex. His task is to discover a new motivation—or develop new and subtle uses for his old conditioning.

If anyone knows the keys to your sexual desire, it is you. And if you don't, it's only because you haven't taken the time to find out.

If you are facing sexual desire problems, keep a sexual diary. Record your fantasies. Watch how you turn yourself on and off. Record the activating events and images that spark feelings. Record all your thoughts about your feelings of desire. Do you meet an interesting woman—arousal, excitement, interest—and then tell yourself that she's taken, or wouldn't be interested in you anyway—system OFF? Describe in as much detail as possible what happens exactly while you are in bed. Do you ever get slightly turned on? What happens when you do? Do you feel yourself going through the motions? What are you telling yourself? Watch the patterns and discover how information liberates.

Every man knows that special way he likes to be touched to get penile blood flowing. Discover, through self-stimulation, your favorite moves. And then communicate these moves to your partner. And notice what you're imagining when you're turned on and learn to reproduce it when you want. In truth, as Harry Reems, the star penis of *Deep Throat*, has said, "The technique of getting and maintaining an erection is really an acting lesson."

Steve shared with us his ongoing struggle with lack of sexual drive. He seemed to have a common male problem: tremendous excitement the first few times, then no interest whatsoever. Steve had a sense of humor about his difficulties. "The most beautiful woman in the world could walk into my bedroom, take off her clothes and offer herself to me. I'd be excited but by the third time I might have to imagine a fat woman I rubbed against on the bus to set afire my sexual desire . . . Am I weird?"

Wayne had a similar experience. "I know that thousands of men would break their legs to spend fifteen minutes with my wife. She's gorgeous. That fact keeps my penis hard: I got what they want. But I've been with her so much; she's always there. She's always ready for my throbbing penis. She loves my hungry hand, my unbored finger. But that's just the point: She's *always there*. The spice and variety has gone out of my sex life."

Steve and Wayne looked at the movies in their mind that turned them on. The story was the same—conquest as fantasy. Could sex be intimate when one's fantasy was impersonal? I went for years turning myself off because I mistrusted my impersonal fantasy until I realized several truths.

1) *You Turn Yourself On:* Many men think that a particular woman gets them hot. In fact, men turn themselves on, using the woman. It is more accurate to say, "I sexually arouse myself in your presence" than "You arouse me." On one level, it doesn't make any difference whether you're in bed with Marilyn Monroe or a board of wood—you tell yourself what is beautiful and attractive, and you sexually motivate yourself.

Imagination is key to sexual desire. The fantasizing of a sexual event creates excitement. Romance and passion come into the play. Imagination inspires arterial action to the caverns of the genitals.

Imagination flows blood throughout your system and heightens hyperventilation, the breathing of sex. Many a fifty-year-old man has regained his "potency" by seducing a woman in her twenties. Is it the body of the twenty-year-old woman that works? (With eyes closed? In the dark?) Or is it your imagination which is telling you, "Look, how potent I am. I'm with a woman half my age. Whatta man!" Is it the woman, or the self-message, that is creating and sensationalizing the man's sexual desire?

2) *You Can Mobilize Male Chauvinism for Sexual Desire:* Effective fantasy uses the age-old myths of the culture, even if they are chauvinistic. In fantasy, we may still be enjoying the power-oriented roles of traditional man and traditional woman to excite ourselves, even when we are, in our behavior, challenging those roles. The woman in our male fantasy might be making no demands or requests of her own, only aggressively showing total interest in our sexual mastery, actively fulfilling our needs. She exists only in our head to serve us in fantasy. And some women motivate themselves sexually through submission fantasies.

Masters and Johnson see fantasy as serving the role of assisting the individual in confronting and letting go of his inhibitions. However, many men and women in this period of female sensitivity hate and repress themselves for their internal rapist or rape victim. A lot of people become screwed up about sex because they feel guilty about the fantasies that turn them on. This disapproval costs some men and women their sexual excitement. But you cannot censor your fantasies and stay turned on. The solution is not to worry about male chauvinist fantasies that excite. Realize that you are not your fantasies. So use them.

Albert Ellis writes, "You can be thinking sadistic thoughts and be acting with love and affection in sex."

Men and women discover that they often have to maintain the excitement of intimate sex by imagining impersonal sex. Most of our fantasies need never become real. Others are acted out—as a game—through suggestion, play, teasing, and conscious role-playing. We must find a partner relaxed enough with her sexual fantasies to allow us to be our total selves in all parts of our wild imagination.

3) *You Can Be in Bed with One Person While Fantasizing Another, and Still Be Loyal:* Wayne worried over the fact that he was fantasizing the airline stewardess when he was sleeping with his wife. He secretly visited a therapist to discuss this peculiarity. "Does that mean I don't love my wife anymore?" he asked the therapist. "Nonsense," she said. "After all, who are you with? Who do you want to be with? You can

fantasize anything for sexual excitement. It's who you are with physically that is most important."

A graduate student from Southern Illinois University told us, "I sometimes fantasize another person in the act of lovemaking. Sometimes it is a real person whom I know; other times it is a stranger whom I don't even know. Sometimes I prefer my imaginary lover to the real thing. I am a white male and sometimes I get terribly excited by a good-looking black female. I remember as a teenager getting hard after looking at an album cover with the picture of Tina Turner on it. The unknown, forbidden fruit can be a real psychological turn-on, and the psychological creates the physiological."

Masters and Johnson discovered that the married male's most frequent fantasy was the substitution of another woman for his wife. But many married people have made love for years without ever revealing to each other what they are fantasizing. And for a good reason. The woman—or man—might feel secretly rejected. But a loyal man can imagine "satisfying" another woman while satisfying his wife. The man, however, often has a double standard of fantasy. Each man has to face this cornerstone of his male chauvinism. How does he feel if his female partner fantasizes another man while screwing him? "If I can fantasize the maid," says Dick, "my wife Susan can fantasize the doorman." Paradoxically, the more intimate we are with our partners, the freer we are to be ourselves, which includes being nonintimate in our fantasies.

Zen Paradoxes About the Erection

Every man must wonder at some deflated moment in his life, "Could it be physical? Something I ate or didn't eat?" Morning and dream erections prove that nonerections are not physical. Every physically normal man gets an erection every ninety minutes during sleep, without conscious direction. Doctors have invented a nocturnal erection machine to separate the physically nonerect from the psychologically nonerect. You hook two ends of the machine to the end point of your penis. And you forget it and go to sleep. All night as your penis rises, the result shows in the machine. If the man has an erection during the night, but not when conscious, the likely conclusion is that he is blocking his own waking erection through the magic of *anxiety!*

Some say that erection anxiety is the modern fear of man. In a society that is fiercely competitive sexually as well as economically, a man must perform to succeed as a man. And the need to perform always brings along with it the anxiety of not performing.

As a man with erection anxiety, I looked for answers from therapists and solutions in the women I dated until I discovered that the true solutions *lie in my own head*. True, I had to find a genuinely loving woman, because the penis is sensitive to the hostilities of a bed partner. (Unless you've become a mechanical performer who could get hard in a traffic jam; then it frankly doesn't make a difference who you are with.) But the basic truth comes in one's expectations of oneself: one's personally constructed prison.

Zen Paradox: Not seeking an erection often produces one. Julie and I jumped into the sack and our clothes are off—except for my underpants, which I keep on to keep the suspense up. A totally naked body leaves nothing to the imagination. The undies give my tiny penis security for his grand entrance at the appropriate time. But some women just don't understand a man in bed with his underwear on.

There are times when you are so turned on your erection arrives without an ounce of awareness; you couldn't stop your erection if you tried, and there are other times when you've got to motivate, coax, coo and seduce your own erection. This was one of those times. Julie was one of the women I wanted to impress. My desire to impress her made it sure that I was making the wrong impression. I just knew she wanted my hot cock inside her pussy. And my cock was pulling one of his stubborn numbers. "You want me, huh, well try and find me! Ha ha!"

Finally Julie shocked me out of my underwear by saying, "Hey Jerry, let's not fuck. I don't think that I want to have intercourse with you the first time we're in bed. Let's just get to know one another." I agreed, with a huge inaudible sigh of relief. My penis responded to her announcement with a sudden sharp rise. I had an erection in thirty-five seconds, and I was ready for action. But I knew it was a conditional erection. Should she announce that she did in fact expect me to penetrate her—now!—my cock would respond to that news with a sharp decline.

This lady had me psyched out. She played to my psychological coyness while at the same time turning me on with light, delicate touches on my neck, my back and across my genital area. She knew that I, like many men, drive women crazy by always asking for sex when I do not want it, and then backing off when they want it. A clever female seducer would announce, "Let's not make love, let's certainly *not fuck* at least this time," while putting her arm around your waist and running her fingertips up your spine, and softly kissing your shoulders. As she repeated that we were not going to have intercourse, I felt a chill up my spine and my penis harden.

Of course, Julie and I did have intercourse that night. Her declaration of "no fucking" created the stage for the fucking.

The secret weapon in the arsenal of techniques that sex therapists sell to patients is the banning of intercourse. It's the expectation of intercourse—and the demand that the man produce the erection that is essential to penetrate—that creates the fear that often results in sexual paralysis. So therapists get patients to agree that they will engage in prolonged physical contact with the agreement of no intercourse.

You eliminate the pressure, and encourage the natural feelings. The couple often breaks the ban, and in achieving intercourse without pressure, they teach themselves how to do it.

Sex therapy produced a mini-revolution in the psychiatric world. Masters and Johnson transformed the way people look at sex and in the process freed millions of people. Until the Masters and Johnson-engineered change, most shrinks felt that a "sex problem" was an expression—a symptom—of a deeper psychological mess. Only by cleaning up the mess could one truly "cure" the symptom. People went to head doctors for years to deal with their sexual fears without ever talking about sex. The success rates were very unimpressive.

Sex therapists in the 1970s concluded that one could treat the sexual conditions independently—as a habit. The major technique was called "bypass." The successful performer is often no healthier psychologically or sexually than the unsuccessful performer. He has learned to repress negative or fearful thoughts and feelings. It's almost as if, sometimes, a person must become less sensitive to perform well. The troubled sexual partner relearns his behavior, following the rules of performance—concentration, attention to goals, self-confidence, practice and focus on what's working—rather than self-blame.

Three Zen Sub-Principles: *First Sub-Principle: In search of a lost erection, stop looking.* "Oh my god, wouldn't it be awful if I didn't get it up," is almost guaranteed to keep the nonerection. Awareness of Murphy's Law ("If something can go wrong, it will"), applied to male sexuality, often creates the problem. I must, I must, I must—I better—I will—am I—aren't I—I'm not?

As one New York advertising man we interviewed said, "If the whole time is spent worrying, 'Is it gonna work this time?' then it takes all the fun and spontaneity out of sex."

Second Sub-Principle: As your erection subsides, let it. Each man has his own response to a fading erection. An anonymous man from Brooklyn suggests, "If my penis starts getting soft, trying to reverse it will not work, even if it's only half hard after being hard. My penis wants to go soft entirely and stop internally, before the erection cycle can begin again."

Third Sub-Principle: Be where you are. You find yourself naked in an embarrassing situation—well, just be there. Hang out with it. Accept it. Don't apologize to yourself if you are not "producing" or living up to some standard. Be where you are. Such a principle often prohibits embarrassment; if you are embarrassed, then you hang out with your embarrassment.

You've got to be willing to make a fool of yourself in bed. Nothing is happening with the penis, or you came too quick. So what? Be there. Be vulnerable. Be willing to be hurt. Be without power. Give up control. Stop performing or apologizing. You've got to be willing to "lose."

It is a natural process to have an erection. The body is made to work that way. When people "try," they tense their muscles, strain, and put pressure on themselves. They overdo, mobilizing too many muscles and putting too much tension in the body.

A soft penis can sometimes reveal an inner hardness, an unwillingness to let go.

Reality Principle #1: You deserve as many erections and orgasms as you desire.

Reality Principle #2: Erections and orgasms are delicious fun.

Reality Principle #3: There is always another erection—erections are plentiful.

A therapist treating a man who kept losing his erection asked him, "What was your exact thought the second before you felt yourself go soft?"

The man thought for a second. "It was," he said, "I goddamn hope I don't lose this erection."

He feared it was It, his one-and-only erection. He convinced himself that his erections were scarce. He fell into the trap: *What I do not have enough of, I am insecure about.* Belief in scarcity leads to the pressure and the fear that causes the tightening anxiety that results in scarcity—a self-contained vicious circle in which the problem perpetuates itself by its own inner logic. And that leads to a second trap: *Use it before you lose it.* Otherwise called premature ejaculation.

The truth is that there is no scarcity. Erections are plentiful. Practice getting and losing them. If I don't use this erection, fine, I can see it disappear and there's always another. The erection becomes a metaphor for our life: the fear of loss creates the pressure which creates what we fear: the loss.

Enjoy nonerectness. Can we say, "I'm having a nonerection" and enjoy it? Enjoy touching your penis with no expectation of a result, but for the sheer joy of touching. How comfortable (nonanxious) are you in bed with a nonhard penis? Imagine in your mind and body all the things you can do making love with a soft-on!

Welcome Home, Mr. Anxiety

The new situation in sex today is that it's no longer acceptable for one sex to treat the other as an object. Today people go to bed as autonomous beings who make agreements. Yet there is a paradox here, because in sex, while we respect the other person, it is sometimes necessary to objectify the other person as you focus completely on your sensations. Therefore equals can objectify each other in a framework of equality.

Yet this ambiguity in sex has created more anxiety in bed today. Rather than reaching for the bottle of Valium, what is the right attitude toward anxiety? *Welcome it.*

Stephen and Cathy ended up in bed, where both began feeling nervous and tense, when what Stephen called "the moment of truth" arrived. They responded to their anxiety differently. Stephen freaked out and panicked; Cathy thought to herself, "There's that old anxiety feeling again. Well, welcome home, Mr. Anxiety." She replayed in her mind the statements she'd heard Stewart Emery make the previous week in a human potential seminar when Cathy stood shivering in front of a hundred people, afraid to make an impromptu speech: "Cathy, you're never going to be completely free of anxiety. Make it your friend," said Stewart. "The people who are making it in the world are making it *with* their fear. The losers are blaming fear and anxiety as an excuse." So Cathy immediately shared her fears with Stephen and they lost their "heaviness." Meanwhile, Stephen had become sexually paralyzed and stiff. He was allowing himself to become immobilized by his fear.

Other "head masters" suggest that we begin to look at the ghost of anxiety differently. Gestaltist Fritz Perls said that energy can be interpreted as either anxiety or excitement; that they are sides of the same coin. So anxiety is only excitement in disguise and is, actually, a sexy source of energy.

Other therapists, though, remind us that anxiety takes place when the system overmobilizes for action. We try too hard and tense up. Too much energy too fast can immobilize.

As one woman puts it, curing her own uptightness, "When I begin to feel insecure or tense and frightened about sexual contact, I find the best cure-all is a warm close hug which often brings release of tension through tears."

An airline stewardess suggests relaxing by changing the environment or direction of behavior. "First you should spend some time together in a nonsexual way. That works wonders. Try a good heart-to-heart sharing. Or a wrestling match, for fun and sharing. A massage can work wonders. In order to be released sexually and achieve orgasms, I must feel warmth and emotional safety with my partner."

For the man to feel relaxed and free, and for the woman to feel comfortable and open, the Sex Bed must be the Safe Bed rather than the Blame Bed. The key words in the airline stewardess's advice were "warmth and emotional safety." The man wants to be erect. The woman wants to lubricate. Both want to be free of guilt, worry, pressure.

Of course a little anxiety, in fact, may be a good—even necessary—thing. A little nervousness adds an edge, a spiciness, an existential doubt to the lovemaking, and makes it a less rehearsed, professionally produced performance, and more of a human interaction.

How to Respond to a Nonhappening

How men respond emotionally is sexually more important than what happens to their penis physically. Pam from Massachusetts had two experiences with "impotent" men on two straight nights. Their reaction was 100% different, and so were the results. "One man frantically worked on his penis. Anytime it got a little hard, he tried to jam the thing in, banging my pubic bone in the process. That hurt! I felt helpless. We stayed up the whole night trying. I went down on him until my mouth was tired. Finally I went to sleep but he kept waking me up with his hands all over me."

The very next night Pam went to bed with another new lover. "He didn't get hard and he didn't get uptight. We made love other ways. I really respected him. He didn't even ask for reassurance. There's a real man: sure of himself and with good concepts of what's necessary in sex."

And other women said the same thing. "I'm not hurt or offended by the lack of an erection, but I'm sometimes irritated by the man's reaction. A man's erection is not important to me if he can handle the situation without becoming depressed," said a female New York stockbroker, summing up the view of about half the women we sampled—that the issue is not the penis but the man's personality.

Sadly, women do not think that many men can handle the nonhappening of such an expectation. "I believe a man can be sexually turned on without the physical dimensions," wrote a thirty-five-year-old woman from Philadelphia. "However, mentally, after a period of time, he would become aware of his limp member, and his lack of erection. And then it would begin to distress him, starting a domino effect of sexual self-hatred."

One experienced woman divides men into two groups: the rational and the crazed: "The Rational Man says, 'Look, I'm having trouble, I don't know what it is, maybe I can't get that business deal off my mind.' We acknowledge and discuss it. The Crazed Man pretends nothing is happening, gets hostile, accuses me of being too impatient if he doesn't have an erection, or too slow if he comes fast, and they keep trying. The Crazed Men are very hard to deal with."

What should a man do when he is in bed and first gets the inkling that he might not get an erection? Should he share his fear and confide in his partner, or should he ignore his paranoid negative inner voice and begin "trying"—and pretend nothing unusual is going on?

Share your fears. If something is bothering you, share it in a positive way—immediately. "One big key to helping him with his anxiety," writes one woman, "was his own openness. He never hesitated to tell me what he was thinking, and this immediately eliminated any communication barrier. Men who are able to be honest about their feelings—the anxiety bursts like a balloon and disappears almost completely."

Female Gossip and Sympathy

The fear of women gossiping behind your back about your failure to deliver can be crippling. Sam, a construction worker in Buffalo, read our call for men to speak honestly about their sexual emotions and wrote his story. "Sex was going very well," he says, "until my wife thought I wasn't giving her enough. She wanted it day and night and I had to slow down because I was getting weak. So when we get ready to have sex my penis wouldn't come erect. Instead of taking it easy and encouraging me, my wife would laugh at me and call my penis a dishrag, and push me away from her."

Sam was sixty. He felt humiliated. But more horror was in store. The male nightmare: "The worst part of it, she told all her women friends that I couldn't get a hard-on. Lots of these women I could have sex with. But they told me what they heard, and that was that."

Sam felt surrounded. His secret was out. He went to the doctor, seeking reassurance from a white coat. He had no men to talk with about it. All his male friends would have said, "Hey, well, satisfy her for crissakes." The doctor told him to find another woman.

"You need a woman who will encourage you, not blame you," the doctor said. Sam felt encouraged. But he was struck with virtually immobilizing shyness to ask a woman for sex because of fear of rejection. But he tried. "It wasn't easy. Very hard," he said. He kept living in fear that the woman would say the wrong thing when he was having difficulty getting an erection.

"Well, they were good to me, they moved their hips to one side and then another. It encouraged me and my penis got bigger and harder. I am sixty-eight years old now and have a wonderful woman who understands Mother Nature. She is sixty-five and a good sex partner in bed. She never says a word if it takes time to get it up."

Sam shared his fears openly with a woman, and discovered that he did not have to be tested. He let go of his defenses. He stopped setting up an external standard he needed to measure up to. When Sam began to relax with himself, he found a woman he could relax with. In his sixties, he developed healthy attitudes about sex.

Telling the Truth in Bed—Is It Possible?

Although women tell the truth to other women they often systematically lie to men to make male egos feel good. One woman said, "A girlfriend who has slept with at least three hundred men described her worst lay to me, and she said that *of course* she told him he'd been good in the sack, because she wouldn't dream of demeaning a guy's ego when he was lousy by telling him the truth. Most women feel the same way—we're going to be as supportive as possible, knowing how sensitive men are about their performances."

Male terror combines with female sympathy (or fear?) to create even deeper problems through deception. Unfortunately, many women are scared to challenge a man's impenetrable defenses against honesty and vulnerability.

Many men will often fail to raise their sexual anxieties with a woman for fear she will not understand, when all the time women are trying to bring it up themselves without flattening the guy's sensitive ego.

Women have gone from faking orgasms to faking their honest feelings about male sexual performance. As long as men approach sex competitively, feeling that their performance determines their manhood, women are on the spot. To avoid a confrontation, a bad scene, or deflating a man's ego, women often lie.

Telling a man that he is not good in bed can be an act of cruelty, creating scars that will last for years. However, not telling him sets up a distortion that can eventually undermine the entire relationship. Women therefore deprive men of the information they need to grow and learn.

Women are confused. How to behave? How to restrain one's disappointment? Is it fair to be dishonest? How to be honest and not hurt, or at least not add to the pressure? Some women use the kind of cruel honesty that wreaks havoc on a sensitive ego. Other women are compassionate, and the insincerity is subtle—but they're insincere nonetheless.

"I felt concern for the man who couldn't get or keep an erection," writes a female New York television producer, "but you can't be overt in your concern or the man may get angry. And so I acted normally, continued conversation, suggested a break, took the emphasis off the situation at hand."

This understanding attitude is helpful to a man, but her silence also indicates this woman's collusion in her partner's embarrassment. But then, the "good girl" in women is challenged and embarrassed by a male no-show. After all, the male traditionally leads the female into sexual excitement, implicitly giving her permission to give in to her sexual impulses. When a man does not have an erection, the woman must risk being the sexual leader, just what "good girls" have been trained not to do.

One woman confesses how in this situation she didn't want to threaten the man, but felt she had to accept her role as sexual follower. "We tried and tried," she says. "I was disappointed but never let him know. But I became inhibited, afraid my expression of desire would make me seem too scary, and be became more inhibited. We never made love again."

*   *   *

What a Woman Should Not Do: Female inhibition is a natural but inappropriate response to a man's temporary paralysis. If the man is not revealing his sexuality, women, trained to follow, may not allow themselves their own sexual expression. And by ignoring the obvious, they help to create a dishonest, noncommunicative environment.

"If a man is nervous and tense," writes S.B. from Rochester, "I try to make him realize that I have no expectations—which I really do, but I'd never let him know that."

There it is—the limp nonparticipating penis that everybody notices but nobody mentions. Such embarrassment! Change the subject—do anything! It would be funny were it not so sad. Or as Bonnie from Charleston wrote, "My actual feelings during these situations are disappointment and sometimes, 'What did I do wrong?' but I cannot express myself because the situation must be handled so delicately." Women should not hold back their feelings this way. It cuts off the communicative process which is essential at times when people are feeling vulnerable and worried.

What a Woman Can Do in Moments of Crisis: She should encourage communication and take the pressure off the need to prove oneself during intercourse. But she *must communicate.* A woman from Dallas, Texas, wrote us, "A woman needs patience and imagination during these moments. She must always suggest, never demand. She must never ridicule; a man's sexual ego is too fragile to withstand the pain. He will never feel comfortable with a woman who makes fun of his sexual difficulty. But she cannot lie. All humans need reliable feedback from those who are important to them."

A Wisconsin secretary-typist writes, "The three things that are most important in dealing with any problem are emotional honesty and accessibility, physical closeness with just touching and holding each other, and a genuine affection for one's partner."

Two other women offer similar advice from similar results. As one woman from Maine wrote, "He was afraid he wouldn't be able to please me, because he *wanted* to so much. We talked, kissed and held each other all afternoon. The next day it happened." And a woman from Wyoming added, "It took about two weeks of just letting him know I just liked him being there and—damn!—he got it up, and kept it up."

Until the "heaviness" leaves sex, and the concept of failure becomes illegitimate, women must navigate between being sensitive and giving reliable, honest information about their feelings.

Shy Men

The problem today is that men don't know whether they're supposed to be aggressive or sexually receptive. Myth and past prejudice says: Be aggressive. As a sixteen-year-old male high school student from Massachusetts wondered aloud, "Why are men always expected to be 'the heavy' in sex?"

The tables are now turned. The pressures of performance and the mystique of the female orgasm have resulted in millions of shy sexual men. They seek initiating women.

And the women are there. Some females seem to love it. Wrote a woman from Kansas, "My reaction to shyness is that I gently take the initiative, usually with good results. You let the men know what you want to do—and do it! As a matter of fact, shy men often end up making the best lovers!"

The shy man gives the woman an opportunity to feel powerful—a feeling often rare to women in sex. "It gives *me* a good chance to be the aggressive one finally," writes one woman. "It's kinda neat because I am able to feel equal, if not superior, to him sexually."

One woman wrote us who said that she has slept with more than one hundred men. She said that more than half were shy. And she offered acute advice for the woman with the inhibited man: "Encourage him to talk. Help him to understand this is no rat race; there is oodles of wonderfully, blissful time. Massage is great—start with a regular, get-acquainted backrub. Use oil and lotion all over the body in gentle, smooth strokes. Love that body with your hands and tongue. Treat his penis as if it had its own special, individual personality. Learn to massage it, caress it, love it with your hands. Put lotion on it. And remember, men like soft words and praise as much as women do. Take your time. Make it count for caring's sake."

Another woman, D.H. of Charlotte, North Carolina, writes, "Teaching a man about sex can be rewarding and fun. Women, take the lead. Take him by the hand, kiss him, feel him, give him a bath and massage, and then proceed. I have given so many baths to my lovers. I love it!"

Some men realize the benefits of sexual shyness. A football player from Southern Illinois University insisted, "It's an asset, not a liability. If you are genuinely moderately shy, it's a turn-on for the sexual partner."

Since for many men the moment of extreme shyness comes at the time of entrance, men and women have come up with a solution that seems to work most of the time. One man put it simply: "Let the woman put you in."

Does "Roger" Know Best?

Men are fond of saying so. "Trust your penis," they say. One "growth guru" in Esalen, California, faced the dilemma of two people in his workshop, both married to other people more than three thousand miles away, wanting to sleep with one another, but tortured by doubts. He said, "Stop asking your minds and start asking your genitals. Go to sleep with each other and see if your penis wants to respond. Let him decide."

Should your penis lead you? This deificication of penis self-responsibility is most often used as an excuse for sport fucking. The man blames his penis. "I couldn't stop him," he says, making a distinction between himself and his penis. It's been a male ploy for centuries to shrug one's shoulders when caught with a wandering penis.

Yet one must listen to his penis. The penis is often a sensitive barometer of how you feel about another person. If you're scared, your penis might reflect your sensitivity—before your mind realizes it. I never before thought of my penis as a separate person with thoughts and feelings until a therapist heard about my two years of nonalertness with a dominating woman, Rosalie, and concluded, sharply and simply, "Jerry, no doubt about it. Your penis is a hell of a lot smarter than you."

The answer is neither to dictate *to* the penis nor blindly follow its dictates. Rather it is to accept its behavior, learn from its feelings, interact with it, develop a give-and-take relationship with your own genitals.

I had been at war with my penis. I was a penis beater. I blamed it, judged it, set goals for it, judged myself by it. I'd hear a compliment about myself and I'd think, "Yeah, but you've never seen my penis." I refused to listen to reason. Once I complained to sex therapist Michael Quagland that my penis was too small to get automatic, nonstop erections. Michael smiled.

"I just received a phone call," he said, "from a man who was very desperate. He was complaining that his penis was too big to become erect whenever he wanted it to. He said that he needed too much blood to fill the space!"

Our attitude toward our penises is similar to all of our attitudes and expectations to all parts of our body. But the penis is also different, because it is considered so symbolic of one's masculinity. Men must liberate themselves from dictatorship by the genitals. They need a Penis Liberation Movement, to free them from concerns with size, performance, and other competitive obsessions. Too many men can have intimate relationships with women only when their penis is involved. That proves the woman loves him—that she accepts his penis into her vagina, her mouth or her hand, and that he is a real man.

It's the "I'd like to be your friend, but you'll have to accept my penis first" syndrome. A forty-two-year-old counselor from Gainesville, Florida, told us during a group interview: "I could not have any woman for a friend that I have not fucked." Then he thinks and muses, "At least once." The "one fuck" is symbolic. It means that she allowed herself to be the subject of his conquest. It means that she accepted his most private, secret and intimate weapon. "Now we can become platonic friends," the counselor said. "Once is enough."

Except for the Good Reason. A twenty-eight-year-old teacher participating in the interview added that he doesn't need the "one fuck" if there is a good reason why it can't be. And what would qualify for a good reason? "One of us is married, or she's going with a close friend."

Gay men, however, voluntarily freed of penis pressure with women, are often more capable of nonsexual, nondemand, relaxed friendships with women than heterosexuals, who feel they must first conquer every female sexually.

Platonic friendships are spreading among male and female teenagers across America—a sign of the evolution of Penis Liberation among youth—indications that the offspring of the Sexual Revolution are capable of making sexual friendships without genital demands or preconditions.

Don't Play Games with the Other Guys: Don't play the silly game of comparison, competition, judging and rating. And accept your penis exactly the way it is, never comparing again.

Sex occurs between human beings, not machines, and to concern oneself with measurement means that you are reducing sexual feeling to a standardized, detached statistic. We make sex an interaction between tools, rather than people. Each penis, like each vagina and clitoris, is unique and special, beyond comparison.

Because I victimized myself with reactionary beliefs about the penis, male-female responsibility, and sex itself, I went around feeling ashamed about my penis. If *I* was embarrassed about its size how was I going to find a woman who would be happy about it? The man's attitude toward his penis determines his mate's attitude; when a man is satisfied, he will then find a mate who shares his penis and sexual self-esteem.

It was my insane expectation about power and bigness that created my disappointment with myself. In fact, 1) Smallness is good, 2) Smallness is functional, 3) In some economic quarters (admirers of philosopher E. M. Schumacher) Small Is Beautiful, and 4) I was not as small as I thought I was.

Strange to say, but maybe I was, at times, insufficiently macho. I visited a very macho therapist who taught breathing, energy flow, and body pleasure. He said, "Be proud of your penis, no matter what its size, Jerry. Show it proudly to your woman, and say, 'Is it big enough for you?'" Maybe, in a way, he was macho, but right.

Change Your Sexual Consciousness: Stop reducing everything in sex to the penis. Stop thinking of your penis as your weapon. Stop seeing it as an instrument, although that is its function. Begin seeing its humanness; it is part of you. Reduce the importance of the penis in your head.

Both men and women need to go through these changes about the symbolism of the penis. Women, as well as men, worship and make symbols of the penis. Maybe men force women to look at the penis the way they do. It's important for both to change—with men in the vanguard.

Many women are going through changes about the relationship of penis size to female pleasure. "I used to think men's bodies were just appendages to their cocks," writes one woman. "But as I grow and mature, I feel the exact opposite, that it depends completely on the man who is attached to it."

A woman named Sue from Texas points out how an attitude toward the penis can affect an attitude toward the definition of sex itself or the role of self-responsibility. "It used to be very important to me for the man to have a huge penis; the bigger, the better. I think I held that opinion at a time when I was insecure about my own femininity. It went along with the idea of 'What can this man *do* to make me come?' rather than the one I now hold: What can *we* do to make each other feel good?"

Sue's insight reveals how equality in bed, female self-confidence and changing sexual attitudes can help free men from their fratricidal competition over tool and technique.

It was my penis obsession plus my tendency to live by comparison and competition that brought me to the door of a behaviorist therapist. I had just met Mimi and I was ready for personal transformation. I had tried all kinds of Freudian childhood speculation for years, but had gone nowhere. I was ready. It was time to change. I decided to go to a behaviorist.

Dr. Herbert Fensterheim buzzed me into his apartment and I waited nervously for fifteen minutes in one room while he finished a session with another patient. I hated the assembly-line procession of patients through therapists' offices, and I felt jealous that when my forty-five minutes were up, he would turn his concerns to a completely different set of characters. How can a therapist care about me when he goes by the clock? And even takes my money? I paced nervously, my heart beating loudly.

He told me to stop looking for causes or reasons. To just *stop* the behavior.

The rules were simple: Look at negative thoughts as bad habits. Every time you think a negative thought about your penis, say to yourself: STOP. Keep saying STOP every time a negative thought appears. I don't care how often. Eventually the thoughts will stop coming.

Nothing works in isolation, but combined with an open communication with Mimi, I stopped having negative thoughts. My fears disappeared and my attitude changed. And the "stop technique" became useful to me in other areas of my life: neurotic thoughts about myself, about me and money, about obsessions. I was no longer the victim of a mind that acts like a drunken monkey.

I broke my next appointment with Fensterheim because it was unnecessary. That's the nicest compliment that I can pay him—that only one appointment was necessary. A good therapist eliminates his own work. The best therapist is the one who makes himself unnecessary. He creates results for you, and you leave him.

Another Peter Principle

Masters and Johnson provided some consolation to the "small man" discovering that the smallest-looking flaccid penis can grow nearly as tall and wide as a penis bigger and fatter in the unexcited state. The flowing bood extends the caverns, and serves as an equalizer. Therefore differences when nonerect are greater than differences with an erection.

Although there are women, as we have seen, who do not agree with the sex experts, there are a number of good scientific reasons why erection size should not affect the female partner's sexual pleasure.

Most sex researchers reveal that the reason size does not matter is that women have no nerve responses in the upper two-thirds of the vagina. All the nerves are at the entrance, which any penis can reach. I felt good after reading the soothing words of the sex therapists, yet thought, "Could this be a conspiracy of shrinks against big macho cocks?"

The vagina is elastic. "The problem is misinformation," said one woman at our workshop. "Most men and women believe myths and have little information regarding their biological systems. The vagina, actually, is potential space. It accommodates whatever goes in, and the nerve endings that stimulate the woman are right at the beginning. So whatever goes in is going to feel nice."

If the man and woman are communicating positively, they can take positions which deemphasize size. A woman can close her legs tight around a thin penis, and the resulting fit will be tight. Size is minimized if not eliminated. The woman feels "possessed and conquered."

It's not what your penis is, it's what you do with it. But even a well-trained penis twirled by a fantastic sexual dancer would be empty if it were not accompanied by communication and feeling. Meaning it's not my penis—it's *me*, the total person, in bed.

One woman who says she's had sex with more than one hundred men reports, "The best sex I ever had was with a man who was about four inches fully erect. He was versatile and lusty. The worst sex was with an inexperienced man whose penis was two inches fully erect. He was devastated by it, had guilt associations about the sexual act and would not read literature about physiology."

It makes sense to ask your partner what she expects and thinks. Since men are so dependent on the female opinions of their equipment, why not ask the woman whenever appropriate? As a Wisconsin man says, "I once worried about the size of my penis. No more. My wife likes it and that makes me like it even more." And then in an afterthought he says, "I'm no longer even self-conscious about group showers with men."

For years I thought that in order to love me, a woman would have to love my penis. Then I finally realized that a woman will love my penis when she loves me. And to do that, she must love herself. So the choice of woman was all-important. Choose a woman who is confident of her own femininity, not an insecure woman. Choose a partner who loves you for you, not for your penis.

Love and Trust Your Own Penis: A man meets a beautiful woman in a singles bar. Their eyes connect. After a drink, they decide to go to her apartment. They undress and she looks at his naked body. She does a double-take when she sees the size of his member. "And who," she asks, "do you intend to satisfy with that?" He looks her in the eye and smiles. "Me!" he says.

In transactional analysis terms, instead of being a "punishing parent" to your child (the penis), be a "nurturing parent." And the nurturing parent inside you says, "I drop all expectations and judgments of you. I support your behavior as it is, and create the best conditions for your growth." I forget and fall back into blaming, judging behavior. Then I remember and move back into nurturing behavior. The important thing is to be flexible, to move from negative to positive as soon as the negative behavior is noticed, without blaming yourself or lapsing back into the punishing parent role.

A man's relationship to his penis is similar to a woman's relationship to her clitoris and vagina. The sexualization of women in the past decade has resulted in the inevitable Orgasm Competition. Now women, like men, make demands of their clitorises and their vaginas: "Why aren't I lubricating? Why can't I relax? Why isn't my vulva erect? Why am I not coming? Why can't I come more?"

The competitive pressure creates miscommunication, which compounds the in-bed confusion. We've got to change the way we play the game—competition, performance, grading, rating, comparing.

The solution for men is the same as the solution for women—to develop attitudes of nondemand, nonexpectation, nurturing oneself—so that one can then reflect the same attitudes toward another person.

8

WHAT WOMEN REALLY WANT IN BED

Love Me, Love My Pussy

Peggy, a partner in a growth seminar, called to say that she wanted to come and see me. To me that meant, of course, to make love. And sure enough we were in bed. I caressed and kissed her face for ten minutes until she mumbled, "Let's start."

I thought to myself, "Let's start?"

I said to her, "Don't you like to be kissed? Don't you want foreplay? I didn't think women liked it when men went right to the genitals."

"That's your idea of a woman, not always the reality." she said. She pointed to her pussy. I had forgotten the New Woman. She wants to be eaten. Properly chastened, I wet my lips and put my hand on her genitals. Then my mouth.

Many women that we interviewed identified sexual love with being eaten. As one woman said, "If you can't love my pussy, you don't love me. Being eaten makes you feel like you're really being loved. It's much more intimate than intercourse."

Oral sex has become the front line in the war between men and women. Women who prefer being eaten to intercourse feel that if the man wants intercourse or fellatio, she deserves some special consideration for her genitals by the man's tongue. If he won't, what is he saying? "When I encounter a man who does not want to engage in oral sex," writes a Seattle woman, "I feel dirty, ugly, hurt and frustrated."

Feeling dirty and unloved results in hurt, which can release itself in anger. "My boyfriend won't go down on me" writes a woman from Mobile, Texas. "He loves my blow jobs and delights in getting them, but he has made quite clear how he feels about eating me: 'Tuna fish.' I love to be eaten. It is so wonderful! I miss it so much. I refuse to be made to feel guilty because a man thinks my vagina smells and tastes bad. I resent the double standard."

When a man refuses to engage in oral sex, the whole sexual relationship can suffer. As one woman said, "If our relationship becomes deeper and he's still not willing, I have this feeling that my anatomy is nasty, and my pleasure wanes."

Is women's love of oral sex a new, subtle castration? Or a true liberation for the male sexual organs? Some men see oral sex as a Trojan Horse for male castration. They are threatened that it is a disguised attack on their genitals. The result is a growing population of women who are scared to tell their husbands or boyfriends that intercourse alone is not that satisfying to them and that they want oral sex, or a more direct contact with the clitoris, too.

Others, though, are more assertive: "I am surprised by the number of men I know who have never experienced oral sex, and these are fairly well-rounded men in their late twenties and early thirties. I'll never have a long-term relationship with a man who won't eat me."

For many women, the rules have changed. Being a good lover no longer means being able to fuck like Picasso paints. The penis has, to them, been put into the background. Listen to one woman on two subjects, the half-mast penis and the inactive tongue and finger:

> Men who view sex as play and not as performance can be very sexually turned on and not have an erection. Soft penises are as much fun to play with as are hard ones. Although I don't know how to cope with a lack of desire, the lack of an erection is not necessarily even a problem unless it is perceived as such.
>
> If I was in an exclusive relationship where the man didn't want any oral sex at all, I would probably just get out of the relationship. It is too important to me. I spend a lot of time fantasizing about finding a person who would genuinely enjoy licking me until I come.

Some women point out that it is their own belief—however unconscious—of the dirtiness of their sexual parts that men reinforce. One woman became upset when the man "wiped his fingers and mouth fastidiously after they were inside me. That brought up feelings in me that I must be unclean or undesirable. I want to feel totally lovable and accepted."

Women are influenced by men to find their vaginas distasteful. The women, then, in turn, teach their children, mostly in nonverbal ways, that the vagina is a dirty and mysterious place. The male distaste for the vagina, ironically, then has a karmic result, because most men adopt, on a deep emotional level, the attitude of their mothers. The historical asexuality of women thus punishes men by influencing them to dislike female sexuality.

Many men will not put their tongues where they will put their penises. It's an age-old tradition, the disrespect to female genitals by male religions, governments and cultures.

The liberation of the vagina will result in the liberation of men. Women and men are changing their attitudes about the alleged dirtiness of sex.

"Sex is not dirty," said one person we talked to, "sex is intimate."

Until the "dirty" issue is resolved, the war goes on. A New York lawyer told us how it broke up his marriage. "My wife constantly wanted me to eat her, and one day I said, 'This is dirty! I won't do it! You're a whore!' She never forgave me, and our marriage was never the same afterward."

My mother saw her pussy as foreign territory and I adopted her discomfort. My mother's vagina was mysterious. I never heard her talk about it. I had no idea what went on down there. It was none of my business. Her vagina needed to be cleaned, deodorized, sweetened, hidden. I avoided women sexually for years because I disliked female genitals, even though I didn't know that I did.

Men who feel nervous about the cleanliness of the vagina can become especially offended during the woman's menstruation. "Frankly the thought of putting my cock, finger or tongue inside you now repels me," Richard said to Winnie. He thought that his sharing of deep feelings and fears would bring them closer. Was he wrong! Tears welled in her eyes. "That is the deepest rejection of me I have ever experienced," she said. "If you cannot love me during my period, you cannot love me. I've listened to your problems now for months and I've been sympathetic. But I've got feelings too. I'm sensitive. And this is too much."

My sexual ignorance of women for years kept me thinking that women did not want vaginal contact while menstruating. I never bothered to ask—instead I consulted my own prejudices, formed by centuries of religious propaganda against a menstruating woman. Orthodox religious Judaism sees a menstruating woman as mysterious and untouchable. The Christian, Moslem and Hindu religions all agree on one thing—a menstruating woman is "unclean." Religion is largely responsible for giving the genitals a bad PR.

Was I due for some sexual reeducation! I learned that many women get more turned on during menstruation. An orgasm reduces possible cramps. And hormonal changes brought about by menstruation may increase the sexual drive. How shocked out of my naivete was I when one female partner told me that the idea of blood in her pussy mixing with my tongue, finger and penis turned her on. I shuddered to myself the first time I pulled my fingers out of her and they came out full of blood. It scared me and excited her.

A man from San Francisco wrote, "I never found going down so exciting until I read in Herb Caen's column in the *San Francisco Chronicle* that a man put bourbon on his wife's pussy and drank it. Wow! I put strawberry spray on my girlfriend's vagina. I sucked it up deliciously. If the woman goes along with you, it solves all your male oral sex hang-ups."

As Joanna from Sacramento says, "Some men I've been with haven't liked the taste of pussy, but a washcloth, fruit-flavored douches or peppermint oil has always remedied the problem. One man always brought a supply of warm, wet, soapy and nonsoapy washcloths to bed for us to use in a variety of neat ways."

There are men who love oral sex. "The very thought," says Bruce, "of oral sex for another's pleasure is stimulating, and sometimes even breathtaking." I began to enjoy oral sex when I felt, in my heart, love for the woman. The feelings in my heart taught my taste buds to enjoy the taste and smell of the vagina.

Learning from Lesbians

Male fear of lesbianism, ironically enough, is a sign of respect to women from men. In Northern Africa, for instance, the men take sex between women lightly because after all, "What can women do with each other? Without the penis, it's not sex." Chauvinistic men disregard interfemale sexual play. The man has all the power anyway. With the growing independence of women, lesbianism becomes symbolic and threatening, so much so that in America today, many men fear losing their lovers to other women as much as other men—a new paranoia satirized by Woody Allen in *Manhattan*.

At first lesbianism threatened me as I feared losing my female companion to another woman. ("Are they?" I wondered.) Then I realized that women who successfully pleasure each other without penises have a lot to teach men.

Lesbianism becomes sexual liberation for men, enabling men to relax from their oppressive sexual performance demands. Lesbians who kiss each other's breasts for more than an hour at a time have much to teach orgasm-minded, intercourse-directed men, who see sex as a linear process. Masters and Johnson suggested in their recent book on homosexuality that heterosexuals can learn how to become better lovers from lesbians and homosexuals.

In contrast to the slow and relaxed lovemaking of homosexuals, they found that, for instance, straight men usually begin stimulation of the breasts within thirty seconds of the initiation of sexual activity. They then continue to "hurry sex, misread signals and communicate poorly. Men usually assume, wrongly, that lubrication of the vagina means that the woman is ready for intercourse. Many women have no idea how men like to be touched sexually, and most men massage the female genitals in a straightforward gung-ho style that women find harsh. And enjoyment of sex is clouded by the fear of not reaching orgasm."

The "Right" and "Wrong" Female Orgasm

"Grrrr," said the wolf, leaping at Little Red Riding Hood, "I'm going to eat you."

"Eat! Eat! Eat!" Red replied, "Doesn't anybody screw anymore?"

A man has his pleasure and reproductive sources in the same place, but for women, the pleasure and reproductive sources are split physically into two different places. The penis for the male is the source of sperm and orgasm. For the woman, the vagina is the reproductive source, but the orgasm zone is the clitoris, which exists outside the vagina. This fact was known for years, but not widely understood, because women rarely wrote about their own sexuality.

Men created sexual consciousness. Male domination of the female sexual reality resulted in a loss for man, since men deprived themselves of biological, physiological, and psychological information about women. And then they had to prove themselves "real men" by providing women with orgasms through intercourse.

Shere Hite criticized male-dominated sexuality for its unresponsiveness to female sexuality. "The sequence of 'foreplay,' 'penetration,' and 'intercourse' (defined as thrusting), followed by male orgasm as the climax and end of the sequence, gives very little chance for female orgasm, is almost always under the control of the man, frequently teases the woman inhumanely, and in short, has institutionalized out any expression of women's sexual feelings except for those that support male sexual needs."

The controversy over the location of the female orgasm—clitoral vs. vaginal—has not been decisively settled in the minds of women. A movie actress showed us her private diary in which she suggested that the women who promote the clitoris are secretly crying over the lack of a hard penis in them. One New York fashion photographer suggested to us that the powerful myth of the clitoral orgasm was a political move by lesbians; that she personally much preferred intercourse. "The clitoris," she said, "is a small, imitation penis. My vagina and my womb—that's what makes me uniquely female." She, like many women, insists that she does receive orgasms—and good ones—from penile intercourse in the vagina.

Women are competing over the right way to enjoy sex. Both sides of the vagina-clitoris orgasm debate are saying, "I am more female than you." Some feminists have gone so far as to say, "Intercourse is a man's trip." In *Sex For Women*, Carmen Kerr writes, "As study after study has proved, the majority of women do not experience orgasms through intercourse. Intercourse is for men." And Shere Hite points to the fact that only 1.9% of the women in her study used insertion for their orgasms through masturbation. The most common female masturbatory method, in Hite's survey, is through hand manipulation of the clitoris. So, she concludes, that is the most natural female sexuality.

Many women resent being told by sex therapists, feminists and others that they have not received a "correct" orgasm, because it involved the vagina rather than the clitoris. The reverse is also true. Clitorally oriented women resent being told by men, traditionalists, and the establishment that an orgasm without intercourse is not a "right" orgasm.

To the intercourse-oral sex debate about female orgasm, the appropriate answer in this age of sexual equality might be pluralism. The source of orgasm is the clitoris, but the penis (or finger) can create orgasm by its pulling in the vagina which thus creates indirect pulling of and friction on the clitoris. One of the reasons for women's reputation for taking longer to climax than men is that intercourse is not the most efficient way to create female orgasm. Left alone, a woman can come as fast as a man—within seconds.

In one stand-up comedy routine on sex during his recent filmed stage tour, Richard Pryor tries everything to give his lover an orgasm. He starts with traditional fucking, then moves to the vibrator, then to oral sex ("mouth-to-mouth resuscitation"), and finally concludes, "Look, I'll be the bitch. *You* get on top. And she came, too! She say, 'Ahhhh . . . I'm COOMIIIIING!'"

Shere Hite put it this way: "The women who had orgasm during intercourse were usually those who, in a sense, did it themselves. They did not expect to 'receive' orgasm automatically from the thrusting of the partner."

When Pryor says, "I'll be the bitch. *You* get on top," he is illustrating that orgasm is an active, not a passive, process and penile thrusting into the vagina may not be the most effective way for women to reach orgasm.

Many men can become quite macho when challenged on the question of female orgasm. At one of our workshops, one man stood up proudly and said, "What's the average distance between the clitoris and the opening of the vagina? Three inches? If you've got the end of your cock in the hole and you've got the base of your cock against the clitoris, the two pubies are in contact. That's all there is to it. The result is clear: Multiple orgasms!"

Many proud men deny even the possibility that some women cannot receive orgasms from intercourse. As one man said, "The essence of sex is fucking—the penis inside the vagina. Eating a woman's pussy is something else, it is not sex. Fucking is lovemaking."

Edward, a movie producer, told us of a recent experience: "She was great! She had the most incredibly alive and responsive vagina ever! The nerves were really cooking there. And you know why? She just spent eighteen months fucking the Tibetan Buddhists in Nepal. To them oral sex is unnatural, and prohibited by their religion."

The pressure for sexual activity to emphasize intercourse comes from millions of years of the definition of sex as procreation. Most, if not all, religions ban oral sex and promote controlled intercourse as the sole modus operandi of sex. Since the traditional role of religion is to control and diminish the sexual impulse, restricting sexual activity to reproduction becomes an effective weapon. But the religious ban on oral sex is fast losing its power.

However there are other, nonreligious interpretations of oral sex today. Many see the popularity of oral sex, with its emphasis on pleasure now, and its lack of responsibility to the future (children), as an essential sexual ingredient in the narcissism of our times. And some think that it is man's contemporary anxiety about his erection and its durability that has led to the widespread popularity of oral sex. Many women, however, have a different viewpoint.

"Intercourse is so—usual!" writes M.K. from Cleveland. "I don't expect a good fuck. I'd rather save it for holidays, birthdays and anniversaries. Save it, please. It takes away from the sensuality of being together. I come so much better from his touching me—I can come from having my breasts played with. I expect him to try to be more aware— to feel up everything, every part of my skin—not his penis, please."

In the 1978 movie, *Coming Home*, the character played by Jane Fonda enjoys sex more with a man without the use of a penis than she does with a man with a penis. She endures while her warbound husband humps and humps. But she gasps for breath and excitement when a paraplegic without a penis eats her to orgasm, at which point, she says, "This has never happened to me before." In Jon Voight's research for the film, he spoke to many men without penises, victims of the Vietnam war. Voight later told an interviewer that he learned a tremendous amount about pleasing women from these men. "It's ironical," suggests a sex counselor, "that we have to wait until we're handicapped to learn how to make love."

A twenty-six-year-old woman from California said, "There are so many ways to please a woman without penetration. Erection is just an added attraction. Oral stimulation and manual stimulation are by far more pleasing to me sexually and, in all honesty, the only real pleasure I get out of penetration is the emotional excitement I get from my partner's satisfaction. This is not to say that I don't enjoy penetration, I do. But it's more an emotional than a sexual excitement."

"Intercourse is only a form of mental satisfaction," writes M.B., a woman from Tallahassee, Florida.

In fact, many of the women who wrote us were very angry over the male emphasis on intercourse. Pam, a twenty-three-year-old Chicago woman, wrote of her experiences with men. "When the crucial time arrived, it was quite obvious: a few of them had no expertise—they jumbled and groped at me mechanically, hoping that going through the motions of petting would turn me on, get me ready for the big moment. I don't need extensive foreplay, but honestly! Just a kiss on the breasts, an inserted finger and climbing awkwardly on top of me, does not excite me at all. Finally I ask him to slow down, take some time."

An anonymous thirty-three-year-old woman from San Anselmo, California, wrote, "The majority of men I've met hide their lack of desire and don't allow themselves to tolerate the experience. They seek to bolster their self-image of manhood by objectifying me and proceeding with intercourse."

"Women have been serving men orgasms like coffee for years," Shere Hite told the American Association of Sex Therapists and Counselors in their 1978 Washington convention. "Well, now women are saying, 'My coffee days are over.' The man uses the vagina to stimulate his penis without asking—why can't a woman get a man's leg or hand to stimulate her clitoris? We need a new definition of physical relations. Why is there no word for manual clitoral stimulation?"

Hite's book was deflating for men who consider the penis the headline actor in the sex movie. Hite said that only one-third of all women experience orgasm through intercourse. She actually said nothing that had not already been said by Masters and Johnson, Ellis, Kaplan and other sexologists, but her book was the first compendium on how women orgasm—story after story, with little talk of the penis. Some people defensively called Hite's work lesbian-motivated, because if a tongue or hand were primary in creating female orgasm, then a woman's hand or tongue could be as good as a man's.

Ironically, Hite's book adopted some male values in making orgasm the goal of sex, and judging all behavior in terms of the goal.

Leave it to Germaine Greer to defend intercourse to women for its emotional rather than orgasmic possibilities. (Even Hite, in a footnote, wrote that women said the greatest single sensation in sex was the precise moment of penetration.) Greer aptly warns women against overemphasizing the clitoris in sex lest the clitoris become the tool to the woman that the penis has become to the man.

Hite's emphasis can be understood, because men have been dominating women sexually for centuries, and many women have sacrificed their orgasmic pleasure and orgasmic independence in exchange for feeling good through making their men feel good. Hite and a score of other authors and philosophers of female sexual response in the late twentieth century are applying the political themes of affirmative action to the bedroom.

However, for many men, sex without intercourse feels—on some deep, emotional, unconscious level—incomplete. After all, we men have defined manhood historically as the ability to penetrate. "I would not feel like a man if I did not have intercourse at some time during sex," wrote an auto mechanic from Detroit. The penis is the sword of our manhood. And, we think, the source of sexual pleasure. Now men must learn that sex is more than the penis.

And the demand for intercourse comes not only from deep in the man but also the man's expectations of the woman's expectations. One man shares his view that he feels his partner is waiting for "me to put it in. I feel her unconscious thinking, 'Well, what is he waiting for?'" Intercourse represents centuries of sexual conditioning. Intercourse has been the definition of sex itself.

Secrets of Female Arousal

Most men that Ursula meets come on to her. She is constantly dodging grabby hands and listening to lines. She's been to bed with hundreds of men, and the verdict is clear: "Most men are sexually anxious, unsure, not confident. Men have not been educated to make women come. Men think they know how to, but they don't. Women are too scared to tell men what turns them on. So most women leave sex frustrated."

Many men have their hearts in the right place—they don't want to be selfish—but they simply do not know what makes a woman tick physically. "It's easy, but then again, it's not so easy," says Ursula.

"Every woman is different. It's often hard to find the buried clitoris. Most men do not know where it is or how to manage it. It takes knowledge and experience. And it's very hard for a man to know unless a woman tells him exactly how."

Some women are critical of how men treat the clitoris. One woman writes, "I will get off better by skillful oral sex than intercourse. However, most men think oral sex is simply sticking the tongue into the vagina and wriggling it around a little. I am constantly amazed at how few know the magic the clit can work."

Another woman says, "Speaking of the ever-popular clitoris, most men treat it as if it were a Grecian goddess statue—beautiful, but cold as stone. They 'massage' it as if they were trying to erase it!"

Dave put his hand on Ann's clitoris. Ann then put her hand over his and rubbed, "See, I like it this way." Dave got turned on by Ann's sexual assertiveness. David knew how difficult it was for Ann to tell him what to do. She was breaking her own barriers.

For many women, even the most liberated, asking for what they want sexually scares and offends them on some deep, conditioned level. They think they are being a "bad little girl." Men have got to demonstrate to women that they want to be shown what turns them on. I get really excited when a woman takes my hand and directs it.

Every man should go to an "orgasm school" taught by women. Every man should seek a woman teacher to guide him through to female orgasm. Men, especially, should ask their female friends to take them on a tour through their intimate anatomy. Men learn from the locker room and street corner, and from the centuries of prejudice against sexual women. Men have been in the habit, historically, of telling women what turned women on. Asking implies weakness. Asking admits: I don't know. The problem with women leading men to the promised land of Sexual Intimacy is that it conflicts with a Law of Manhood—that men must not admit any ignorance of sex.

Because there are so many men out there hiding their ignorance, they are more ignorant than ever. Nobody can learn anything if he is not willing to reveal that he does not know, says one woman. "I'm open enough to say, 'Here's how to do it, do it this way.' Some men, however, really resent it when a woman says this and feel their masculinity is threatened. I think that's bullshit."

A thirty-four-year-old barber from Ft. Dodge, Iowa, agrees, "Let the woman lead you. You will enjoy it more."

I've had to ask a number of women to direct my hand to their clitoris. And you know what? There was nothing embarrassing about it. There are many men out there who don't know where the clitoris is because they're not willing to reveal that they don't know. But it's not written in stone somewhere that men must know everything about sex without asking.

Sometimes, even when men ask, women won't respond. Writes one man from Texas, "I wish more women would tell us men if they were getting off or when they want to get off. Why are we men supposed to be psychic about women in bed? I know there must have been times when my partners didn't feel moved to orgasm and just wanted to snuggle or pleasure me, but they never told me, and I never feel comfortable. Do women think it would insult our manhood if they volunteered their sexual preferences? If women were more verbal, it would make it easier and freer for me."

However, one must watch out how we ask another person what they want, avoiding the tone of one man who "inquired about pleasing me in a manner suggestive of a waiter taking an order." A rule book with instructions on which buttons to push when will never satisfy communication needs. An interchange of loving and caring discussion before, during and after sex, though, will open up the sexual isolation chambers.

Don't Ask, Look! A psychiatrist credits one woman with his sexual breakthrough. "Most women would have showed me the door because, let's face it, I was a lousy fuck. I can say that now only because I've learned the difference. This woman was willing to take responsibility for the part of our relationship she didn't like. She took the chance of me rejecting her because of my hearing something that I didn't want to hear."

This psychiatrist says that he is a refugee from the "How was I?" fraternity. "I kept asking her," he said. "How am I doing?" "She finally said, 'Do you really honestly want to know?' I said, 'Yes.' She said, 'Then just look at me. Really look at me. Do I look like I had a good time?'" He looked at her eyes, her breathing, her vibration. Words of reassurance were redundant.

Body language is the key to communication in sex, often more important than verbal directives or questions. "I had never before," he said, "thought of a woman except as a bunch of parts. I stopped asking and started looking. And found myself getting much more in touch with women than I had ever been before."

Many women complain that during sex men seem removed and distant. As one woman puts it, "I can't stand 'silent sex'—not a word passed between us. It makes me feel like a disposal vessel—for his pleasure only."

Another woman agrees, saying, "If a partner closes his eyes, I feel shut out mostly and there is a large loss of intimacy. I don't want to make love unconsciously. I like it if we can talk to each other while we make love. Sounds are as good as words. But the more I express with my partner, the more intense and touching the experience."

A man must be directive and clear in telling a woman *exactly how* he wants his penis stroked as a woman is clear about her clitoris and vagina. We're always open to new moves but we know what we usually like best. And how's the other person going to know if we don't tell her?

The Performing Tongue

My first interest in oral sex was in performing well, not necessarily enjoying it. I often went right for the orgasm. If it took, at the most, ten minutes, that was okay; I don't know what I would do if it took one hour. My tongue would have gotten very tired.

A new competition among men reflects the new reality. Men, of course, still compete over their pump's power throbbing through the vagina. But the "in" sexual competition of the seventies and eighties is the generosity and enjoyment of the man performing cunnilingus on the woman. Even men who are bored by oral sex stick it out so long as possible, like the radio interviewer who said that he keeps saying to himself while bringing a woman to orgasm with oral sex, "All right, already, come, have you come yet, all right, all ready, come, let's go, hurry up."

The man who can last and *genuinely enjoy* oral sex is also the "real man"—he wins the love and adoration of the woman. "Jim could arouse me through oral sex like no one else could or ever has since," writes a twenty-year-old Colorado college student. "I really appreciated him for that. He was one of the best lovers I've ever had because of his willingness to perform oral sex."

A woman will be sensitive to *why* the master eater enjoys it. The competitive-performance man who enjoys only because his ego knows how well he is doing can turn a woman off sexually. Men forget that women distrust men who are obviously performing and waiting for the rave reviews. Or insecurely asking, "Didja come? Didja come?"—about the unsexiest question one can ask at such a crucial time.

Let us not fall into the same foolish competition with our tongues and fingers that we play with our penises. But we already have. Men are so proud these days of the size of their tongue. And their finger.

And the yo-yo tricks that we have learned with these, displaced from the penis to the tongue and finger.

We can now hint about the size of our tongues. "How much circumerence does my tongue take?" one man asked, rhetorically. Reports of men doing secret tongue exercises may be highly exaggerated, although the lion position in yoga classes—an exercise of the tongue—may indicate the implied sexuality of yoga exercises.

Can you imagine—tongue exercises? And tongue advice: "Don't use your tongue like your penis," says one sage. Adds another, "It's crucial to keep your tongue relaxed."

At a party of uptight academics in a university town, one graduate student stuck out his tongue as a joke. It was huge, and fell down to his chin. Its shape was sculptured, well formed and heavily textured. One of the wives of a young professor said, "Look at that tongue." People gathered in groups to admire the student's tongue. It became a joke for the rest of the party, although nobody mentioned the obvious sexual allusion to the whole experience. Was everyone thinking it and nobody mentioning it?

Three Cheers for the Tongue and the Finger

"Men can do with their mouths what a foot-long penis cannot do," writes one woman to our survey. A man's ego can go bananas when he realizes that it's not his hard penis but his finger and his tongue that determine his masculinity and his skill as a lover. Wow, think of that. My finger makes me a man! Albert Ellis says the hand is the most useful sexual tool. "I often shock people," says Ellis, "by saying that you can gain a reputation as a wonderful lover if you have no cock whatever."

The Victory of the Mouth and Finger over the Penis Liberates the Penis: If you are concerned that your penis may not respond on command, you can always turn to your mouth or hand as primary sexual tools—as the mouth and hand are subject to control of the will, unlike the pesky penis.

The finger and tongue are often better sexual tools for female orgasm than the penis anyway:

The finger does not ejaculate and go soft.
The finger stays sturdy.

The finger is tough.
The finger has great flexibility.
No problem keeping the tongue wet or the finger hard.

"Jim was tense and had trouble getting a good erection when we first met," writes one woman, "and it was awhile before he was convinced that my pleasure wasn't totally dependent on his erection. If a man is concerned about the woman's climax, he may stay limp as a dishrag. If he has taken care of her with a good tongue, finger, vibrator—anything at all to get the pressure off—then he is in an easier frame of mind and can enjoy himself. Once the pressure is off to take care of the woman, the man can often get and keep it up more easily. And have a satisfactory climax himself."

Feminism Reduces Male Sexual Anxiety: Some observers have pointed to the rising demands of feminism as a chief cause of male sexual uptightness, but in truth feminism contains the secret that is the true liberation of men. From expectations. From the need to perform. From the need to be a sexual athlete. Feminism releases the penis from pressure. Intercourse, instead of being an expectation, is now a choice. And the freeing of the act increases the pleasure.

The fact that many women prefer oral sex to intercourse for *their* pleasure is a blessing in disguise for the man concerned about his sexual performance. My penis is not needed by the women anyway, except as a symbol, for her ego. My penis is just for me and *my* personal pleasure. Our cocks have been unchained—no longer carrying the responsibility of manhood or the responsibility of female pleasure, but now free to play!

You Don't Need an Erection to Have Fun in Bed

As sex moves from penis-dominated to body/person-oriented, we must free ourselves of the dogmas stated in sex magazines, sex textbooks, sex gossip, and general sexual communication—even the most enlightened—that enough blood in the penis for a constant erection is a necessity for potency, manhood, masculinity, intimacy or exciting sex.

Erection or nonerection is irrelevant to the *true* climax of the sexual experience—the intimate sharing of feelings. We asked men and women whether a man could be sexually aroused without an erection. The answers surprised us: overwhelmingly no. As one woman wrote, "I thought an erection was the definition of sexual arousal." Men especially still equate their sexual turn-on with the blood flow in and out of their penis.

Erection is easy to measure. There it is. Sexual arousal is more open to interpretation. There's the breathing rate, the tingling of skin, the altered state of consciousness, the color in the face. But most important, there's the feeling inside the head and heart. And how do you measure a feeling? You can't.

Enough women have left bed unsatisfied—with men who used their penises as instruments—to know that sex is more than a hard and throbbing instrument. In fact, an erection can be a block to sexual intimacy. (As can be a nonerection, if the man is obsessed or even too concerned with it.) "We're in bed," she says, "and there he is with that erection. We've got to do something about it." The erection writes the sex script, and sets the tempo and pace of sex.

What is sex? Is sex looking? Is sex touching? Or orgasm? Intimacy? Or conquest? Closeness? Heavy breathing? Cuddling? Is masturbation sex? Is sex kissing? Is sex ego? Or is sex a hard penis in a wet vagina?

We are living in an era where the purpose of basic activities like sex are being redefined. Sex historically has been for one purpose—to produce babies. Pleasure was without God's permission.

The reproductive ideology of sex perpetuated the idea that sex was bad; pleasure needed to be earned; the family must be maintained at all costs; the sex impulse controlled; men enjoy sex while women don't; women became nonsexual once their baby-producing days were over.

Those who define sex as reproductive can't understand that children have sexual sensations; they see masturbation or "spilling the seed" as sinful; and they think sex always had to lead up to the big bang of male ejaculation.

Naturally, the reproductive definition of sex perpetuated the vaginal orgasm at the expense of the expendable clitoris.

Professor John Money is a well-respected sexologist known for his careful research and thoughtful judgments on the effect of sexuality on society. He waxes enthusiastic about the change, saying, "The ability to separate the bait of sexual pleasure from the hook of reproduction sparked a revolution more momentous for the human race than any in history. . . ."

In a keynote lecture in April 1978 to the meeting of the American

Association of Sex Therapists and Counselors, Professor Money said, "The transition from procreational to recreational sex is the most important change in human history since the wheel, so important, because it affects *everyone* in their daily lives."

Sex has historically been interchangeable with intercourse. Penetration was necessary to complete the act. When a person says, "We had sex," he usually means, "We had intercourse." We asked people in our workshops what they mean when they say, "We just had sex." The most frequent answers were, "Penile-vaginal contact . . . Fucking . . . Just physical intercourse . . . The intimacy of intercourse." One person said, "Orgasm." Another said, "Physical and emotional closeness." But most people agreed with the traditional equation of sex with intercourse.

With the change from reproductive to recreational sex, the position of the penis has changed. The penis used to bear total responsibility for manhood which equalled fatherhood—the fulfillment of the male sex role. Fathers feel potent. A friend, a father of two months, pointed to his crotch and pushed his thumb in the air gleefully as he relayed his pride of accomplishment.

Today the purpose of sex is more often pleasure and intimacy. Parenthood is optional, and if anything, sometimes a block to sexual expression. The end of the procreational ideology can lead us to see intercourse and erection as exciting aspects of many sexual possibilities.

The procreational definition of sex resulted in such perverted concepts as "impotence," meaning that sex has a purpose, and unless a man carries out his part of the purpose, he is powerless.

Never again should people use this concept which victimizes men. The fear of "impotence" is even more stark than the situation itself. For the sake of *all* men *and women*, people must drop a key part of the baggage of male chauvinism—the potent/impotent dichotomy in sex, which means: *You are or aren't up to standard*. We need a new process-oriented definition of potency, so that we can stop judging ourselves and each other in terms of performance, and start relating to each other as lovers.

It is not only for the millions of men with erection sensitivity that the word "impotence" should be outlawed from use. But for the sake of all men and women. All men have fears, however buried, of "impotence." Once we all stop fearing "impotence" or "powerlessness," we can stop oppressing ourselves and others with our pressures for "potency."

The most important change that has accompanied the definition change is the change in power relations in bed. Today in sex we have

Equal Opportunity for Orgasm. Women have changed from orgasm providers and consumers to orgasm creators. And that equal opportunity has created the potential to deemphasize orgasm pressure, competition and other "shoulds" during sex—has created, in fact, Equality Sex which is enjoyable and loving.

A NEW SEXUALITY

Equality in Bed

Sex has been transformed from a male-directed, female-following act to a two-person communication. Men have no choice but to give up the director's role in sex and learn how to interact, and learn the role of follower.

Equality Demands Communication! Sex is no place for psychics. Because of male pride and female fear—and female pride and male fear—an astonishing number of couples in this country have never had a basic conversation about sex.

If men and women have difficulty communicating out of bed, imagine how difficult it is *in* bed in the middle of the confusion. Neither one knows what the other wants. Each is concerned with his or her own needs.

We have certain ideas about sex, such as: It must be spontaneous. We expect each other to be mind readers, sexual psychics who can intuit each other's individual preferences. We're afraid we'll lose all the mystery and romance if she told us how to turn her on. And from our Puritan anti-body tradition comes the idea that sex talk is dirty, embarrassing, and self-indulgent.

One woman from the Midwest captured the difficulty of communication during sex in a very self-revealing way: "Sexual activity was bizarre and overwhelming for me. I was too consumed with my own fears of inadequacy, too much on guard against possible rejection and too lacking in sexual confidence to perceive what was happening with my male partners. My own inexperience prevented me from seeing or understanding what was going on, from seeing the games, from seeing the panic. The consequences of no communication were disastrous."

Sex works best without rules, but with an agreement between the partners to completely communicate and support each other's enjoyment. Both the men and women can have the appropriate attention and time paid to their genitals the way they like it, and also the freedom to be nongenital. Sex equality means that each person has the opportunity to determine the content and pace of sexual activity.

In Equality Sex, each person gets what each wants. Maybe the man wants quick sex leading to orgasm. In this era of the promotion of the prolonged sexual experience, a man may be ashamed to reveal that. But he deserves quick sex. Let him enjoy it, and then ask his partner what she wants. If she wants forty minutes of his tongue loving her clitoris and vagina, that might be equal to his two-minute explosion. Sex becomes a fit between two personalities.

In egalitarian, communicative sex, we can harness our old habits to our pleasure as we create the new vision. Men and women do not have to be ashamed of their old patterns in New Sex. The resulting roles are played like a game or exercise, and enjoyed completely.

The New Woman of Equality Sex ends the unequal division of responsibilities. She takes responsibility for sexual initiative for her experience in bed. She knows what turns her on and lets the man know. She directs the moves, while he follows. She can give herself her own orgasm.

Historically the woman's role has been to support the man in his chosen identity. Today the view is spreading that both men and women have the right to choose and develop their own identities. And then comes the growing success of women in becoming economically independent—the only true independence—another slap at the masculine image of their genitalia.

Many men have begun to see the tremendous opportunities for freedom hidden in the expanding definitions of female roles. Men are beginning to realize that they don't have to be responsible for whatever happens in sex. They don't have to be Mr. Know-It-All. Men can finally smell actual Sexual Freedom from the rules and from one's own conditioning.

Ironically, the women's consciousness movement—in the early seventies, a weapon in the hands of women—bears the seeds for the liberation of men. Women basically are telling men that they no longer have to maintain their male facade—for them—and men can speak honestly about themselves. The rebellion of women enables men to overthrow their own oppression—the self-oppression of false, limiting beliefs. The solution for men is a change in masculine consciousness to affirm their inherent self-worth and stop using sex to prove their masculinity.

In discovering themselves, women reduce the pressure on men. The equal woman allows the man to step down from his oppressive provider role. Freed from the strait jacket of a particular script, the man can play many different roles, enjoy a wide range of experiences, and relax from performance demands.

Jonathan

Jonathan gave the impression of being hot with women, always surrounded by the most interesting women in high school. He was captain of the football team, president of the class. He was always smiling, and quite handsome. People naturally assumed he must be a Jack-of-all-trades in bed.

"I was a virgin all through high school," he said. "I was scared. Lois wanted to. But I didn't know what to do down there," he confided. "And so I kept making excuses, like, 'We better be careful. I don't want to make you pregnant.'"

Jonathan married his college sweetheart, Susan. The Male Sexual Revolution of the sixties came, and he made sex his favorite sport. Then feminism arrived with the Female Sexual Revolution of the seventies and Susan began to initiate, enjoy and experiment. At first, Jonathan loved it. They "fucked and sucked deliriously" for five years until "the roof fell in."

"My wife became a feminist activist. She refused to do the laundry any more. She refused to cook. Everything in our house became an issue. She started staying out late all night going to feminist meetings. We argued all the time. I lost all my control over her. The implicit agreement we had made when we married was that she would support me in my life. She reneged."

Sex, however, got better. "The friction between us added anger to our sex, and made it spicier. I was really out to fuck her ass off. It gave me a feeling of power I had lost in our outside life. But even though mechanically our sex life improved, I resented her on a deep level and the feeling left me. And then something happened that I will never forget. It scared the shit out of me. I had a power failure."

Jonathan went momentarily crazy while Susan stayed calm during his sudden but persistent electrical blowout. She pointed to his mouth and her pussy. He began licking. He found his interest in sex dwindling, and the more apathetic he became, the more turned on became Susan, the new pursuer.

The experience shook Jonathan to the soul of his masculinity. He felt himself a failure and threw himself totally into his work. He began coming home from work "very tired" to avoid sex.

Jonathan, part of the transitional generation of the sixties—taught one thing and experiencing another—found himself an early casualty of the women's consciousness movement. He and Susan separated and then divorced. Jonathan entered therapy and there he learned to apply the insights of the women's movement to his own life—to rescue himself through the principles of the same movement that almost destroyed him.

"I can speak up for my needs and be myself," he said. "I went on a vacation recently with one woman and all she wanted to do was fuck. I came five times in one night. By the fifth time, my come was very weak. Now I know not to ask too much of my penis. I've learned that as a man it's okay for me not to be perfect. I'm being strong; I'm being myself. I'm being me."

Like many men today, Jonathan developed a greater sense of himself. No longer did he have to perform like a bull in bed. No longer did he have to worry about not getting erect. No longer did he have to worry about maintaining his male image. He learned from women to accept himself as he is, and not twist himself into some form to fit a male stereotype.

The women's consciousness movement was freeing women from fixed images of what it means to be a woman. And male consciousness was freeing men from fixed images of what it means to be a man.

People Liberation

Abraham Maslow said that the self-actualized man does not differentiate between male and female roles in bed, but freely *interchanges them.* The liberation of men sexually will take place when men discover the female side of themselves. Jules Feiffer put it this way in a 1971 *Playboy* interview: "The women's lib movement, with all its nuttiness and perversity, is much more important than the sexual revolution, because what it will basically do over a period of years is make both men and women stop dealing with each other as objects."

In addition, equality of power in bed allows people to switch roles. The female dominates; the male dominates. We throw away all previous sexual scripts and expectations. We can even begin to reverse our own programming. We can play—in bed—both the roles of the man and woman in each of us.

In reality, the differences among people may be greater than the differences between men and women. A woman from Pueblo wrote, "I don't think men and women are actually too far apart in their emotional concerns with sex. Women are beginning to admit that interest in technique and experimentation are good, and men are beginning to realize that they don't have to hide their feelings. Both sexes need to drop the conditioning that society has put on us when we are in the bedroom."

Within every woman is a man. Within every man is a woman. When we go to bed, there are four of us, interacting with each other, the males and females in each of us. We can take turns playing the tradtional male and female roles. She allows me to play out my masculine conditioning as a game, and then the roles are reversed. He allows himself to be female in bed with the women who experiences her internalized man. A woman says, "He enjoys us changing our dominant roles. He likes to lay back and 'be done to' and he admits it." Men learn passivity, just being there, being pleasured, doing nothing.

One woman put it this way, "I don't expect the man always to be dominating, the 'strong' one; I can expect that a man needs to be held and let cry occasionally. I would hope that a man could accept my need to be held and let to cry."

Thanks to the change in women, men are able to redefine sex away from one-way, conquest-domination, role-playing performances to a shared experience of intimacy. One woman wrote, "I reject the myth that a woman likes to be subdued by a raging beast and finds animality perversely pleasurable, that somehow she's made to feel more like a woman when the battle is over. Sex to me is not merely the sexual act but the intimacy that is shared by a man and a woman in bed. Sex should be a dialogue, with the language tenderness."

It means the male must give up control—often a difficult psychological move. One psychiatrist told us: "In my sex therapy sessions, a strong objection by women about not going down on men was the fact that men are not willing to give up control and let the woman please the man. They insist on holding the women's head, thrusting and pushing it down and manipulating her face. The women even feel that they are being literally fucked in their face and they are not able to give pleasure to a man, he feels he must direct and control his own pleasure-giving."

What's needed is a redefinition of sexuality, to go beyond fixed role-playing, traditional male-dominant, female-submissive games, and to move to a definition of sexuality in which people take turns satisfying and being satisfied, dominating and being dominated. Nobody's femininity or masculinity is at stake, and nothing is expected except consideration. Sex becomes affection, communication, play.

Female sexual equality is the friend to all men, because it enables men to liberate themselves. But a deeply ingrained male belief system memorized from birth does not die easily, either in the media of the country or the psychological process of any individual. And while it dies, men experience pain. Men blame the women for that pain, unwilling to accept the obvious fact that they are the creators of their own pain because they believe society's nonsense about what it must mean to be a man—Compete, Produce, Compare, Achieve, Overcome.

The more men allow their female side to flow, the better they get along with women. Once men allow themselves to take responsibility for their own nurturing, they can begin to relate to women as people, as friends, as lovers, and as sexual partners.

Women and men today are both deeply involved in a transformation of the consciousness of the sexual act. On the way to that transformation we are finding ourselves changing positions, playing out old conditioning, and making wonderful, perfect fools of ourselves, as we find out who we really are. By overthrowing men sexually, women are doing them a favor, enabling men to liberate themselves from themselves.

I and Thou in Bed

Who Comes First in Equality Sex? Today the sex ethic often dictates that the woman should come first in sex—part of the affirmative-action attitude of sexuality. "I won't let a man enter me who doesn't eat me and get me off first," says one woman. Since some men feel like ending sex once the physiological letdown begins after their orgasm, women rightly seek their attention first.

But one disadvantage of this contemporary practice is a loss of interest in sex by men. It does not work for a man to routinely put women's pleasure first at the expense of his own. Sexual self-denial leads to sexual indifference, and that does not serve the interests of the more sexually turned-on partner. In addition, the woman-first rule can even be an example of reverse machoism, treating the female as a delicate object that the man still protects.

Affirmative sexual action on behalf of women may be necessary, but eventually we must move to the position of each partner enjoying enlightened selfishness and noncompetitive altruism in sex. Can one be both completely selfish and completely altruistic? Yes—in sex.

Do what turns you on.

Take care of your own orgasm.

Don't be dependent on the other person.

In Equality Sex, the emphasis is on people, not sex roles. Little will be gained sexually if men and women simply switch sexual roles. Men can learn from women sexually. Women are asserting themselves and learning to ask for what they want. Two people asking for what they want in bed, and willing to create the environment for the other person to get what he or she wants—that makes sex play, not work.

In Equality Sex we play in the environment of paradox—living two opposite, and apparently contradictory, principles at the same time.

Put Your Own Pleasure First. This is a risky principle, because it is exactly what men have been doing—and most still are doing—for eons. *Absolute* sexual selfishness doesn't work. The failure of the male sexual power ethic reveals itself in the effect it has had on women—creating passive, sexually faking, and nowadays rebelling-dominating women. Today men have begun to repress their own sexual desire in their competitive struggle to bring their female partners to total satisfaction. That struggle may exist only in the heads of the men, but it does not work either. Sexual sacrifice sets men up in the role of victims.

Putting a woman's desires over your own is, ironically, a clever way to avoid intimacy with a woman. A totally "unselfish" pleaser in bed pleases no one, not himself or his partner. It's only the male equivalent of female masochism—"I am here to serve the woman, not myself."

A level of selfishness must underlie support for someone else. If I am not happy in bed, how can I make another happy? If I do not feel good, how can my vibration make another person feel good? If I don't take care of myself in bed, how can I take care of another?

Ultimately, You Give Yourself an Orgasm. You are finally responsible for what happens inside you during orgasm; you choose the fantasy; you feel the excitement and the release. Each person directs his or her own sexual unfolding. By touching, breathing, verbal instructions and sexual feedback, we are leading the other person, even when it looks as if we are following.

Put Your Partner's Pleasure First. Yet the highest form of self-interest may be when you completely forget yourself and lose yourself in total focus on the second-to-second pleasuring of your partner. Use your entire body. And do all this for yourself—for the pleasure it gives you to give her or him pleasure.

In sex, as in life, we usually give to receive. In Transformed Sex, we experience giving as an end in itself. You are the judge of your own giving. Both partners focus on one partner's pleasure, which can go to orgasm. They focus on the other, and in both instances are merged as one; giving and receiving blends into one process.

Taking-Turns Sex

Remember Simultaneous Orgasm—the Great American Sex Myth? The drive for long intercourse to produce orgasm in the woman at the same time as the man's orgasm demonstrates the man's dogged determination to make sex revolve around his penis—and the clock.

Sex used to work on a schedule—both people trying to come together in Simultaneous Orgasm. Men put on their Superman costume: fifteen minutes, thirty minutes, an hour! Still nothing?

Isn't it just like America to measure sex by the clock? Consider all the pain caused by the expectation of Simultaneous Orgasm. That institution of sexual expectation has cast a dark cloud over many a bedroom. There're the people who've "failed," the women who've faked, the men who've faked, the furious trying, the missed orgasms, the excuses, regrets, accusations, comparisons—all the thoughts that take one out of the experience of the moment.

And then there's the inevitable muttering under one's breath: "Next time . . ." or "If only she came quicker." Ah, how many times have we gone to sex in search of the Big S.O. and left unsatisfied.

Simultaneous Orgasm is fine if it happens, and its rarity should not increase its value. As a goal, S.O., like most goals, can destroy the process.

Partners who know each other well can—if they want to—discover how to combine their individualized orgasm patterns into an orgasm at the same time. Different rhythms can combine; methods can be discovered. And there may even be first-time moments of beginner's luck. But, in this transitional, groping time of sexual redefinition, the most common form of sexual expression is called Taking-Turns Sex.

It is necessary to be completely selfish and completely giving in sex. We are all completely idiosyncratic. We need to pace and shape a sexual event to our own timing. That's why first-night sex is often unsatisfying. As a TV actress told us, "It's hard to ask for what I like from someone I don't know so well. I like some weird things. So I like sex only with people that I've known for some time."

In sex, as in life, the goal is to turn what too often is a win/lose game into a win/win game. Asking for what you want and giving your partner what he or she wants makes sex a win/win game.

Taking-Turns Sex acknowledges the essential narcissism of sex. Albert Ellis puts it this way: "You probably wouldn't reach climax at all if you didn't focus almost exclusively on yourself for at least a few moments." Letters to our survey indicated the same. One woman said,

"I want all the attention of men when I am having an orgasm. If he's coming too, I can't have his full concentration on me."

In fact, even the hallowed technique of "69" has come under criticism. A twenty-six-year-old Minnesota woman sums it up this way: "This may sound silly, but I find it hard to concentrate on both acts at the same time."

The best feeling about Taking-Turns Sex was expressed by the woman who said, "I want his total support during my orgasm, so I can give him the same support during his orgasm."

Instead of Simultaneous Orgasm, we need Simultaneous Affection.

Who Does What to Whom, How and Why: Historically, men and women have believed that sex is something that the man does to the woman. Today, sexual activity is more democratic and roles and responsibilities are shared. Even the man who still takes responsibility for the female orgasm says, "No matter how good a job I do, there's no way I can give somebody an orgasm who isn't into taking it from me."

Many men feel liberated from the pressure of being orgasm producers. A man from Whittier, California, says, "I'm pleased when 'we' have an orgasm in her, but if she doesn't, I feel that's in large part her decision." That freedom for men could, however, turn into a rudeness or coldness—"Let her take care of herself. I'll take care of me."

Taking-Turns Sex can be alienating, especially if it is seen in terms of the man who says, "I'll do her if she does me." A sociologist calls it the "exchange theory of sociology." As soon as sex becomes mechanical, then taking turns—or any set form—can be mechanical, without feeling, with the clock reinstated in a position of power over the sex experience.

The fact is that orgasm is a cooperative venture which requires the participation of both partners. The Whittier man understands that because he says, "I want to be sure, of course, that I haven't done anything to turn her off, or failed to do something that would turn her on, but I don't assume guilt automaticlly, as I used to. It's her responsibility to tell me what she wants—and how."

Sex is environment, and orgasm comes more from feeling than from technique. (Although good technique is important.) As an Oregon woman says, "I never achieve orgasm through a certain kind of technique or stimulation, but always when I'm relaxed, open and emotionally safe and excited."

A woman from Berkeley waxes articulate about the process of cooperative participation in sexual excitement: "My ideal lover has a true, not a fake, interest in helping me achieve sexual satisfaction. He listens to what I need and *remembers* it. This is predominantly mental and not physical. Men need to learn that it is not the specific physical technique that is a turn-on but the way a man feels about a woman that really turns us on. When the caring is there, the physical part takes care of itself."

Women are discovering that they can relax and orgasm—or hold back—based not on what the man does but on what vibrations he is communicating. And men are becoming more subtle in their role during female orgasm, as the thirty-one-year-old man from Rochester who said, "I don't feel really responsible to *make* her come, any more than she is responsible to make me come, but I feel I can do a lot to make conditions right for her to achieve her own orgasm."

Does this mean that mutual lovemaking (or sexual equality) excludes the dramatic "taking" aspect of sex, most often the male-takes-woman play? No. The exchange of roles means that both men and women can play at being traditional man and traditional woman.

Paul was confused about the meaning of female sexuality to men so he enrolled in a class on women's sexuality taught by a woman. "My teacher is liberated. But she described how much she enjoyed love-time with a man that 'took' her once without regard to her pleasure, squeezing her with his arms and legs, starting intercourse with her lying on top gripping her legs tightly together between his. What I'm learning is that even the liberated woman is still traditional enough not only to want her man to be tender, swet, gentle and thoughtful but— underneath these characteristics—virile, forceful, strong and suppor- tive at the same time."

And then another time, the roles can be reveresed, and the man can play passive receptor as the woman "takes" the man, with the man serving as a total "love slave." There is part of each of us that enjoys both overpowering and being overpowered.

The Sexual Radicals Have Become Sexual Conservatives

The Sexual Revolution of the late sixties made it "in" to go to bed quickly. Sex became the fast way to "meet" someone. And men used to ask each other, "Is she fast? Or slow?" Sex became impersonal. People discovered that the one-night or one-week stand could be explosively memorable. Anonymous sex could be gripping. Since the fantasies of most people—female and male—feature sex with strangers, it became a time when people could live their fantasies.

Women responded at first by balking at being thought of as sex objects. Then some women began seeking impersonal sex like men. In *Moment by Moment,* John Travolta refuses Lily Tomlin's offer of nonemotional sex. "I've had enough casual sex," says John. "I've never had casual sex," says Lily. "I was kinda looking forward to it."

Despite the myth of the New Sexual Woman, however, women have not become as casual as men with sexual flings. Sex still means more to most women than it does to most men; sex still cannot be so easily separated from emotion as it is with a man. Many roaming men heard that we were writing a book on sex and intimacy, and said, "Is there any difference?" To these men, sex itself *is* intimacy. And, ironically, many of these men are often the most nonintimate lovers in bed.

A reaction has set in against the nonintimacy of impersonal sex. Many of the early advocates of sexual freedom in the sixties have become the sexual conservatives of the eighties. People reported to us that they have passed the initial excitement of discovering sex. The search for the pure physical pleasure of the sixties and seventies has turned into the present search for emotional contact and meaningful relationship.

A woman from Berkeley writes:

> I feel people today jump into the sack far too soon, and I am convinced that I enjoyed sex so much more during the early 1960s and even heavy petting in the 1950s because of the taboos. I am responding to the "sexual revolution" by getting more conservative in my recent years. I never have sex the first night I meet a man anymore. I never have one-night stands anymore.
>
> If a relationship is developing, I try to postpone having sex for as long as possible. You'd be surprised how enjoyable this makes the eventual sex for me and my partner. I adore it when a man tells me he is sexually interested but wants to postpone it so we can get to know each other better.

It takes time to be intimate. With a stranger in bed, we never know how much to reveal. We hold onto our defenses and our games, and go for the results—orgasm and performance. First-night sex often leads to more conquest than intimacy. A woman from San Diego writes, "I feel personally that a lot of sexual pain would be avoided if each partner began by telling the other what we didn't like about ourselves. Then we wouldn't have to hide from each other," she said.

And what happens when we don't go to bed the first time? Barry McCarthy, psychologist at American University, suggests to men worried about their sexual skill that make an initial contract with the woman at the first suggestion of intercourse. The contract stipulates that they agree in advance "not to fuck" the first time they share bed together, but to explore each other's bodies. What's important is that it's an agreement, verbal, and completed in advance.

Actually, this sexual attitude gives a man an opportunity to please a woman—but in a different way. "I spent a lovely evening with a man recently," says one woman from Virginia. "At his suggestion we spent the night together nude without sex. I was extremely impressed with this. And happy."

Who Makes the First Sexual Move?

"Women are not meeting their responsibility in the equality game," said one psychologist during one of our group discussions on male-female courtship roles. "How many women have called you out for dinner recently?" he asked, rhetorically. "Most women are still playing their hard-to-get, call-me, passive games. And it's always the men who put their ass on the line."

A male social worker from Georgia agreed. "Many sixteen-year-old boys in Atlanta get rejected more times in one week than a woman does in her life," he says.

Some women in the group pointed out that a telephone invitation for dinner to a man might be interpreted as an invitation to bed. So women have to be hesitant. And women don't like being rejected either; so the passive role gives comfort.

In most sex today, the man still makes the advances. The dynamic is still the woman's surrender to the man's desire. Most women remain passive. A thirty-year-old woman from Pasadena, California, said, "I only once gave an overt invitation to a man. We were very stoned. He was so shy that it made sense. And it worked. But the rest of the time I let the man go out on a limb a little to indicate interest. I'm not secure enough."

A Macho Man believing in biological determinism responded to that idea by saying, "Of course, because during the moment of truth, the man has to produce while the woman doesn't, so naturally women let a man make the first move."

In every relationship I've been in, it's been a source of tension: who initiates sex? If she initiates it, I may, as a man, feel put up against the wall.

A woman spoke up. "I find that men get scared when women come on aggressive," she said. "It's like we're making a demand for a sexual performance."

A shy man agreed. "I feel threatened when a woman comes on to me," he said. He is a twenty-year-old Princeton University student. "I actually become quite frightened. And then the woman sees me so frightened that she gets frightened herself. She runs away. I'd love to find a woman who would stay with me during my fear."

Many men would prefer some more passivity for themselves. "We need some nurturing too," said one man. "I'm tired of the burden of always starting everything. I want to be on the receiving end, too. Women must share the risks. Underneath, we're all the same—sensitive and scared to be hurt."

One Way to Initiate Sex: "Let's take a hot bath together, or may I give you a massage?" It's logical, whether or not a man is sexually nervous. Why shouldn't people get to know one another's bodies before attempting performance? Why shouldn't people get used to each other's smell, touch and rhythm before rushing toward intercourse or orgasm? An all-body massage or hot bath together are intimate ways for people to get to know one another in nonpressured physical loving.

A woman from Iowa writes, "If people weren't hurried to have it all so good, all at once, and all the hip way the media so subtly makes us believe it should be, maybe there would be time to let the passions rise to the point where lovemaking can no longer be contained! The old courting days! Bring back romance!"

The Sex Date: For couples who live together, starting sex may be more difficult than it seems. Since there's so much time, it's never "now." Avoidance is easier than confrontation. Spontaneity often fails as a sexual inducer.

One solution that works is to agree in advance when to have sex. One couple sets aside Sunday afternoon every week—no matter what—as their sex time. The "sex date" lessens misunderstanding, crossed signals ("But I thought you didn't want sex." "But no, I thought *you* didn't want sex.") and makes up for the limitations of spontaneity. Then, during the week, spontaneous sex will be less pressured, and therefore more likely.

Sex therapists theorize that the source of all sex deprivations might be touch. We are touch-handicapped from childhood. Start a sexual seduction by offering to give your partner a detailed, vigorous foot massage. Some physiologists say all the nerves of the body are located in the foot. A foot massage is a good way for two people to say hello to each other.

The Female Vibrator and the Male Ego

Since sex is so tied into masculine ego, it was no surprise that Roy, the president of a small corporation in the Midwest, became "physically sick to my stomach" when his wife mentioned her desire for a vibrator. The idea struck at his genitals. He imagined her pulling it out for a nightcap after their furious intercourse. "Just one more orgasm, dear," she'd say. His masculine mind would go crazy. "Wasn't I enough?" He felt sicker to his stomach.

He pictured another night. He wouldn't be in the mood for sex. She was. She went into the bedroom with her vibrator "to relax." His masculine mind tortured him: "If I was really a man, and had sex with her now, she'd throw that damn machine away."

Roy stared at himself in the mirror when his wife insisted on her right to experiment with a vibrator. After all, her girlfriends were doing it. Roy came face to face with his male mid-life crisis. He knew his ego depended on his wife's sexual dependence on him. Roy mused, "If she gets orgasms from me, she's dependent on me. If she gets them from a damn vibrator, I'd be unnecessary. Beaten by a machine!"

Roy was not alone. The numbers of men who walk the streets of America dispirited because they fear they are losing their masculinity to a machine now produced and sold by such responsible manufacturers as Norelco and Clairol are multiplying daily.

Roy made an appointment with a female therapist who sees many women. "You should be happy that your wife is expanding her sexual pleasure," the therapist said. "You should support her. You are not responsible for her sexual pleasure. You are responsible for your own. And for god's sake, a vibrator says nothing about your manhood. Let her be!"

Partially satisfied, Roy sought out a male therapist who sees many males. He sympathized with Roy and agreed that it might be "the most difficult thing" for a man to accept. Yet the therapist gave the same answer: "It says nothing about your masculinity, her femininity or the quality of your sexual relationship."

Roy knew that we were writing a book and giving occasional workshops on intimate sexuality, so he called us up. We met for lunch. I shared with him my first how-do-you-do with a vibrator. I was in bed with a lawyer. Her artist boyfriend was out of town. Just as we started getting relaxed with each other, she reached into the drawer of a night table and, without saying a word, produced a pink plastic vibrator with a long cord which she plugged into the wall. To make matters worse, the vibrator was off-key and made a huge buzzing noise as it worked. I stared at it as if it were the final victory of women's liberation over my manhood. I was conquered by the machine, cut to the quick, demoralized.

"But I adjusted, Roy," I said, "and I grew to like it. It made sex less work for me. The vibrator is a liberator of your masculinity. After all, if the name of the game is producing orgasms, then science can always discover something even more powerful. So the vibrator gives you a chance to relax and stop pushing so hard. And how can one be jealous of a machine, really?"

By the end of lunch, Roy had decided to buy his wife a vibrator as a demonstration of his support. He had decided that he was not chauvinistically responsible for every one of his wife's orgasms, and that her need for him would not weaken if he was not the sole source of her sexual pleasure.

"She'll turn herself on, and I'll turn myself on," Roy said. "And we'll enjoy each other. A vibrator may be able to give my wife an orgasm but it can't give her intimacy," Roy said. "Only I can do that."

Months later we saw Roy again. "Once I accepted the vibrator," he said, "everything became fine. We are more relaxed with each other. You know, I think sex is often an excuse for people to touch, to be physically close—a socially approved form of touching."

Resolving the Male-Female Crisis over Time of Orgasm

One of the biggest complaints by women about male sexual behavior is related to time of orgasm. Men who stop sex prematurely after they orgasm leave women overstimulated and frustrated. Women are only now beginning to express their anger at such behavior. As one woman wrote us, "He was a real case of premature ejaculation. He rolled over and went to sleep immediately after. This pissed me off. I don't mind dealing with his problems, but if you have nothing else, at least give me a finger . . . I woke him up and finally he realized that he had left a job undone."

The New Sexual Man is busy learning to last longer. It's considered the essential of male sexuality—to be able to control, direct and maintain your orgasm. From experience, from interviews with sex therapists in New York and California, and from interviews with men, we have come up with Five Solutions for Premature Ejaculation.

The First Solution: Enjoy the Process of Arousal. Actually, the most fun in sex is not orgasm—it's getting there. The period right before orgasm is considered by many men to be the hottest and most alive times of sex. The orgasm often is an anticlimax—in fact, killing all sex energy for a period of time. The male orgasm signifies for most men the end—or death—of the enjoyable sex act.

The Second Solution: Don't Stop Sex. An orgasm is premature if you play the traditional male role and ignore the female pleasure centers before or after you are satisfied. Do you say thank you and go to sleep? Or put all your unselfish attention on her? "Nothing is wrong with premature ejaculation," writes a nineteen-year-old Warrensberg, Maryland, woman, "as long as the man isn't ashamed of it and continues to pet and touch."

Ursula, one of the women we interviewed, describes this typical sex scene, in a mood of resignation rather than anger: "We affectionately touched for ten minutes. He put his hand on my clitoris and excited me. Then we fucked, regular, face-to-face, for ten minutes. We went down on each other. Finally, we went back to fucking, and he came right away—in less than five minutes. We kissed and hugged some more but he called it a night and fell asleep. I loved the physical closeness of the experience. But I felt very frustrated because he took me to the peak of sex and stopped there, leaving me without an orgasm."

A New Mexico woman put it this way: "A woman wants something real from a man. Not the same basic techniques of kissing lips, fondling breasts, some oral-genital contact, and *voila!* Penetration! Orgasm! It would be great with me if a man said, 'Hey, I can't hold back long, can I come, and then continue from there?'"

What do you do if you want to come? Ask, "Is it okay with you if I come now?" Duane, a male model, knew that he could not control his orgasm. His follow-up statement, "I'm coming now," was more of an announcement, but it at least gave the woman an opportunity to participate in the orgasm.

Ironically, the point seems to be to let the man have his obligatory orgasm-release so that we can get the male orgasm out of the way, and make love together. One woman put it this way, "I was married and faithful to a man for twenty-one years. He always prematurely ejaculated. Every time—he wanted that orgasm in sex. Usually I'd wait about twenty minutes, arouse him again and get myself off—not necessarily at the same time, but number two was my time, at my speed. We both became quite satisfied with this arrangement."

What you do *after* you come can be as important as when you come. Duane's ejaculation meant that his penis wilted. He could no longer stay inside in such a floppy state. "I oozed myself out," he said, "and stuck my finger in. I moved my finger like crazy. I began licking her too, while continuing the movement of my hand. Within a few minutes she was panting, screaming, and finally squeezed her legs together, forcing me to stop."

The Third Solution: Find a Woman With a Positive Attitude. If you blame yourself, you're likely to choose a woman who will be critical. Instead, choose a woman with a positive attitude toward you. One woman expressed a positive attitude toward early ejaculation: "Is it right to put a negative label on something which is sometimes just as satisfying an experience for the man as prolonged sex? Never put a man down. The best thing to do is wait awhile and try to arouse him again. Use a little imagination, sense the mood and state of your man, and it shouldn't be difficult."

The Fourth Solution: Communicate. One Los Angeles lawyer discovered that if he tells the woman in advance that he may come quick, he doesn't. "The pressure is off," he says. A twenty-seven-year-old female French exchange student says, "Once I slept with an older man for whom I felt much love. He came almost as soon as he was inside me and he felt badly about this. I remember holding him. I felt so much warmth and compassion for him. He cried. He had never received this kind of response before. He was warmed by my acceptance. We touched and shared deeply. It was a sexual experience I'll never forget."

The Fifth Solution: Learn Penis Control. Men in a passion these days for self-improvement keep sex therapists booked with more patients than they can see. The analysis of the condition varies from anything from suppressed hostility against women to simple bad habits. The solution has become standard: practice.

Burt, a poet, compares sexual intercourse to surf riding: "Premature ejaculation is when you get on a short little wave, ride it all the way in very quickly, and the wave breaks up." He adds, "The secret of screwing at length for me is to be able to get off a wave before it takes me all the way to the beach. If I'm with a woman who digs me sexually and turns me on with caring, I can go from bigger wave to bigger wave, each time finding myself further from shore and with bigger waves. To get off the wave when it hits, I stop penile-vaginal movement. Then when she's ready to come, you ride the wave all the way in."

Masturbation becomes the time to retrain an uncontrolled ejaculation reflex. Make a commitment to spend a certain amount of time each week practicing getting hard. Just before you reach the point of inevitability—the second before—put your release on hold. Stay there. Practice tolerating the stimulation. Enjoy the feeling of ejaculation suppression.

Control over the ejaculation reflex—so you can decide to orgasm when you want to—is a skill to master, learned by repetition, step-by-step, with positive reinforcement guiding the individual in his process.

Once you have mastered your reflex, then apply the lessons learned to partner sex. Share exactly where you are. Enlist her support in the game of teaching yourself to maintain the energy of sexual excitement.

Don't hoard all your sexual energy in your penis. Sexual energy can flow from your genitals down to your legs to your toes, then up through your body to your heart area, where there is a second energy explosion. Penile and heart energy join in a synergy that sends feeling to the arms, the back of the neck, the face, and all of this flows out of you to your partner. And the entire process happens in your mind. The control of ejaculation can make the eventual orgasm more of an all-body—rather than tip-of-the-penis—experience as energy is synthesized and distributed all over the body.

Ecstasy and Baseball Scores

Let's not leap to the other extreme, though, and make sex a lasting-longer sport. Despite the fact that orgasm through intercourse takes a long time, many women object to greatly sustained fucking as painful—and even slightly inconsiderate. One woman wrote to us, "In a recent incident with a twenty-year-old he insisted that I allow him to continue thrusting, even when I was completely worn out (and it takes a lot to wear me out!). Finally, I simply had to make him stop, and he seemed very put out, as if he eventually would have come if I hadn't stopped him. I think he would have gone on all night with no results. Why do men always have to orgasm?"

Another woman, from Thunder Bay, Ontario, shares a recent experience. "He seemed to want to prove he was Mr. Stud—he'd stay hard for hours and never come . . . I think he really had a problem. He claimed he wanted to satisfy me, but it was a bit much. A girl can get pretty sore after two hours of screwing . . . I tried to talk to him about it, but he didn't think he had a problem."

One man writes, "My wife doesn't like a guy that will screw her for too long, because she gets sore, so she plays with my balls, which she knows gets me to come."

Is there a relationship between length of time of erection and power of orgasm? Reichian fundamentalists, sex promoters and Taoists all agree on the myth that the longer the period of penile excitation, the more powerful the orgasm. From personal experience, I'd have to suggest the opposite. I've pumped for forty minutes to end up with a weak ejaculation, and some of my most powerful comes take off like a rocket. Tony, a writer, agrees. "They say the longer you hold off your orgasm, the more powerful it is. I've found that to be true sometimes. But just as often I'll be hard as rock and then when I come, it's nothing, just a little pop, and fizz, with a very flat feeling. I know that orgasm would have been more powerful had I come immediately upon getting hard."

As men age, it's said that erections take longer, and that orgasms decline in power. In one of our workshops, a man moaned that he's lost his "stuff," that he used to be able to ejaculate over his shoulder. America's dean of sex journalists told us that as he hit his fortieth birthday, "My orgasms are not as pleasurable as they were when I was younger, so naturally I'm getting more and more into foreplay."

Some women are very much impressed with a man who simply *experiences* his erection, riding its energy, choosing not to end sex by *using* his erection—and then ending sex when he's hot, not when he's depleted.

"On the few occasions I have fucked for more than two hours of continuous fucking," says one man, in a casual example of sexual bravado, "the session will eventually be ended by me losing my erection without ever having an ejaculation. That's okay with me, because the long period of fucking was as—or more—rewarding than the missed orgasm."

Leo had been merrily pumping inside Jane for twenty minutes. The consummate fucker. The magic sex-dancer. At one point he came to a crisis: he started coming. He bit his tongue, and fought back the flowing rivers of passion. Like Superman, he won. He held off his orgasm and pumped on. The audience cheered! He bowed. The woman smiled.

Then suddenly Leo the performer realized the absurdity of his journey. His wife had already climaxed with the aid of his tongue. He was doing all this for his sexual image! Ah, enlightenment struck: "Am I going on because I want her to think I could last forever?"

Renewed thrusting brought Leo to another peak. This time he decided to go over the mountain, to pull the cork out of the bottle, to let it loose. Boom. Phzzz! Yikes—no feeling! "Shit, oh shit." All he felt was a little bite of pleasure at the tip of his penis. A spill, not a launching. All that work for nothing.

An ejaculation is really "premature" if you do not enjoy it: that's the ultimate male cheat. Boy, do you get furious. You'd like to rap that little rascal. You're seeping—and absolutely no feeling! Why come if you can't feel anything? I mean, after all, it is not waste material. There is no medical reason to ejaculate. So we ejaculate to get the pleasure, and when there's no pleasure you feel your life-energy ebbing away— and for no kick! Shit!

In addition to encouraging orgasm at the end of *every* sexual interaction, fear of orgasm scarcity often leads to a "premature" takeoff and landing. And continues the growing dissatisfaction of men with sex, and lack of enjoyment in the experience itself. Can you enjoy yourself when you're feeling guilty about coming too soon? Orgasm is a personal, self-involved, selfish act. The apologizing, guilty ejaculator often ends up not experiencing and enjoying the pleasurable sensations of his orgasm.

Men rarely admit these intimate limitations. Traditional American- ism says: "Never testify against yourself." Yet women are the spies: "I know men hide the fact that they came before me, while trying to bring me to orgasm," says one Baltimore woman. "I hate it because part of the beauty of lovemaking is knowing what's happening to the man you're pleasing." However, it's amazing how easy it is to fake and fool each other when we are in the most intimate, naked times of personal revelation. Ego plays such a dominant role in bed that it blinds us to even the most obvious, even physical, realities. I know that a number of times I did, in fact, convince the woman that I did not come when I did. To hide you cannot give in to the sensations of your orgasm; you must maintain control.

Enjoy Your Orgasm, Premature or Not. If you do come, enjoy it completely, and start again. Avoid becoming an A.M.—Apologizing Man. No matter when you come, you have an absolute right to your self-enjoyment. Put your consciousness on the pleasure centers in your body—and leave the explaining for much later.

Lately, I've begun to experience long erections—and erections that are so hard that they lack feeling. I've now had to moderate my erection for the maximum feeling. Each man must choose the level of arousal that is appropriate for him—and not adopt someone else's expectation.

Five Ways Masturbation with Another Person Adds to Equality and Ecstasy in Sex

The emphasis in sex today is creating new conditions. The rules and requirements are gone. And unheard-of practices are becoming respectable.

You Can Touch Yourself During Sex with Another Person. The permission to put one's own hand on one's own genitals during sex with another widens sexual possibility. That goes along with the change in the role of the man during sex. The man no longer is Mr. Expert in bed. The woman can rub her own genitals while enjoying sex with the man.

The acceptance of the many uses of masturbation has changed the sex act for the man and woman. In at least five ways masturbation has improved and deepened interpersonal sex.

1) *Learning How the Other Gets Turned On:* The man can encourage the woman to masturbate in front of him so he can learn exactly how she likes to be touched.

2) *An Easy Way to Launch Touching:* Some women do not like to put their hand on your penis right away; it might be interpreted as a demand. The man can put his hand on his penis and manipulate himself. Or he can take her hand and put it over his, so that he teaches her exactly how hard, how fast, and with what rhythm he likes to be touched.

3) *Turning Yourself On:* It was not without some small embarrassment that Bart, thirty, began losing his erection with Helen, so he took his own hand and began to masturbate himself while they were kissing and holding each other. Bart felt guilty. He was too shy to even ask Helen if it was okay with her. "If anyone had told me five years ago that it would be okay for me to touch my own genitals during sex with a woman, I would have thought: never. And here I just did it. I just did it."

Helen did like it. As Bart recounts, "As a matter of fact, without saying anything herself, she then put her own hand on her pussy, and we got ourselves hot together."

Such sexual heresy! A woman from Ohio writes, "I feel free enough in sex now to touch and rub myself until my ache for orgasm is soothed and wrap my legs around him so that I can press my genitals against him and feel the comfort of that contact . . . I don't want to ask him to do anything but the support for me to touch myself in couple sex is important."

4) *Overcoming Inhibitions:* What if the man is just too overcome with anxiety to relax? Men can use masturbation to turn themselves on and keep themselves hot. One woman gave a vivid description of an experience in which the man couldn't orgasm. "I know he was more used to the hand of the master, even though that's the last taboo in sex. When we became comfortable with one another, I said, 'Hey, let me just hold and snuggle with you, and you just take care of business.' I feel I'm participating, even though it's his hand."

5) *Resolving the Vaginal-Clitoral Dilemma:* For men stuck on the question of whether intercourse causes female orgasm, the acceptance of self-stimulation provides a way out. The man can be inside and the woman can be loving her own clitoris simultaneously. Or the man can be inside and using his loving finger at the same time.

At our workshop a woman described her integration of masturbation into exciting sex: "You can have great simultaneous orgasm this way. When I developed the self-confidence to touch myself, it usually blows the man's socks off. But once the man becomes used to it, wow, what a relief, you can have all kinds of sexual positions, and all kinds of vaginal feelings, and I can still take care of whatever clitoral activity I want."

A man gives his version of the same experience: "I've noticed a couple of women who couldn't have an orgasm with me. So I said, 'Could you flick yourself?' 'Yeah.' So while we're having intercourse I said, 'Okay, go do it with yourself,' and she had a great orgasm."

You Don't Need an Orgasm to Have Fun in Bed

My definition of sex had always been the Quick Thrill. Sex was orgasm. And the orgasm was timed for the most explosive knockout.

My interest in sex awakened, paradoxically, when I stopped making orgasm the goal, and when I began to experience fully each sensation of sex. For practice I recently enjoyed two hours of sex without coming. I made it a game: sex without orgasm. It was the most fun I had in sex! Knowing that I wouldn't orgasm took the edge away, and I enjoyed sustaining the energy without release.

America's fastest growing in-bed activity is sex without orgasm. As one woman advises men, "Let sex be an event in your life and not just an orgasm." A woman from Newport Beach, California, writes, "The importance placed on having a good orgasm causes people to think if they don't have one, they didn't have a good time. That to me is rubbish."

Intimacy is the passion of the eighties. Orgasm is only as important as its contribution to intimacy. One man writes, "I can remember the way a woman's eyes looked when I held her longer than how many times I went off or in how many different ways. Intimacy is melting into the other person." Unfortunately, men, and now women, are so into orgasm these days that they sacrifice what they really want—intimacy—for what they think they want—orgasm.

Peter was such a person. A midwestern farmer, he never had any trouble with erections—in fact, his problem was keeping it down, especially in high school and college, fantasizing screwing the teachers. Yet, he never enjoyed sex, not till he was forty-one.

"An orgasm is only a split second of pleasure," he said. "Big deal. And I feel selfish when I come and the woman doesn't. Awful. So better avoid sex."

For years Peter avoided sex, while making love to his pillow at least once a day. "But that wasn't sex. That was masturbation. Masturbation is not sex." His average tension-release masturbation was, at most, two minutes.

Then, at the age of thirty-eight, Peter was pumping inside a woman when she said, "Look, I don't get off through intercourse, so don't expect me to come."

Peter felt his erection suddenly wilt. He pulled out. "This had never happened to me before. It was the first time I ever lost an erection. I got scared. In fact, I panicked."

The woman calmed Peter down. "It's okay if you don't get hard," she said, beginning to massage and kiss his penis. He decided to lie back and enjoy it. For forty-five minutes she rubbed and kissed his genital area, his ass, legs, and lower stomach. He never got the hint of an erection, yet, "I never experienced such sexual pleasure in my life. It was soft, warm, cuddly, without pressure, and with total sensitivity. She kissed me all over, soft and tender kisses. It felt good—and opened up my head. That's it for quick orgasms after perpetual erections. I never enjoyed sex before that experience."

Orgasm may actually be a way to avoid intimacy. Orgasm ends the anxiety of free-floating closeness. Orgasm peaks sex; what comes up must go down, whether a penis or a clitoris. The anxiety of simply being physically with another person is alleviated by the sexual explosion.

The goal of orgasm gives purpose to sex. Otherwise, it might be frightening to be in such deep contact with another person—for no reason, with no script, and with no requirements. Orgasm often ends the contact.

Intimacy, in fact, means that two people are sharing one another at a particular time. However, if people are absorbed by thoughts of disappointment or "How big was my orgasm?" or "How great was I in bed," how can they be there for their partner? Expectations in sex, especially around orgasm, endanger intimacy.

The real problem with orgasm is the pressure. Orgasm is over-emphasized. It starts as an expectation, perhaps innocent enough. That expectation becomes pressure. The pressure leads to the Orgasm Olympics which establishes the tyranny of orgasm over sex.

We must put the orgasm in perspective. We expect too much of it.

Roger, twenty-eight, was having a good time with Patty. "I had been eating her out for a long while. Finally I felt she had enough, and we just snuggled together on the floor. I felt very happy. I had an erection all this time, but I really had no desire to come. I just wanted to be with her and enjoy the moment."

Yet Roger felt a nervousness in Patty. "She decided to reciprocate my attentions and began giving me head, but when she realized I wasn't coming—although I was enjoying it—she tried harder by deep throating until she gagged. After several gags, I stopped her and told her not to worry. I just wasn't in the mood to come although I was hard. I just wanted to be with her. Within three minutes she began sobbing. I told her not to be upset, that there's nothing wrong with her or me, but it's just the way I feel at the moment."

Sometimes the female pressure for male orgasm can be as great as the pressure the man puts on himself. The expectation that male orgasm must complete sex was deep in Patty's psyche. "I hugged her closer," Roger said, "stroked her hair and kissed her all over gently, but she insisted on leaving, and that I was not to look at her when she left. I felt like shit. I had let her down because I hadn't come."

Patty took Roger's "failure" to have an orgasm as a condemnation of her attractiveness, and a statement about his unwillingness to relax with her. What is this experience of orgasm that its absence can turn an otherwise exciting sexual experience into a so-called "failure"?

Men, especially, have a hard time fully accepting the end of sex without orgasm. Sex educator Sol Gordon says we've got to convince men that "Nobody ever died from an unused erection."

I still go to bed today thinking on some level that sex is not complete if I don't have an orgasm or if my partner doesn't. I have to recondition myself out of that thought every single time.

One man says, "During my last sexual encounter, I had a beautiful night of making love to a special friend of mine. Neither of us had an orgasm, although she at one point said that she had a small one. We were both satisfied and happy just being close to one another for the night, holding each other, touching, kissing, talking. There was no pressure from either of us to move to orgasm."

Then, he adds, "I don't think I would feel the same with a woman I was going to bed with for the first time."

Michael, a literary agent, wonders aloud, "How many exciting sexual experiences have I missed in my life because of my belief in the formula: erection to orgasm equals manhood?"

Sex historically has been an ends-over-means proposition. The means is foreplay to the end: intercourse-orgasm. Now that both men and women expect orgasm—or expect that the other expects orgasm—sex has temporarily become even more mechanical and technical. One male friend satirizes himself, "Go back to the breasts? I played with them five minutes ago. I'm on my way to intercourse—watch out!" A thirty-one-year-old engineer reflected the old sexual consciousness when he wrote us, "Foreplay is pleasurable, but it's still foreplay, not intercourse. Same goes for postplay."

Fear of Orgasm: The fear of the power of the orgasm keeps many people away from sex because they make the absolute identification of sex with orgasm. (And if they don't, their partner will.) And that link of sex itself with potentially threatening orgasm keeps many people in a constant state of touch deprivation. And unfortunately relationship scarcity.

I heard the myth that my father, who died at forty-nine of a heart attack, suffered one of his heart attacks while involved in fucking. That doesn't make me feel good for my ticker when I'm rolling in the sack. In fact, sometimes an orgasm feels like a simulated heart attack.

A woman reveals her discomfort at orgasm pressure:

I believe too much pressure is put on people to have an orgasm. In a way it's making sex become mechanical. Everyone is so intent on where to touch and how hard or lightly to touch, that the spontaneity is going out of making love. I find exploring and trying different things much more satisfying, even if it doesn't lead to orgasm. If my partner and I are enjoying each other mentally and emotionally as people, it makes the sex act a bond between us. If there is no mental-emotional stimulation, I may as well be in bed with a mannequin because nothing he does will satisfy me.

Orgasm Comparison: During sex, ask yourself, "Am I trying to keep up with the Joneses *(Playboy* or *Penthouse)* in terms of orgasms?" Or, "Do we ever orgasm to please or prove something to our partner?"

Following the example of women, I discovered that I have the most explosive and uninhibited orgasms during masturbation. For years I enjoyed masturbation more than fucking. In masturbation I can time my ejaculation and when I feel that it is time I can scream, grab the pillow tightly and hold on—and if I remember especially not to hold my breath at the optimal time—I have five seconds of heaven, perfect happiness!

Tony came to us, concerned. He worried why his orgasms during intercourse do not leave him screaming. "Many of my female partners tell me that their other lovers make more noise than I do when I come," he said. He began to worry that he was having "inferior orgasms . . . because I don't feel like screaming. I like to enjoy them silently. Is there something wrong with me or my orgasms?"

How I Faked—The Male Faked Orgasm. It is not surprising that in this era of pressure for orgasm (for The Result), rising expectations toward orgasm and the increasing popularity of the female organ, men would begin to act like traditional women. Historically women have faked orgasm. More and more women are discovering the phenomena of the male faked orgasm, theatrically produced to prove virility.

I discovered that sometimes women don't know if the man has ejaculated. I was astonished when after a wild ejaculation, my partner asked me, "Did you come?" I thought that was my question—my question to ask her about her mysterious orgasm. But no. She honestly didn't know. So men and women aren't so different after all. Since sometimes women can't feel the spurt of sperm against the vaginal wall, they've got to deduce from breathing, shaking, sound-making—the exact same signals men use to measure female orgasm.

I was lying on top of a woman we'll call Louise, feigning that I was having an orgasm. After all, she wanted it so much. She wanted to know that I was coming. So I moved and gasped, and then turned over on my side, resting.

She bought the act. Sex was over—for a good reason. Orgasm.

Another man shared his faked orgasm with the other people at our workshop. "I've never heard a man admit this," he said, "and I know it happens. Once in a while I fake an orgasm. If I'm enjoying being with the woman and I sense the woman feels it's important, no hassle, I'll just fake it."

"How?" somebody wondered.

"Sigh, yell, anything I feel like doing. Then I relax."

"And what about the lack of semen?"

"Some women will discover that."

Erotic Cuddling

Orgasms are great. Lasting only a matter of seconds, orgasm is the one period of a time in a man's life when he stops being a goal-oriented animal and completely loses himself in the moment.

Orgasm is an expression of deep intimacy. For that brief flash of time, we are defenseless, revealing our body's animality. Yet the expectation of orgasm can make sex mechanical and pressured. In competitive sex, orgasm is the reward—and the judge.

But orgasm is not what sex is all about. Sex is about relationship and communication with another human being.

The comparative and competitive attitude toward orgasm destroys the experience of sex. It brings the questioning mind into bed, where it does not belong: Is this activity worth my time?

The Quantitative Mind in Bed: Check the results measured in orgasms. Bigger and better. More. Different women. Conquests, new heights. It's a male hang-up, putting the goal first and then rushing to the goal.

Making orgasm the end-all climax of sex makes sex a goal-oriented activity, rather than a second-by-second experience.

Nothing kills Intimate Sex more than falling into the pit of comparative thinking when naked. The mental man must leave his mind at the door when he takes off his clothes. While orgasm is a body experience, comparison is a mental one. There will always be a Bigger and Better Orgasm. Each orgasm is itself, defying comparison. Comparisons leave us in a permanent state of striving for more. According to the Zen of Orgasms, there is no orgasm better than the one you are having *now*.

I had to remind myself to slow down when in bed. Savor the

moment, the touch, taste, smell. Take small bits. Chew. Swallow. The end will come soon enough.

Sex is not an achievement; it is not a job well done; or the biggest ever, or the best. Sex can be a deep expression of intimacy between two people, in which the fewer secrets kept the better—the greater freedom for the animal and child within and for the passions.

Sex becomes nonintimate when people play secret roles in bed with each other. In the intimacy-starved times of the 1980s, people crave intimacy, and look for it in sexual intercourse. Yet they remain strangers to each other. People can't admit the truth—that sex was just a good reason for touching. Some people think they want sexual intercourse when what they *really* want is to be held.

Sex Is Really an Excuse for Touching. Sex today requires a completely new language and set of categories. Under the definition of the New Sexuality, the statement "I can last for hours," would mean that the partners could last for hours kissing, cuddling, rubbing hugging, feeling each other all over. Sensuality and sexuality are integrated into one organic experience.

The next Sexual Revolution will be one of physical touch and erotic cuddling without orgasm requirements. Physical pleasure and intimate conversation will geometrically increase as we deemphasize the genital-orgasm pressure on sex.

Questionnaire for Men on Sexuality

We published questionnaires in magazines and distributed them at college lectures and human potential workshops. Although the questionnaire went through a number of changes, the following is typical of the questions we were asking to induce men and women to talk honestly about what happens between them on an intimate level.

You do not have to include your name. Anonymity and confidentiality will be strongly observed. Please be as honest and as *specific* as possible. One of the purposes of our book is to open up communication channels between men on sexual doubts, difficulties or problems. Your participation in this questionnaire will be very valuable in reaching this goal. (Women—please see that a male friend of your fills out this questionnaire.) You may answer *any one or all* of these questions, as you wish.

1. Is there any aspect or occurrence in sex which makes you uncomfortable or unsatisfied? Have you ever experienced what you

consider to be a "failure" in bed? Do you find or have you ever found that although you were functioning normally, you were not receiving any pleasurable feelings from sex? If so, please describe specifically what happened or happens. How did you feel? How did it affect you afterward, in sex and in other aspects of your life? How did you communicate with your partner about it?

2.   In what sense does sex result in intimacy for you? Describe a non-intimate sexual experience. What happened and how did you feel? Describe an intimate sexual experience.

3.   How does your sexual behavior relate to your sense of manhood or self-esteem? What happens if you do not have an erection at some moment or times when you expect one? How do you feel? What do you say? Are your erections automatic or do you need to motivate them? If the latter, how do you motivate erections? Can you be sexually aroused or turned on without an erection? Explain specifically.

4.   Have you ever had any sexual inhibitions, hang-ups, doubts, problems which you have overcome? How, specifically, did you overcome them? If you still have a sexual fear, please describe it specifically, and how it relates to your sexual and other self-image.

5.   Do you feel that you, your partner, or both of you must have an orgasm for you to feel that a sexual experience has been a good one? In what way do you express your thoughts about the importance of orgasm in action? Would you consider a sexual experience complete without (a) orgasm (b) intercourse (c) erection? Explain specifically.

6.   Do you ever find yourself "performing" sexually. If so, how do you "perform" sexually?

7.   What is happening inside your mind during sexual activity?

8.   What would you be most afraid of other men or women to know about your in-bed sexual behavior? Specifically, what would you not want a woman to say about you sexually?

9.   How has the new women's demanding consciousness in bed specifically affected your sexual behavior, attitudes? New problems? New benefits?

10.   Do you talk about sex with other men? Do you talk about sexual successes? Sexual failures? Do you compare yourself with other men? If so, how?

Bibliography

We researched widely in the area of male–female relationships and found the following books and articles to be the most helpful to our study and conclusions.

Annon, Jack S. "The Behavioral Treatment of Sexual Problems." *Brief Therapy*, vol. 1. Honolulu: Kapiolani Health Services, 1974.

Apfelbaum, Bernard. "Does Turning on Mean Always Saying Yes?" Mimeographed. San Francisco: CSPA Convention, January 8, 1978.

———"On the Etiology of Sexual Dysfunction." *Journal of Sex and Marital Therapy*, vol. 3, no. 1 (Spring 1977).

———"The Enemy in the Bedroom, or Say I Love You." Mimeographed. March 1979.

Atkins, John. *Sex in Literature*. London: Calder and Boyars, 1970.

Bach, George R., and Peter Wyden. *The Intimate Enemy*. New York: Avon Books, 1968.

Barbach, Lonnie Garfield. *For Yourself: The Fulfillment of Female Sexuality*. Garden City, NY: Anchor Books, 1976.

Bean, Orson. *Me and the Orgone*. Greenwich, CT: Fawcett Publications, 1972.

Bengis, Ingrid. *Combat in The Erogenous Zone*. New York: Bantam Books, 1973.

Berne, Eric. *Games People Play*. New York: Grove Press, 1964.

———*What Do You Say After You Say Hello?* New York: Bantam Books, 1976.

Bieler, Henry G., and Sarah Nichols. *Dr. Bieler's Natural Way to Sexual Health*. Los Angeles: Charles Publishing, 1972.

Boston Women's Health Book Collective. *Our Bodies, Ourselves*. 2nd Ed. New York: Simon and Schuster, 1976.

Brecher, Edward M. *The Sex Researchers*. Boston: Little, Brown and Co., 1969.

Brenton, Myron. *The American Male*. Greenwich, CT: Fawcett Publications, 1970.

Chesler, Phyllis. *About Men*. New York: Simon and Schuster, 1978.

Diagram Group. *Man's Body: An Owner's Manual*. New York: Bantam Books, 1977.

Ellis, Albert. *The Art and Science of Love*. New York: Bantam Books, 1969.

———*The Sensuous Person*. Secaucus, NJ: Lyle Stuart, 1973.

———*Sex and the Liberated Man*. Secaucus, NJ: Lyle Stuart, 1976.

———*Sex Without Guilt*. North Hollywood, CA: Wilshire Book Company, 1973.

Ellis, Albert, and Robert A. Harper. *A Guide to Rational Living*. North Hollywood, CA: Wilshire Book Company, 1966.

Farrell, Warren. *The Liberated Man*. New York: Bantam Books, 1972.

Fast, Julius. *The Body Language of Sex, Power, and Aggression*. New York: M. Evans and Co., 1977.

———*The Incompatibility of Men and Women and How to Overcome It*. New York: Avon Books, 1972.

Fasteau, Marc Feigen. *The Male Machine*. New York: McGraw-Hill, 1974.

Fellman, Sheldon L., and Paul Neimark. *The Virile Man*. New York: Stein and Day, 1976.

Felton, David. "(Portrait of the Godhead as a Young Dog) Richard Pryor's." *Rolling Stone*, May 3, 1979.

Fensterheim, Herbert, and Jean Baer. *Don't Say Yes When You Want to Say No*. New York: Dell, 1977.

Fisher, Seymour. *The Female Orgasm*. New York: Basic Books, 1973.

Frankfort, Ellen. *Vaginal Politics*. New York: Times Books, 1972.

Friedan, Betty. *The Feminine Mystique*. New York: Dell, 1963.

Gagnon, John H. and William Simon. *Sexual Conduct*. Chicago: Aldine, 1973.

Gillies, Jerry. *My Needs, Your Needs, Our Needs*. Garden City, NY: Doubleday & Co., 1974.

Ginsberg, et al. "The New Impotence." *Archives of General Psychiatry*, vol. 26, no. 3 (March 1972).

Gittelson, Natelie. *Dominus: A Woman Looks at Men's Lives*. New York: Farrar, Straus and Giroux, 1978.

Goffman, Erving. *The Presentation of Self in Everyday Life*. New York: Doubleday & Co., 1959.

Goldberg, Herb. *The Hazards of Being Male*. New York: Nash, 1974.

———*The New Male*. New York: William Morrow and Co., 1979.

Gordon, Sol, and Roger W. Libby. *Sexuality Today—and Tomorrow*. Belmont, CA: Duxbury Press, 1976.

Greer, Germaine. *The Female Eunuch*. New York: McGraw-Hill, 1971.

Hacker, Helen. "New Burdens of Masculinity." *Journal of Marriage and the Family*, August 1957.

Hite, Shere. *The Hite Report*. New York: Dell, 1974.

Hoffman, Bob. *No One Is to Blame*. Palo Alto, CA: Science and Behavior Books, 1979.

Holt, Patricia, ed. *The New Sexual Etiquette for Women*. San Francisco: San Francisco Book Company, 1977.

Hunt, Morton. *Sexual Behavior in the 70's*. New York: Dell, 1974.

Jong, Erica. *Fear of Flying*. New York: Holt, Rinehart & Winston, 1973.

Julty, Sam. *Male Sexual Performance*. New York: Grosset & Dunlap, 1975.

Kaplan, Helen Singer. *The New Sex Therapy*. New York: Brunner/Mazel, 1974.

Kassorla, Irene. *Putting It All Together*. New York: Warner Books, 1976.

Keen, Sam. "Some Ludicrous Theses About Sexuality." Paper read at Conference on Religion and Sexuality, July 9, 1974, at Syracuse U. Mimeographed.

Keill, Norman. *Varieties of Sexual Experience*. New York: International Universities Press, 1976.

Keleman, Stanley. *Sexuality, Self & Survival*. San Francisco: Lodestar Press, 1971.

Kerr, Carmen. *Sex for Women*. New York: Grove Press, 1977.

Kinsey, Alfred C., Wardell B. Pomeroy and Clyde E. Martin. *Sexual Behavior in the Human Male*. Philadelphia: W. B. Saunders, 1948.

Kinsey, Alfred C., Wardell B. Pomeroy, Clyde E. Martin and Paul Gebhard. *Sexual Behavior in the Human Female*. Philadelphia: W. B. Saunders, 1948.

Komarovsky, Mirra. *Dilemmas of Masculinity*. New York: W. W. Norton & Co., 1976.

Kriegel, Leonard, ed. *The Myth of American Manhood*. New York: Dell, 1978.

Kupferberg, Tuli. *The Book of the Body*. New York: Birth Press, 1966.

Laing, R. D. *Do You Love Me?* New York: Pantheon Books, 1976.

———*Knots*. New York: Pantheon Books, 1970.

Lakein, Alan. *How to Get Control of Your Time & Your Life*. New York: Signet, 1974.

Lasch, Christopher. *The Culture of Narcissism*. New York: W. W. Norton & Co., 1978.

Lazarus, Arnold. "Overcoming Sexual Inadequacy." In *Handbook of Sex Therapy*, LoPiccolo & LoPiccolo, eds. New York: Plenum Press, 1978.

Leonard, George. *Man & Woman Thing & Other Provocations*. New York: Dell, 1971.

———*The Ultimate Athlete*. New York: Viking Press, 1975.

Lowen, Alexander. *Depression and the Body*. New York: Coward, McCann & Geoghegan, 1972.

McCarthy, Barry. *What You Still Don't Know About Male Sexuality*. New York: Thomas Y. Crowell Co., 1977.

———*Pleasure*. New York: Lancer Books, 1970.

Maltz, Maxwell. *Psycho-Cybernetics*. New York: Pocket Books, 1969.

Marks, Carole, "Heterosexual Coitus as a Cultural Symbol." Paper read at A.A.S.E.C.T., April 1, 1978, Washington, D.C.

Maslow, Abraham. "Dominance, Personality, and Social Behavior in Women." *Journal of Social Psychology*, vol. 11 (1939): pp. 3–39.

Masters, William H., and Virginia E. Johnson. *Homosexuality in Perspective*. Boston: Little, Brown and Co., 1979.

————Human Sexual Inadequacy. Boston: Little, Brown and Co., 1970.

————Human Sexual Response. Boston: Little, Brown and Co., 1966.

Masters, William H., and Virginia E. Johnson, in association with Robert J. Levin. The Pleasure Bond. New York: Bantam Books, 1976.

May, Rollo. Love & Will. New York: W. W. Norton & Co., 1969.

Mayer, Nancy. The Male Mid-Life Crisis. New York: Signet, 1978.

Medical Aspects of Human Sexuality. New York: Hospital Publications, Inc., June 1979.

Money, John, and Patricia Tucker. Sexual Signatures. Boston: Little, Brown and Co., 1972.

Neville, Richard. "Living With a Small Penis." Penthouse Magazine, April 1977.

Nichols, Jack. Men's Liberation. New York: Penguin, 1976.

Offit, Avodah K. The Sexual Self. New York: J. B. Lippincott Co., 1977.

O'Neill, Nena. The Marriage Premise. New York: Bantam Books, 1978.

Peele, Stanton, with Archie Brodsky. Love and Addiction. New York: Taplinger Publishing Co., 1975.

Pietropinto, Anthony, and Jacqueline Simenauer. Beyond the Male Myth. New York: Times Books, 1977.

Pion, Ron, with Jerry Hopkins. The Last Sex Manual. New York: Wyden Books, 1977.

Playboy, Editors of. New Sexual Life Styles of the 70's. Chicago: Playboy Press, 1975.

Pleck, Joseph H., and Jack Sawyer, eds. Men and Masculinity. Englewood Cliffs, NJ: Spectrum Books, 1974.

Rathus, Spencer A., and Jeffrey Nevid. BT Behavior Therapy. Garden City, NY: Doubleday & Co., 1977.

Reuben, David. How to Get More Out of Sex. New York: Bantam Books, 1977.

Rosenberg, Jack Lee. Total Orgasm. New York: Random House, 1973.

Rossman, Michael. "Masturbation and Consciousness-Raising Groups as Adjunctive Therapy in the Treatment of Male Sexual Dysfunction." Cowell Hospital, University of California, Berkeley, CA. Mimeograph.

Rubin, Theodore Isaac, with David C. Berliner. Understanding Your Man . New York: Ballantine Books, 1977.

Russell, Bertrand. The Conquest of Happiness. New York: Bantam Books, 1968.

————Marriage and Morals. New York: Liveright, 1970.

"Secrets of the New Male Sexuality." Ms. Magazine, April 1978.

Shain, Merle. Some Men Are More Perfect Than Others. New York: Bantam Books, 1978.

Shanor, Karen. The Sexual Sensitivity of the American Male. New York:

Ballantine Books, 1978.

Sherfey, Mary Jane. *The Nature and Evolution of Female Sexuality*. New York: Random House, 1973.

Slater, Philip E. "Sexual Adequacy in America." *Intellectual Digest*, November 1973.

Snodgrass, Jon, ed. *A Book of Readings for Men Against Sexism*. New York: Times Change Press, 1977.

Steinmann, Anne, and David S. Fox. *The Male Dilemma*. New York: Aronson, 1974.

Strage, Mark. *The Durable Fig Leaf*. New York: William Morrow and Co., 1980.

Tripp, C. A. *The Homosexual Matrix*. New York: Signet, 1976.

Vanggaard, Thorkil. *Phallos*. New York: International Universities Press, 1972.

Warhol, Andy. *The Philosophy of Andy Warhol*. New York: Harcourt Brace Jovanovich, 1975.

Wetzsteon, Ross. "What Men Fear Most About Sex." *Redbook* Magazine, May 1978.

Zilbergeld, Bernie. *Male Sexuality*. Boston: Little, Brown and Co., 1978.

About the Authors

Mimi Leonard is an account executive with one of the largest and most prestigious commodity brokerage houses in the world. She graduated from Columbia University summa cum laude and Phi Beta Kappa with a B.A. in sociology. Ms. Leonard became a senior market research analyst for B.B.D.O. advertising agency and later worked for ABC News. She has wide experience in the field of human potential. Ms. Leonard founded The Living Forum with Jerry Rubin and co-produced The Event in November 1978, a 14-hour experience with Masters and Johnson, Wayne Dyer, George Carlin, Buckminster Fuller, Werner Erhard and others. She is the daughter of philosopher-author George Leonard.

Jerry Rubin is securities analyst and creative financier for solar and other environmentally positive companies for John Muir & Co., an investment banking firm in New York. Mr. Rubin, son of a Teamster Union official, worked for five years as a journalist for *The Cincinnati Post and Times-Star*. He graduated from the University of Cincinnati with a B.A. in American history and sociology. Mr. Rubin organized one of the first antiwar activist groups in the country, the Vietnam Day Committee. He finished second in a 1966 race for Mayor of Berkeley. Mr. Rubin co-founded the Youth International Party (the Yippies) and went on trial in Chicago as a member of the Chicago 7. In the 1970s Mr. Rubin became a therapist and helped popularize the human potential movement. He has written five books, lectured on more than 500 college campuses, and continues to be an innovator and promoter of cultural, psychological and economic developments.

If your organization is interested in contacting Mr. Rubin for lectures, please write:

Jerry Rubin
New Line Presentations
853 Broadway
New York, New York 10003